Vietnam, Hồ Quý Ly, and the Ming (1371-1421)

ACKNOWLEDGMENT

The publication of this second volume in the Lạc-Việt Series is made possible by continued support from the Henry Luce Foundation, whose initial grant helped to launch the Yale Southeast Asian Refugee Project in 1981.

JOHN K. WHITMORE

Vietnam, Hồ Quý Ly, and the Ming (1371-1421)

The LẠC-VIỆT Series — No. 2

YALE CENTER FOR INTERNATIONAL AND AREA STUDIES
COUNCIL ON SOUTHEAST ASIA STUDIES

YALE SOUTHEAST ASIA STUDIES

James C. Scott, Director

* *

Copyright © 1985 by Yale Southeast Asia Studies

International Standard Book Number: **0-938692-22-4**

Library of Congress Catalog Card Number: **85-51296**

The LẠC-VIỆT Series

No. 2

O. W. Wolters, Senior Editor

Huỳnh Sanh Thông, Executive Editor

M. Kay Mansfield, Business Manager

Nguyễn Mộng Giác, West Coast Representative

Price: US$10 (including postage).

Your check or money order should be made payable to: Yale Southeast Asia Studies.

Please address all inquiries to:

Yale Southeast Asia Studies
Box 13A Yale Station
New Haven, CT 06520 USA

Printed in the U.S.A.

iv

CONTENTS

INTRODUCTION   vii

I. ĐẠI VIỆT IN THE FOURTEENTH CENTURY   1

II. THE SUCCESS OF LÊ QUÝ LY   12

III. QUÝ LY IN POWER   37

IV. THE HỒ REGIME   58

V. DESTRUCTION OF THE VIETNAMESE STATE   77

VI. CHIAO-CHIH AND MING COLONIALISM   97

NOTES
     Introduction   133
     Chapter I   136
     Chapter II   145
     Chapter III   156
     Chapter IV   162
     Chapter V   168
     Chapter VI   175
ORIGINAL SOURCES   198
SECONDARY SOURCES   200

ABOUT THE AUTHOR

John K. Whitmore is a scholar of premodern Vietnam and Southeast Asia who is working on survey research among Southeast Asian refugees. He received his B.A. from Wesleyan University and his M.A. (cultural anthropology) and Ph.D. (Southeast Asian history) from Cornell University. He has taught at Yale University, the University of Michigan, and the University of Virginia.

INTRODUCTION

The establishment of Confucianism as the official ideology and historiography of Vietnam in the fifteenth century has deprived scholars of a true rendering of the role of Hồ Quý Ly in history. Though a major figure who helped resurrect Vietnam in a critical time of weakness, Quý Ly received short shrift from the official historians of the Vietnamese state over the following four centuries.

Phan Phu Tiên and Ngô Sĩ Liên of the early Lê dynasty, reflecting a strong anti-Hồ bias, compiled the first edition of the Đại Việt Sử Ký Toàn Thư in the 1450s and 1470s respectively. Phu Tiên, while seeing some merit in Quý Ly's strengthening of the state and his opposition to the Chinese, joined Sĩ Liên in condemning the general evil of the Hồ regime. To these Confucians, a Chinese-style morality outweighed service to the state of Đại Việt. Quý Ly's grasp for power and his seizure of the throne, among other unethical acts, meant more than his reconstitution of central power, and the subsequent Ming occupation (1407-1427) with its horrors was thus, according to Sĩ Liên at least, a divine judgment placed upon the Vietnamese as a consequence.[1] The eighteenth and early nineteenth century historians, Ngô Thì Sĩ and Phan Huy Chú, continued this line of moral criticism, stressing the lack of propriety and correctness in the Hồ efforts.[2] In the middle of the nineteenth century, as the power of the state weakened and the French brought more and more pressure to bear on Vietnam, the Tự Đức Emperor of the Nguyễn dynasty could only quote old sayings and maintain the moral condemnation of Quý Ly.[3]

Those who held such moralistic views saw the Hồ maneuvers as a grave threat to the legitimacy of the Vietnamese Throne and, under French colonialism, Vietnamese historiography merely retained, without much vigor, those expressions of the Confucian historians which reinforced such legitimacy. If the Chinese model had been emasculated, its impact on the writing of history remained. Trần Trọng Kim's Việt Nam Sử Lược [A short history of Vietnam] is the major example of this phenomenon. Originally published in the 1920s, this work went through many editions and remained a semiofficial text down to the fall of the Republic of Vietnam at the end of April 1975. Although Kim's book contains a description of the Hồ reforms, it stresses that Quý Ly was a usurping court minister whose acts brought on the Ming invasion.[4] The consequent view of Hồ Quý Ly as a usurper who used his power for his own benefit appeared in most of the French and later Anglo-American treatises of early Vietnamese history.[5] No change was attempted until the 1950s when Lê Thành Khôi emphasized Quý Ly's reform efforts equally with the minister's "criminal" seizure of power. These efforts, he believed, had actively helped "to resolve the economic and social crisis of the times". Joseph Buttinger, in turn, adopted much of Khôi's approach.[6]

As Lê Thành Khôi was re-examining the role of the Hồ in Paris, the Hanoi historians were moving in a similar direction. Shortly after liberation in 1954, Minh Tranh published an article in Văn Sử Địa which, according to Maurice Durand, argued convincingly "that the reform projects of Hồ Quý Ly (agricultural, fiscal, cultural) corresponded to the necessities of the evolution of Vietnamese society and economy... [and that] Hồ Quý Ly was an audacious spirit and a reformer who advanced the course of history."[7] Nevertheless, the examination of Quý Ly's role continued in the North through the 1960s[8] and by 1971 it was again regarded negatively. In volume 1 of the official Lịch Sử Việt Nam [History of Vietnam],[9] the general assessment is that while Quý Ly had centralized administrative and military power in the state, broken the Trần aristocracy through his social and economic reforms (in land, serfs, and paper money), and furthered Vietnamese cultural development (education and nôm literature), he nevertheless alienated the people, caused rifts among the classes of Vietnamese society, and handled the defense of the country poorly. In sum, Quý Ly was held responsible, both socially and militarily, for the ordeal of the Ming occupation—a reiteration of the centuries-old verdict of the Confucian historians.

My re-examination of Hồ Quý Ly and the Ming, and the place of their regimes in Vietnamese and Southeast Asian history seeks to break away from the Confucian view of Quý Ly as a usurper as well as to gain a broader perspective of the consequence of his rule. During the thirteenth and fourteenth centuries, the early civilization of Vietnam which had begun under the Lý dynasty (1009-1224) went through change as the Vietnamese state weakened in a situation parallel to what was happening to Angkor in Cambodia and to Pagan in Burma. The political system gradually disintegrated as local regions became more and more autonomous, undoubtedly abetted by changes in the central ideology of the state. Increasingly, the old style of state stood exposed due to this weakened ideology and a lack of control over the manpower and revenue of the countryside. Yet, unlike the disintegration of Angkor and Pagan, the Vietnamese, under the leadership of Hồ Quý Ly, moved quickly to strengthen their state. In my interpretation, the main goal of Quý Ly and his supporters was not to gain personal power but to achieve a more strongly centralized state. The late fourteenth century presented the crisis to which these men responded, and the specific historical situation gave them the opportunity to meet the country's needs and, at the same time, destroyed them. To understand this paradox and to appreciate fully Quý Ly's impact on the course of Vietnamese history, we must put aside the ethical arguments of the Confucians as well as the shame of the Ming conquest.

The following study is based upon documentation from the fifteenth century as it survives today. The major source of information covering the period to 1428 is the **Đại Việt Sử Ký Toàn Thư** [The complete historical record of Đại Việt] which was compiled by Ngô Sĩ Liên in 1479, a quarter of a century after Phan Phu Tiên had begun work on it, and which has been incorporated into later editions of the book. The **Toàn Thư** (**TT**), or **History** as we shall refer to it, is a year-by-year record of events in the style of the eleventh-century **Tzu Chih T'ung Chien** by the Chinese historian Ssu-ma Kuang, with Phu Tiên's and Sĩ Liên's separate moral comments scattered throughout the text.[10] Whatever the attitudes of these Confucian historians, the material included is quite trustworthy as far as I have been able to determine. A different work that shares some of the same information and may be used to counterbalance the anti-Hồ interpretation of the Confucian historians is the **Nam Ông Mộng Lục** [Record of the dreams of an old man of the South]. Émile Gaspardone believed this work to have

been written by Quý Ly's son Nguyên Trừng during his captivity
in China (the preface is dated 1438).[11] In the then traditional
Vietnamese style of collected tales Nguyên Trừng gives us a
view, presumably to a great extent from his own memory, of
the events and beliefs of Vietnam in the late fourteenth century.

Other materials supplement the data and interpretations
obtained from the above two texts. The **Veritable Records** (**Shih
Lu**) of the Ming imperial court in China add information from
the official Chinese viewpoint, and the slightly later writings
of the great Vietnamese minister Nguyễn Trãi (1380-1442) provide
interesting detail.[12] Later Vietnamese compilations are of help
in grouping information on similar topics. I have used Phan
Huy Chú's early nineteenth-century **Lịch Triều Hiến Chương Loại
Chí** [Regulated annals of successive dynasties][13] extensively
for a variety of topics, and biographical collections of scholars successful in the Chinese-style examinations of Vietnam
provide valuable material on their careers in Vietnamese government service.[14]

This study was completed in 1976 and few changes have been
made in it since that year. The most important work done on
this period of Vietnamese history over the past ten years
has been the ongoing study by O. W. Wolters of the fourteenth
century and the literati in Vietnam.[15] In his work, Professor
Wolters is examining the Vietnamese scholars of classical
Chinese learning and their place in the history of the age.
I make passing reference to his work in this volume, but I
encourage the readers to go directly to Professor Wolters'
writings in order to gain for themselves an understanding
of his valuable contribution to the study of Vietnamese history.

I wish to thank the many people over the years who have
aided the development of this manuscript, including Keith
W. Taylor for his help in its initial stage and for his map
and genealogy and Patti Brennan for her initial editing. Edward
L. Farmer was kind enough first to publish and then grant permission for me to use my essay, "Chiao-chih and Neo-Confucianism: The Ming Attempt to Transform Vietnam", **Ming Studies,**
4 (1977), pp. 51-91, as the sixth chapter in this volume. Joan
and the boys have offered constant patience and encouragement
in the slow development of this work.

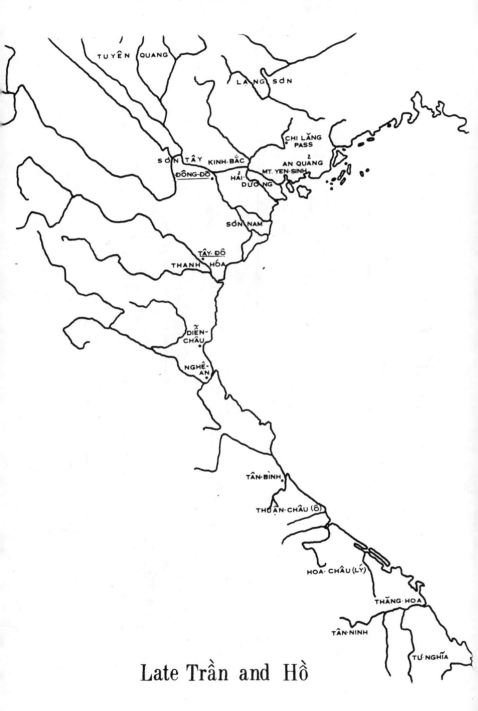

Late Trần and Hồ

The Trần and Hồ Dynasties

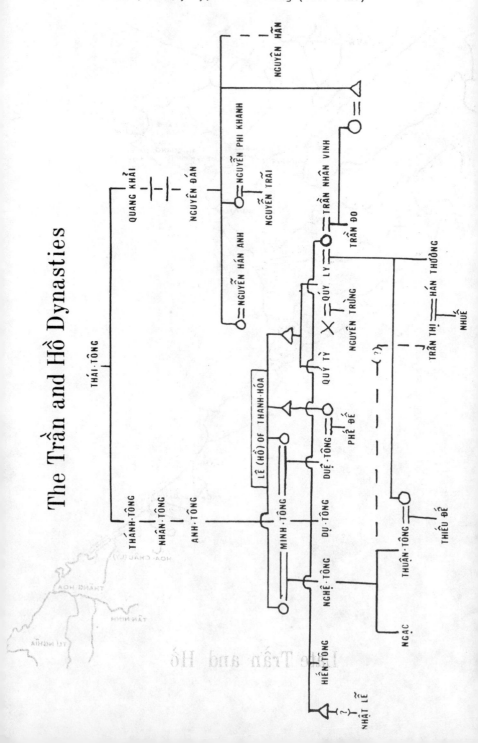

I. ĐẠI VIỆT IN THE FOURTEENTH CENTURY

As the impact of the Mongol wars receded and the fourteenth century began, the Vietnamese reverted to an earlier form of government. Following mid-thirteenth century attempts to tighten the central control of the state by recruiting officials via the classical Chinese examinations and by placing these officials in outer regions of the countryside, the Trần dynasty returned to the framework established by its predecessor, the Lý, three centuries before. This framework, similar to those in Cambodia, Burma, and Java of the same years,[1] was loose in structure, focused its efforts primarily in the region of the capital (Thăng-long, now Hanoi), and controlled the state through the blood oath and the maintenance of direct personal loyalty to the Throne.[2]

The threat of war and the eventual Mongol invasions of the 1280s took regional administration out of literati hands and placed it firmly in those of the royal princes. No examination was held for almost three decades (until 1304), and by then the administrative ideal of the early years of the dynasty seems to have disappeared. As the Mongols approached, the princes received orders to recruit and command armies from their own domains scattered around the Red River Delta and to the south, where the Trần ultimately made their stand.[3] Prince Quang Khải faced the southern Mongol landing at his base in Nghệ-an, while the Hưng Đạo Prince, Trần Quốc Tuấn, struck against the Mongol army in the Red River Delta from Thanh-hóa, ultimately driving the invaders out.[4]

In addition to the preservation of independence, the prime

1

result of the Vietnamese resistance to the Mongols, based as
it was on the princes, seems to have been the change in form
of government. As Ngô Sĩ Liên later pointed out,[5] the princes
initially had little influence on the administration of the
country. For the next century, however, these princes, their
protégés,[6] and their descendants became major components in
the control of the state. The strength which Sĩ Liên saw in
the princes lay in their close personal relations to the land
and people of their local domains. This may be seen most promi-
nently in the Hưng Đạo Prince's famous proclamation to his
officers during the Mongol wars.[7] In particular, it was Quốc
Tuấn's cousin Quang Khải who aggressively led the princes in
holding high government positions and whose descendants would
play major roles in the last century of Trần rule.[8]

Over the countryside, the princely domains began to control
local administration. Prince Quốc Khang, for example, held
sway in Diễn-châu and took to wife the most beautiful girls
of the area. All his children were therefore local natives
who continued to administer the province after his death in
1300. When Quốc Khang's line died out, local men received the
administrative jobs. Much the same occurred in Thanh-hóa where
Prince Nhật Duật married a local woman who brought in others
of her province as secondary wives. The prince's sons were
consequently of Thanh-hóa stock and became the hereditary administrators of that province.[9] In this way, provincial areas
returned to a form of personal rule as the princes and their
families took over the regional administration from literati
officials.

Thus did the bureaucratic innovations of the early Trần
period fade away. The selection and use of officials became
more personal and arbitrary. By the first decade of the fourteenth century, veterans and scholars, top winners in the examinations and students, northerners and southerners rubbed shoul-
ders in the court, dependent upon personal loyalty and favor
for the retention of their positions. As the nineteenth-century
historian Phan Huy Chú noted, "they were used as needed; there
was no formality in selection procedures."[10]

Under the patronage of the Throne and its kin, proponents
of varied patterns of thought—Buddhism, classical Chinese
learning, and mythic beliefs—enjoyed support and status in

the capital of Thăng-long. The first decades of the fourteenth century were a time of vigorous intellectual development. The abdicated ruler, Trần Nhân-tông, returned from a pilgrimage to Champa and took charge of his Buddhist sect, that of the Bamboo Grove (**Trúc Lâm**), which would dominate the religious life of the aristocracy for thirty years.[11] Classical scholars congregated around the capital in the entourage of various princes and aristocrats and served as administrators.[12] Already, in 1272, their opinions may be seen in Lê Văn Hữu's chronicles, **Đại Việt Sử Ký**, the first known indigenous history of Vietnam.[13] With this classical learning, **nôm**, the form of writing adapted to the Vietnamese language, began to emerge.[14] Finally, and most basically, the mythic tradition of the Vietnamese past continued in strength among the populace.[15]

A geographic division appears to have existed at this time between those carrying on the older ideologies, such as Buddhism and the mythic beliefs, and the scholars of classical Chinese learning. The former were located primarily in the capital region and to its north and west; the scholars, a number of whom despised Buddhism, came from the eastern and southern Delta as well as from farther south, especially Thanh-hóa.[16] In the first decades of the fourteenth century, scholar-officials began both to challenge the beliefs of the Buddhist establishment as "supersitition" and to advocate points from their learning for state action. Through ability these men rose to high rank within the court, and a number of them served as Counsellors (**Hành-khiển**) around the throne.[17]

The appearance of these scholars in the court must be viewed not as a "Confucianization" of the state, but as a part of the eclectic acceptance of useful persons and cultural elements which was typical of the Southeast Asian state in these centuries. The Buddhist establishment continued to thrive, and the Vietnamese ruler of the time, the Buddhist Trần Minh-tông (1314-1329), explicitly told the scholar-officials that their moral and governmental preachments would come to naught.[18] Indeed, 1329 is the traditional date for the compilation of the classic Vietnamese mythic history, **Việt Điện U Linh Tập**,[19] perhaps in reaction to the emergence of the more formal and moralistic Chinese style of history.

The pattern of relations between Đại Việt and its southern

neighbor Champa is also indicative of the style of thought
among the aristocrats of the Vietnamese court. Under the threat
of the Mongols, the two countries put aside their warfare
over the hegemony of the eastern mainland[20] and grew relatively
close by 1300, so close that the abdicated king and Buddhist
monk, Nhân-tông, took his pilgrimage to the holy Cham sites.
He had such an enjoyable time there that in 1301 he promised
his daughter, sister of the ruling king Anh-tông, in marriage
to his host, the Cham king Jayasimhavarman IV. The later histories, with their Confucian bias, faithfully record the protests
of the   scholar-officials   against their princess marrying
a barbarian. It was, they shouted, equivalent to giving the
Chinese princess to the Hun. Yet their arguments had no effect
on the 1306 decision by the Vietnamese court to allow the marriage and to receive the two northern Cham provinces in return.[21]

When the Cham king died the following year (1307) and a
Vietnamese raiding party rescued the princess from the funeral
pyre, the Chams demanded their provinces back. The Vietnamese
refusal led to increasing Cham unrest and resulted in the Vietnamese campaigns of 1312 and 1318 to put down the troublemak-
ers.[22] In opposition to the learned   arguments, the Vietnamese
court did not regard the Chams as barbarians and inalterable
enemies, but as neighbors of a not too different cultural tradition who required only minimal force to acknowledge the Vietnamese political sway.

Through the 1360s, as the Yüan dynasty of the Mongols to
the north gradually fell before various rebel attacks,[23] the
Trần dynasty began to feel the resurgence of Cham power led
by the   great king Chế Bồng Nga.[24] The tensions between these
two states which emerged following the episode of the "gift"
provinces in 1307 now came back to bedevil the Vietnamese.
The possibility of friendship formerly offered had ultimately
been brushed aside, as the scholars had urged, and the two
states found themselves at each other's throats. The Chams,
determined to regain their lost northern provinces, carried
out raids of increasing intensity and destroyed an attacking
Vietnamese army before finally, in 1371, overwhelming a Vietnamese capital weakened by a recent succession crisis.[25]

In mid-fourteenth-century Vietnam, the aristocracy ran the
state with the vital aid from powerful ministers, bound in

allegiance by the blood oath. The Trần pattern of the father abdicating the throne for the son was well established and most years in this century saw two rulers, the senior abdicated monarch and the young enthroned monarch, with power actually in the former's hands. This institution has been described in the nearly contemporaneous Nam Ông Mộng Lục as follows:

> The Trần family tradition was that as soon as the [king's] son reached maturity he was placed on the throne and the father retired to the Northern Palace, to be respectfully referred to as Father of the King and to share in governing. In fact, this was no more than a transfer of nominal status so as to fix the succession and take precautions against unexpected eventualities [on the father's death]. Decisions in all matters were received from the father; the successor king was no different than a crown prince.[26]

Thus, from 1329 until his death in 1357, the abdicated king Minh-tông directed affairs at the court while first his young eldest son, Hiến-tông (1329-1341), and then his eleventh son, Dụ-tông (1341-1369), sat on the throne. At Minh-tông's death, however, Dụ-tông became the sole ruler for twelve years. He had no children and hence no heirs.[27]

Surrounding the throne and the young king was the aristocracy, essentially consisting of the royal clan, that is, the princes (vương) and princesses (công-chúa), and those with lesser titles of nobility, referred to in general by the term "marquis" (hầu). A class with special recognition and special duties, at least in form if not entirely in fact, the relatives of the Throne appear to have led an easy life in and around the capital and were not as involved in Buddhist activities as their parents had been. The princes, in the time-honored way, were appointed generals and ordered to organize their own troops and ships, though they seem to have done little fighting. Owning choice estates and followers tattooed with their marks, the aristocratic families took part in the extravagant life of Dụ-tông's court.[28] The king, evidently as fond of literature as of drink and dance, in 1362 ordered the aristocratic families to stage performances of Chinese Yüan-style drama and rewarded the best of them. In addition, time and money were spent on gambling and gardens, including a magnificent one of Chinese

style.[29] To meet its flowing expenses, the Throne confiscated
the possessions of any subjects who died. At least one classical
scholar, Chu Văn An, left the court in protest against the
carousing. In his mountain retreat An would write:

> Fish splash the pond—but where have dragons gone?
> Clouds drench bare mountains—cranes are yet away.
>
> . . . .
>
> My heart is not cold ashes—it still burns.
> I think of our late kings and hide my tears.

Great rulers and wise counsellors no longer, in An's judgment,
graced the capital of Thăng-long.[30]

Only members of the royal clan could fill the positions
of prime minister (thái-tể or bình-chường chính-sự) or general
(tường-quốc). They appear also to have been the only ones allowed to hold the royal counsellor (đại-thần) positions.[31] The
bulk of the talent in the court, however, lay with those appointed to the post of Counsellor (Hành-khiển) in one degree
or another and those who formed the Secret Council (Khu-mật-
viện), very often the same people. The men who held these positions, including some posts not mentioned here, were used to
perform any task deemed necessary by the Throne and often found
themselves performing tasks, such as leading armies, which
ought to have fallen to their aristocratic superiors. The Counsellors were also sent out, sometimes as special commissioners
(kinh-lược-sứ), to undertake specific tasks in one or several
of the provinces. Through mid-century, many of these Counsellors
had a strong classical studies background but carried little
voice in the formation of court policy.[32]

In the capital there also existed a varied array of administrative, scholarly, and palace positions. A number of these
positions were linked with the Secret Council and consequently
were important. The Six Ministries, on the other hand, were
not very significant and, to the limited extent that they
had been established, merely formed one group of administrative
offices among many. Together with other Sinic institutions
such as the Censorate (Ngự-sử-đài), the Hàn-lâm Academy (Hàn-
lâm-viện), and the National College (Quốc-tử-giám), the Ministries and similar administrative offices stood at the beck
and call of the Counsellors, apparently without independent
status or a voice of their own. Recruitment for the bureaus

(quán) and council chambers (các) came from classical examinations, while clerks were tested in reading and writing to fill posts in the offices (sảnh) and institutes (viện).[33] The provincial offices, on the other hand, do not seem to have received officials in any such manner and were probably filled by appointment from the ranks of local members of the royal clan or court favorites (and those out of favor). The chief official of a province was the an-phủ-sứ, literally the pacifier, who was in charge of all matters, civil and military, within his jurisdiction. It was his responsibility to keep peace and to bring in revenue and soldiers for the government. Other local officials, such as defenders (phòng-ngụ-sứ), existed in border provinces to the north and south.[34]

The countryside over which these officials extended their personal power stretched away from the capital at Thăng-long across the Red River Delta.[35] To the north and west, homeland of the Vietnamese aristocracy, the delta met the foothills and then the mountains. To the east and south, it extended across many streams into marshy ground until it met the sea. Farther south lay the narrow coastal plains and small deltas of what are now the central lowlands, closely fringed by the mountains. Several million peasants, carrying their own arms, lived in more than two thousand villages (xã), while some two million persons of various ethnic groups dwelled in the mountains. Wet rice was the basis of the lowland economy. Members of the royal clan and nobles seem to have continued their hereditary control over segments of these lowlands and used the villages, dependent upon them, to produce the wealth of the land. More than two hundred Buddhist temples were scattered over the lowlands though little is known of their economic foundation.[36]

Activity in the countryside, besides the normal duties of the an-phủ-sứ, appears to have been mainly in the hands of private individuals. When troops were needed for a major effort, as in 1353 against Champa, the princes and other nobles were called upon to build warships, manufacture weapons, and train troops. The forces kept in the provincial centers were only capable of handling occasional bandits. The provinces supported their own troops with no help from the capital, as each district took an allotted amount of rice from its fields. A province

might join its forces with those of another province for use
against a major bandit threat, but if the threat continued
the Palace Guard (Cấm-quân) had to be called upon for aid.[37]
If calamities occurred among the populace, as they   often did
during   the 1360s, the Throne could only reduce taxes and
make an appeal to the wealthy of the land to give rice and
alleviate the distress of the poor. In return the donors were,
in one instance, given money and, in another, a title according
to their rank. The only direct government aid during these
years took place when the king left the capital to visit a
nearby prefecture and his entourage distributed medicines.[38]
Nowhere is there any record of central officials taking action.
Economic, social, and legal affairs would seem to have been
the preserve of the locality and the concern of local powers.

   Thus, the government of Đại Việt lay mainly in the hands
of the royal family. By 1369, the major literati Counsellors
of the previous half century had disappeared from the court
and apparently left no protégés capable of carrying on their
campaign for more effective government. Probably only lesser
students of Chinese affairs who served Dụ-tông's wishes remained. Implanted in the capital, the surviving Counsellors
found themselves at the mercy of intrigue within the royal
clan. His death foreshadowed by a solar eclipse,[39] the pleasure-
loving Dụ-tông passed away in 1369 leaving no heir, and the
throne was offered to Dương Nhật Lễ, offspring of a wife of
the dissolute eldest son of Minh-tông. The royal counsellors
(đại-thần) favored Prince Phủ, third son of Minh-tông, for
his "extreme virtue". In the phrases of the **Nam Ông Mộng Lục**,
Phủ was "simple and sincere, filial and friendly, respectful
and restrained, discerning and incisive. [He] possessed a
broad knowledge of the [Chinese] Classics and Histories, and
he did not enjoy excessive luxury..." Yet, according to the
same source, an older brother had no right to be the heir of
his younger brother, and so the Counsellors followed the Queen
Mother's wish to take Nhật Lễ as their ruler.[40] Said to have
been the son of an actor, his mother having been pregnant at
the time of her marriage to the prince, Nhật Lễ was nevertheless
acknowledged by the prince as his legitimate son. Establishing
himself in the court and following its advice, Nhật Lễ selected
the fifty-year-old son of Minh-tông (ostensibly his uncle),

Trần Nguyên Trác, as his prime minister and commander-in-chief and two other uncles, the princes Phủ and Kính, as royal counsellors, while taking Phủ's daughter as his queen.[41]

By the end of the year, however, the new ruler's hold began to slip as other members of the royal clan turned against him. No doubt feeling secure, Nhật Lễ had taken revenge on the kind-hearted mother of Dụ-tông for having misgivings about his accession to the throne. The poisoning of the former Queen Mother, however, seems to have deeply offended the prime minister who had been aided by her in a crisis some ten years earlier. This, together with Nhật Lễ's lack of respect for the royal counsellors and the proper rites, especially mourning, his carousing and acts of favoritism, and his desire to change his family name,[42] seems to have been the cause of Nguyên Trác's attempted coup nine months later. The old prince, joined by his son and two grandsons of the Queen Mother, tried to trap Nhật Lễ in the palace. The latter evaded them and ordered their execution, killing a large number of the royal clan. Fearful that the calamity might overtake him as well, Trần Phủ slipped out of the capital by night to join other members of the aristocracy in resistance among the hills of Thanh-hóa, his mother's home province. Aided secretly by a courtier at Nhật Lễ's side, Prince Phủ, his younger brother Kính, and supporters with their followers destroyed all armies sent against them.[43]

On Kính's strong urging and backed by his fellow aristocrats, the shy Prince Phủ reluctantly returned to purge the capital and to claim the throne less than two months after he had left. Nhật Lễ was demoted and then executed.[44] As Minh-tông's son, the new ruler Nghệ-tông (1370-1372) restored the proper line to the throne and did everything according to his late father's rules. Whereas in the last years of the younger brother's reign (1357-1369) there had been an eclectic pursuit of pleasure with a number of activities drawn from China, now the group behind Nghệ-tông was determined to bring the court back to the old ways it had seen under Minh-tông. Echoing his father's words, the new king proclaimed:

> [When] the earlier reigns established the country, [they] had their own system of law [and] did not follow the [Chinese] system of the Sung. [This] was because in the North [China] and the South [Vietnam] each ruler [had]

his own land and no need to follow the other. During
the Đại-trị reign (1358-69), pale scholars were employed
who did not understand [the depth of] the establishment
of law [in our state] [and] who changed the old customs
of our ancestors to follow the customs of the North entirely, as if [these customs] were clothes, music, [or]
literature. We cannot choose anything [of theirs].[45]

Though pleasure-loving aristocrats might make use of such external attractions as Nghệ-tông listed, the new group was in effect
saying, "We have our own style of life and insist on maintaining
this style in the face of mere imitation of China." Thus Đại
Việt refused to become a miniature reproduction of its northern
neighbor.

Yet, the segment of the aristocracy which held the above
view and was the ruling power in the state shared a common
cause with the reformist literati. As Nghệ-tông made his way
back to the capital, he was met jointly by his fellow aristocrats and by the officials, both of whom hailed him as the
new ruler. The old master of classical learning Chu Văn An
left the mountain retreat he had taken in protest of Dụ-tông's
misgovernment to wish the new monarch well. Soon afterward
An died and was honored by a place of worship in the classical
Temple of Literature (Văn-miếu). In turn, some months later,
Nghệ-tông gave a banquet for the officials in one of the palaces and rewarded them according to their rank.[46] Nevertheless,
the men who held power were those who had actively supported
the revolt--men such as the new king's cousin, Trần Nguyên
Đán, and the semi-literate Nguyễn Nhiên. The former was appointed tư-đồ and prime minister, while the latter became
a Counsellor (Hành-khiển), and other loyal members of the
royal clan received influential positions close to the Throne.
Earlier restrictions on property ownership and wealth were
removed.[47] The literati Counsellors of earlier decades were
nowhere to be seen.

Then the Chams struck into the Red River Delta for the first
time. Once again disaffection within the Vietnamese court led
a Vietnamese, this time Nhật Lễ's mother, to flee to the Chams
and encourage them in their attack on Vietnamese territory.[48]
Chế Bồng Nga, having heard from her of the weak state of the
Vietnamese defenses and of the great booty there, moved unop-

posed straight up through the southern Delta, across an unde-
fended ford, and into Thăng-long as the Vietnamese court left
hurriedly from the opposite side of the city. Nghệ-tông fled
by boat, traveling a short distance to the north and abandoning
his newly won capital to the invaders. Grasping the opportunity,
the Chams burned the palaces and seized women, jewels, and
silks. In the Southeast Asian pattern of warfare, they aimed
at, captured, and destroyed the center of the Vietnamese state,
thus shaking its foundations before withdrawing. The Vietnamese,
despite the earlier Cham raids, seem to have been practically
defenseless.[49]

II. THE SUCCESS OF LÊ QUÝ LY

Following the disastrous defeat at the hands of the Chams,
Nghệ-tông returned to the capital and to efforts at the reform
of aristocratic life in the court. His son supposedly
incompetent, Nghệ-tông formally shared power with his younger
brother, Prince Kính, who became Heir Apparent with the consort
of the Lê family as his official wife. Nghệ-tông also issued
"Royal Instructions" (Hoàng-Huấn) in fourteen sections which
probably served as guidelines for the court activities of the
period.[1] The following month, a man related to the Throne by
marriage, emerged in the key post of đại-sứ in the Secret Council, a position just below the royal counsellor posts held
by the royal clan. Two of Lê Quý Ly's paternal aunts entered
the palace during Minh-tông's reign, produced first the future
Nghệ-tông (Trần Phủ) and then his brother (now Heir Apparent),
and were honored in the years 1371-72. Quý Ly's family's home
province of Thanh-hóa served as the base for the rise of Phủ
and Kính. His first cousin was also the Heir Apparent's wife.
Thus Quý Ly's rapid rise to power within the upsurge of aristocratic influence should be no surprise as Nghệ-tông and his
brother, the future ruler Duệ-tông, proceeded to place much
trust and confidence in him. Before the end of 1371, Quý Ly
had already been sent south to Nghệ-an to soothe its people
and to pacify the border. After this expedition, he was made
a marquis (hầu) and was drawn into the ranks of the aristocratic
élite. In addition, he received a princess, a daughter of Minh-
tông who had been widowed in the Nhật Lễ debacle, as his major
wife.[2]

12

Originally from a Chinese family named Hu (Hồ) which had moved from Chekiang province to Diễn-châu in the tenth century, Quý Ly's branch of the family had settled in Thanh-hóa and taken the name Lê from that of a benefactor sometime in the thirteenth century. This branch had apparently attached itself to the royal service, perhaps at first to the local entourage of one of the Trần princes, and through the decades had gradually risen to a level where its daughters were chosen to be consorts of the king.[3] Thus, the rise of Nghệ-tông and his brother brought state power to this branch of the royal clan and provided Quý Ly with both personal influence and a limited stage upon which to base his own maneuvering for power.

As Lê Quý Ly began his rise under the auspices of the Throne, Nghệ-tông proceeded to carry out varied projects of the aristocratic program before stepping aside for his younger brother at the end of 1372. The twin tactic of purifying the lifestyle of the aristocracy while keeping the officials and the people in their places continued. An order went out that the reconstruction of the palace buildings must follow simple lines and that service would be rendered by the royal clan and retired officials, though in such a way as not to disturb the people. Then, an official was ordered to compile the state statutes and ritual observances. All those holding aristocratic titles were to make a declaration thereof and be recorded in a register. This action was taken because many of the common people were greatly confusing matters by claiming to hold titles they had no right to. At the beginning of the New Year (1372), an examination was made into the merits and achievements of the civil and military officials. Some months later, the provincial registers were ordered redone.[4]

In this way the new group clearly drew the lines between the privileged élite of the court, the officials, and the common people. Matters were set right and every person was authenticated in his place. The only way to gain entrance to the court élite was through royal favor, and in 1372 we see several instances of this occurring: Đỗ Tử Bình, an experienced official and general, was made Counsellor with military responsibilities; next the semiliterate Nguyễn Nhiên, already a Counsellor, received a position on the Secret Council; and Phạm A Song, a proven official on the southern frontier, was honored and given

a title, thus being brought into the lower ranks of the aristocracy.[5] Besides such trusted and experienced officers as these,
two additional figures appear in the historical record for
the first time, both bearing the surname Hồ and both from the
southern territory. The brilliant Hồ Tông Thốc of Diễn-châu
was named a scholar in the Hàn-lâm Academy, and Hồ Long from
Hóa-châu became the district official in his home territory.[6]
Lê Quý Ly had gone south the previous year, and it is most
likely no coincidence that these men entered the government
at that time. We may speculate that Quý Ly's influence lay
behind their appointments, and we may see their presence in
the government as the start of Quý Ly's skillful politicking.
Two trends in the final quarter of the fourteenth century were
Quý Ly's forging of a political base in the south and the strong
emergence, for the first time, of southerners in a power struggle around the court.

When the scholarly Nghệ-tông abdicated the throne at the
end of 1372 to his more forceful brother, he promulgated a
statement entitled "Imperial Admonitions" (Đế Châm). Perhaps
these words, which have not survived, outlined his own feelings
on aristocratic life and Sinic influence. While his brother,
later to be known as Duệ-tông (1373—78), took command of the
state, Nghệ-tông helped to develop the literary and civil side
of affairs. He honored the late literati Counsellor Trương
Hán Siêu by having sacrifices performed for him in the Temple
of Literature. This was followed by the establishment of a
register for civil and military ranks. Apparently once this
definition of status had been achieved, there began a systematic
selection of officials. An examination was held among lower
government employees for the choice of clerks to serve in an
internal record office of the court. Then, at the beginning
of 1374, Nghệ-tông held a palace examination which was open to
students and officials working in the capital and to the aristocracy. The successful candidates were given a banquet and clothing and received offices according to their performance in
the examination. The top three scholars went on a three-day
procession, presumably to their home areas.[7]

In the meantime, the main goal of Duệ-tông and the dominant
theme of his reign was retaliation against Champa. While Nghệ-
tông settled into his palace at the Trần family home in Sơn-

nam, a province south of the capital, his brother began preparations for a campaign to the south. Though a literati official
again and again advanced a decidedly Ming Chinese cultural
line for dealing with the barbarians,[8] Duệ-tông merely turned
his back on such a peaceful approach and continued to consider
the efforts needed for his expedition. These efforts entailed
not just the gathering of men, materials and transport, but
a reorganization of the southern part of the state. Neglected
for more than half a century, the southern provinces had to
be brought back into direct contact with the capital in order
to support the campaign.

Orders went out to fill the ranks of the army and to repair
and build ships. Then, at harvesttime, an appeal was made for
rice, and those who donated it were rewarded titles of nobility
according to the amount given. At the end of 1373, Duệ-tông
declared that he would personally lead the attack on the Chams.
The preparations went on for another two years. Thanh-hóa and
Nghệ-an were first ordered to dredge and deepen their coastal
harbors; then, as the army ranks were filled, military units
were organized in the five southern provinces to supplement
the forces of the capital. At the start of the following year
(1375), an administrative reform took place in the provinces
south of Thanh-hóa as Nghệ-an was broken into smaller administrative units, and two officials came down to direct the people
of Thanh-hóa, Nghệ-an, and Tân-bình in putting the roads in
good order throughout their provinces. The work was finished
in three months. Thus, the central hand came to be felt in
the southern territories, a hand to which the people there
had long been unaccustomed. As the establishment of the military
registers continued, all the households of Thanh-hóa and Nghệ-
an were ordered to provide men for the army.[9]

The problems of preparation may be seen in the fact that
another appeal for rice had to be made during the next harvest,
this time explicitly to the rich in the provinces who also
received titles in return. The Vietnamese state apparently
had no official system for requisitioning such a large supply
of rice and continually had to go to the big landowners to
gain the necessary amount. Despite an overture to the literati,
the government in the capital remained concentrated in the
hands of the royal clan and the aristocracy. When inner court

offices were set up in 1374, members of these groups became
the heads of the offices. The following year, Lê Quý Ly, further
benefiting from his royal contacts, received a high military
rank, though indeed men of ability, "not necessarily from the
royal clan", could become officers. During these years, the
Throne reaffirmed its aristocratic, native stance by forbidding the Chinese style of dress and the imitation of Lao and
Cham speech, and by again setting the pattern for the use of
vehicles, parasols, insignia, and clothes. In this way the
court prepared itself for the ceremony of the blood oath. Meanwhile, amidst marriages and matings within and between the
royal clan and the aristocracy, two major members of the royal
family, Trần Nguyên Đán and Prince Ngạc (the latter a son of
the abdicated king Nghệ-tông) took charge of posts in the northern and western mountains, presumably to provide protection
against China during the prospective southern campaign.[10]

While the Vietnamese prepared for their revenge, the Chams
were expertly playing their role within the East Asian political
scene. This scene was in a state of flux as the Hung-wu Emperor,
founder of the Ming dynasty, attempted to undo the damage of
the barbarian Mongols and to reorient China in a classical
direction. In interstate relations, this meant not only the
reconstruction of the system which had existed under earlier
Chinese dynasties, but also the establishment of a new order
throughout the world under the umbrella of virtue (te), as
symbolized, for example, by the granting and expected use of
the Chinese calendar. Where possible, all states were to be
treated equally, at least as long as they maintained their
virtue and recognized the Chinese order. Indeed, with these
goals attained, the Chinese emperor practically guaranteed
that such states would not be attacked.[11] Thus, when Ming T'ai-
tsu heard of the countercoup in Vietnam, he sent Nghệ-tông
a reprimand for his "usurpation" and the execution of Nhật
Lễ and issued a threat of invasion, though he did not follow
through on it.[12]

What the Chinese Throne required from its vassals was propriety, sincerity, and the maintenance of each other's borders.
Soon after taking the throne, the Hung-wu Emperor called upon
the Vietnamese and the Chams to cease their fighting and to
live peacefully. The emperor's strong desire for impartiality,

however, left him open to the ploys of the Cham king. In 1372, the year after his attack on the Vietnamese capital, Chế Bồng Nga sent a letter to China charging that the Vietnamese were about to invade his country and requested war materials, musicians, and the protection of China. This led the Hung-wu Emperor to question the behavior of both Champa and Vietnam, demanding that each country occupy only its own territory; he insisted that order be maintained and refused to send the musicians because of the cultural differences between the two countries. The following year, Chế Bồng Nga again wrote to the emperor (who was still concerned about the Mongol threat on his northern borders), drawing the irritated response that he was tired of the perpetual squabbling and that, since both sides were complaining—one year the Vietnamese, the next year the Chams —they should both keep quiet and live in peace. However, he did send a decree to the Vietnamese in 1375, repeating his warning against warfare with the Chams, and made a weak attempt to mediate the fight when it took place the following year.[13] Thus, Champa effectively neutralized any Chinese opprobrium for its own aggression, threw such opprobrium on the Vietnamese, and was prepared to receive the Vietnamese attack.

The Chams struck first with a raid on Hóa-châu in June 1376. This act appears to have finally triggered the Vietnamese response. Final preparations were made for weapons and ships to carry out Duệ-tông's determination to crush the Cham power. Opponents in the court tried unsuccessfully to dissuade him from the effort on the ground of the need for internal reform. Pushing aside the argument of his own personal danger, Duệ-tông ordered the mobilization of the expedition. The southern provinces were ordered to transport the necessary rice supply (fifty thousand piculs) to Hóa-châu, and a grand review of the army and navy was attended by both rulers, Nghệ-tông and Duệ-tông. At the end of the lunar year (January 1377), Duệ-tông set out, leading one hundred twenty thousand troops.[14]

The campaign was a catastrophe. Lê Quý Ly received the command of the southern troops from Nghệ-an, Tân-bình, and Thuận-hóa who were responsible for carrying the supplies, while the experienced military Counsellor Đỗ Tử Bình led the vanguard. At first all went well. The Cham forces raided the border and Chế Bồng Nga sent ten vessels full of gold as a gift for the

Vietnamese ruler. Tử Bình kept the gold for himself and told Duệ-tông that the Cham king had been insolent, lacked the proper decorum, and should be crushed. Duệ-tông, infuriated, resolved to push on and to lead the troops himself. However, he took a month out for further training of his troops. During this time, local men from the border provinces of Tân-bình and Thuận-hóa captured some Chams and turned them over to the Vietnamese force. For the inhabitants of these southern territories, immediate power weighed more than any cultural or political loyalty.

In the first month of the new year, Duệ-tông made his move. Plunging into Champa, he led his soldiers directly toward the Cham capital of Vijaya where Chế Bồng Nga had built his fortifications. The Cham king, acting as though he were about to flee, drew the advance Vietnamese forces into what they believed was an empty city. Brushing aside as "womanish" the precautionary words of a general, the headstrong Duệ-tông led his soldiers into the trap. In the resulting massacre, the Vietnamese were decimated, the king killed, and a son of Nghệ-tông, Prince Húc, captured. Đỗ Tử Bình, in charge of the rear guard for the attack, hung back and was able to escape. Lê Quý Ly, in the rear with the supply train, fled immediately on hearing of the king's death.[15]

The remnants of the army gradually made their way back to Thăng-long, while Đỗ Tử Bình returned north in a prisoner's cage to face his countrymen's curses and a trial where he was judged guilty. He escaped the death sentence, however, and was made a common soldier, only to reemerge in his former position of Counsellor within a year. Lê Quý Ly would not reappear until the beginning of 1379, almost two years later, bearing aristocratic and high official titles "as before".[16] The throne being vacant, Nghệ-tông picked as the next ruler his brother's eldest son, sixteen-year-old Prince Nghiễn (known as Phế-đế, 1377-1388) over the objections of Nghiễn's mother, the Lê queen, and proclaimed that same year to be the first of his reign. The new ruler was the son of Quý Ly's cousin.[17]

The Chams rapidly followed up their victory, once more pushing into the Red River Delta to take the capital. When Nghệ-tông heard of the attack, he sent the general and prince Trần Sư Hiền to hold the major river mouth at Đại-an in Sơn-nam province at the southern edge of the delta. The Chams, however,

learning of the defense at Đại-an, chose another river mouth
to the south, and worked their way behind the Vietnamese forces.
Proceeding directly toward the capital, they reached it again
without resistance and plundered it for a day before retiring
by the same route.[18] While the Chams continued to put pressure
on the Vietnamese in the Red River Delta, they were also beginning to gain a hold over the southern provinces of the Vietnamese territory. In the following two years (1378-1380), Chế
Bồng Nga threatened to take over these provinces, not only
the lost territories but also Nghệ-an and Thanh-hóa. This led
the Vietnamese to make another ill-fated effort to drive the
Cham forces back.

As the Vietnamese worked to reorganize their own forces
in 1378, Chế Bồng Nga married the captured Prince Húc to his
daughter and placed the prince at the head of his forces in
an attack on Nghệ-an. With the Vietnamese prince and the power
on their side, the Chams were able to draw support from the
local inhabitants of the southern territories, "many" of whom,
according to the Vietnamese records, accepted the "false" mandate. With such support behind them, the Cham troops again
moved north, attacking northern Thanh-hóa on the edge of the
Red River Delta. The resurrected Counsellor Đỗ Tử Bình moved
against them, but the Vietnamese forces simply disintegrated,
leaving the way to the capital open once more. The Chams promptly sacked the city and left, carrying off prisoners and loot.
One of the captives was the provincial official Lê Giác, a
classical scholar like his father, the Thanh-hóa Counsellor
Lê Quát. Giác predictably refused to accept the barbarian authority, unlike many of his province, and was executed, cursing
his captors, much to the satisfaction of later Confucian writt-
ers.[19]

Again Đại Việt had been drawn into the political vortex
of the eastern mainland. Yet this time incompetence at the
court and the disintegration of the outer barrier formed by
the southern provinces threatened the core of the Vietnamese
state. The resurgent Chams of Chế Bồng Nga were accomplishing
what Suryavarman II had failed to do at the height of Angkor's
power in the twelfth century: the dismantling of the Vietnamese
mandala. Indeed, Thăng-long seemed to be on the same path as
Angkor itself in these years, under attack from external forces

which manipulated feuds within the royal family and took advantage of internal strife and a lack of central control over manpower and resources.[20] Certainly, contending Vietnamese princes were prepared to obtain foreign aid in seeking the throne. Next would come a thriving regionalism that would weaken and seriously damage the Vietnamese state, similar to what would take place in Cambodia in the following centuries.

Under the impact of the repeated Cham thrusts, the authority of the Vietnamese government began to crumble. Nghệ-tông, the scholarly abdicated ruler, remained the chief figure in the state, though he appeared unable to confront the reality of the situation. Drought and famine struck in 1379 and shortly thereafter a man from the northern province of Kinh-bắc revolted and, by using "black magic", proclaimed himself king (vương). He was soon crushed, but the Cham hold on parts of the southern territories remained. At the beginning of 1380, the Chams could call on men from Tân-bình and Thuận-hóa for a raid north into Nghệ-an and Diễn-châu where prisoners and loot were taken. Next they moved again into Thanh-hóa and parts north. Later, the Vietnamese executed a man named Hồ Thuật of Diễn-châu for just such collaboration in accompanying a Cham attack.[21]

The Vietnamese persisted in their attempt to rebuild their military power. Recognizing its weakness due to dependence upon regional and local forces as well as an empty treasury, the Throne accepted a suggestion of Đỗ Tử Bình, borrowed from T'ang Chinese regulations, and levied a head tax on all males of the land. This act began to bring revenue into the capital. New officers were again selected, with the choice for the lower ranks based on merit and the command positions still going to men of privilege. Some of the latter were men who had, in infancy, shared a nurse with the young king. Lê Quý Ly reappeared at the beginning of 1379, bringing with him some of his own men such as Nguyễn Đa Phương, a close friend and son of his teacher, and the official Phạm Cự Luận of Hải-dương. Quý Ly sponsored both of them for new and higher positions, though people at the time commented that such action was like placing square pegs in round holes, a pun on the names of Phương and Luận.[22] Meanwhile, the situation in the country continued to deteriorate. Some of the money in the state treasury was transported to Mount Thiên-kiện, south of the capital at the

site of an old travel palace of Trần Thái-tông, and more was
hidden in the shrine of a Buddhist temple in the northern mountains of Lạng-sơn, all for fear that the Chams would again
burn the palace buildings. Later, in mid-1381, the sacred images
(thần-tượng) of the Trần royal tombs were taken north from
their locations in Sơn-nam province to the Great Tomb site
on Mount Yên-sinh in Hải-dương, also to escape potential dese-
cration at the hands of Cham raiders. The extremity of the
Vietnamese plight in that year may be seen in the royal order
given to the Buddhist Master of the Realm (Quốc-sư) in Kinh-
bắc province to lead his able-bodied monks from the monasteries,
as well as the "wild" ones from the mountains and forests,
against the Chams in defense of the country.[23]

The battles of these years, from 1380 to 1383, left a ravaged
countryside, at least in the region south of the capital, and
increasingly shook the system which ruled the country. As the
aristocrat Trần Nguyên Đán noted in a Sinic allusion,

> The people live like fish in boiling pots.
>
> North and east, Yen and Pan all shattered up.[24]

The Chams, like the northern barbarians in twelfth-century
China, were tearing the political system apart. Only once before, under the Mongol thrust of the previous century, had
the Vietnamese state been as seriously challenged, and then
the corps of strong princes had taken control in the state
and had steered it to victory. Now there was no such group
and the pattern of rule that had first established a strong
Vietnamese state under the Lý reached a crisis point. Power
was slipping away from the old established aristocratic families
surrounding the capital, particularly to the north and west.
Trần Nguyên Đán, a member of this élite, commented in another
poem written during these confused years, "Stealing into Heaven
in broad daylight is easier than discovering a sage king like
[the legendary Chinese emperors] Yao and Shun so as to serve
him."[25] In this situation, a new figure with a new power base
emerged. As we have seen, this man, Lê Quý Ly, gained access
to power via the aristocracy and the coup of 1370. His cousin
Nghệ-tông was his patron. Such royal favor enabled Quý Ly to
set about building his political base. He would not, however,
make his real move for power until his patron passed from the
scene in January 1395.

The Cham attack on Thanh-hóa in 1380 saw a joint campaign headed by Quý Ly and Đỗ Tử Bình, handling the sea and land forces respectively. But one of Quý Ly's commanders turned and fled. Quý Ly executed him on the spot as a warning and ordered an advance, forcing the Chams back. During the campaign, Tử Bình fell ill, leaving Quý Ly in control of the military forces and the administration of the Hải-tây region ("West of the Sea"—the southern provinces) where he executed at least one man who aided the Chams, Hồ Thuật. Tử Bình then faded from the scene as special commissioner (kinh-lược-sứ) of Lạng-sơn in the northern mountains. Two years later, the Chams again attacked Thanh-hóa from their base in Nghệ-an. Quý Ly moved against them and held the passes separating the south from the Red River Delta, posting his lieutenant and protégé, the "spirit" general Nguyễn Đa Phương, on the coast to hold his left flank. As the Chams advanced by both land and sea, destroying many Vietnamese ships in an ambush, Đa Phương put aside Quý Ly's orders and left his positions to attack. Fortunately, he inflicted a serious defeat on the Chams who fled into the mountains, were defeated again, retired to Nghệ-an, and ultimately withdrew to their homeland. When the victory was proclaimed, Đa Phương became the hero of the hour and received a promotion as preparations were being made for another attack on Champa. Men of Nghệ-an and Diễn-châu were ordered to dredge all the harbors in the Hải-tây region, presumably under Quý Ly's supervision. At the beginning of 1383, Quý Ly set out in command of a fleet of large warships, newly built, only to be turned back by a huge storm. Midyear brought Chế Bồng Nga and his troops north again, this time avoiding the passes held by the Vietnamese, outflanking them through the mountains, and coming out on the Red River Delta in Sơn-tây province, southwest of the terrified capital. Nghệ-tông ordered troops out to meet the invaders who defeated the Vietnamese with elephants and captured their commander. As Nguyễn Đa Phương took charge of Thăng-long's defenses "day and night", Nghệ-tông once again fled north across the Red River into Kinh-bắc, ignoring a scholar's plea that he stand and fight. Indeed, heroism seems to have been so lacking that a horse was the single figure worthy of acclaim. Only after a half year of plundering did the Chams withdraw.[26]

During these years of attacks and raids, the Chams continued to make special efforts to keep the Ming court in a favorable diplomatic stance. In all probability part of the loot taken from Vietnamese territory went to China as tribute with the missions of 1377 and 1378 at a time when the Ming court was most unsympathetic with the Vietnamese plight. By 1379, the Chams were in the good graces of the Hung-wu Emperor. Their mission of that year had been interfered with by the Chinese minister Hu Wei-yung, later executed ostensibly for plotting with foreign envoys, and the Chinese Throne had favorably compared Cham behavior with the "deceit" of the Javanese, granting the Cham envoys the calendar and clothes and requesting them once again to remain at peace with the Vietnamese. The raids continued, of course, but the Chams still seem to have retained the upper hand over Đại Việt in their Chinese relations. While the Hung-wu Emperor did not cease to scold the Cham king for his turbulent behavior, he never refused to accept his missions and rich tribute (in 1382, 1383, and 1384) as he did to the Vietnamese mission of 1382, rejected because of a border dispute and their "guile".[27] The Cham attacks did, however, slacken from the beginning of 1384, and Chinese feelings may have had something to do with it.

The shock of the wars and the devastation evidently led Nghệ-tông to reconsider the pattern of administration for his state, and the peace of the next few years allowed time for the state to move in a new direction, one which fit Quý Ly's purposes very well. During the months of Cham pillage at the end of 1383, the sixty-one-year-old reclusive ruler established himself in the Bảo-hòa Palace at the old Buddhist center of Phật-tích in Kinh-bắc, north of the capital, where he was to remain for the next three years. There he gathered around him a number of officials who took turns questioning him on past affairs. His answers were recorded daily and compiled into a book titled Bảo Hòa (Điện) Dư Bút [Learned writings of Bảo-hòa Palace] with an introduction by the classical scholar Đào Sư Tích. The book was intended to be used for instructing the young king. While the instructions themselves may have been for the royal family, the fact that Đào Sư Tích (who placed first in the examination of 1374) wrote the introduction demonstrates the reemergence of the classical scholar in the court.

Though the scholars had remained since the 1360s, they had done so in a very attenuated position. As during the Lý period, they were once again used merely for diplomacy and ritual while royal favor went to the aristocracy.[28] Early in 1381, a **Thái-học** examination was held. At about this time (1383-84) the general Đỗ Tử Bình posthumously received a place in the Temple of Literature, much to the disgust of the fifteenth-century Confucian historians. In the second month of the new year (1384) Nghệ-tông held another **Thái-học** examination in the nearby Buddhist temple of Vạn-phúc on Mount Tiên-du with thirty successful scholars resulting. Three months later, he took a number of other scholars into his palace there as historians (**thư-sử**). In addition, at the beginning of the following year, the registers for the civil and military officials and the attendants were again brought up to date.[29]

With this change in emphasis emerged what had been an undercurrent in the court over the past decade and a half, that is, the literary side of the courtiers and the existence of the literati. This fact became apparent over the next two years, the duration of Nghệ-tông's stay at Phật-tích. At the same time, with the king still quite young and Nghệ-tông in retreat, Quý Ly was beginning to move into a position of power and soon drew a literary response from his opponents in the court. The royal counsellor Trần Nguyên Đán, a member of the royal clan and one of the first to emerge in power under Nghệ-tông, and Prince Ngạc, the son of Nghệ-tông, both used verse to express their feelings on the matter. Nguyên Đán, recently retired to Mount Côn in northern Hải-dương, wrote a friend that what was happening at the court was clear and asked why no one was remonstrating against the situation. Prince Ngạc cryptically replied: "I [who] supported [the activities of] past years have renounced the affairs of the world./ You [who] condemned the Great House (Quý Ly) have a rare talent./ Together [we] are of a kind, old and sick./ The fields and gardens are distinguishable early; [you should] come back home." Nguyên Đán, however, was caught in the situation and decided to avoid conflict with Quý Ly and probable disaster by placing his son, Trần Mộng Dữ, in the latter's care. Quý Ly promptly married Mộng Dữ to his stepdaughter. Meanwhile the adamant Ngạc issued more poetry, this time in **nôm** ridiculing Nguyên

Đán by inference.[30]

At the same time, Nguyên Đán also placed his daughters under the literary instruction of two classical students, Nguyễn Ứng Long and Nguyễn Hán Anh. The students thereupon used nôm poetry, so the story goes, to seduce the girls and one of them became pregnant. Ứng Long fearfully lay low, but Nguyên Đán, swearing that proper rule was lacking in the state ("How is one to know right from wrong?"), excused him with a reference to a classic Han case and, despite Nghệ-tông's disapproval, gave the girls as wives to the students. The two grateful students thereafter conscientiously applied themselves to their studies and ultimately succeeded in the examinations.[31] Thus did Nguyên Đán tie his family fortunes to the rising influence of the literati class as well. Quý Ly appears to have been using his growing personal power to undercut the aristocratic position and to develop a government service that would respond to his control. The literati served his purpose well. Both Ứng Long (better known as Phi Khanh) and Hán Anh came to fill posts in his administration. Similarly, the classical scholar Hồ Tông Thốc of Diễn-châu, who had been appointed to the Hàn-lâm Academy in 1372 shortly after Quý Ly's emergence, was now, fourteen years later, made its director. A scholar of local fame, Tông Thốc was undoubtedly advanced from his service as a provincial pacifier by his ostensible clansman, Quý Ly.[32] Slowly, the graduates of the earlier examinations (those of 1374 and 1384) took posts in the capital and in provincial administration, either via Nghệ-tông's favor or Quý Ly's hand.[33]

The reemergence of the literati brought with it the new popularity of poetry writing. Aristocrats like Trần Nguyên Đán and literati like Hồ Tông Thốc compiled their poetry, some in nôm, some in Chinese, in collections of their own which accurately reflected their times.[34] Nghệ-tông, sitting in his retreat, could write, "Rain brings a torrent of sound through the crevice in the rock;/ the wind sets the shadow of the bamboo in motion on the roof of the veranda,"[35] as the political turmoil built up around him. Nguyễn Phi Khanh, composing within the quiet confines of his family home, could only say,

A leisured heart casts off a thousand cares.

A learned mind relaxes life and limb.

It's a mistake to crave and strive for things.

Follow An-jen, content to live unknown.[36]

At the same time that more men from the Buddhist region north and west of the capital were becoming classical scholars, the literati of the south appear to have taken a greater interest in the less Sinic, more indigenous aspects of their tradition, similar to the author of the Việt Điện U Linh Tập a half-century before, going beyond the limitations of Chinese-style history. While Lê Văn Hưu of Thanh-hóa a century earlier had begun his history with Ch'ao T'o (Triệu Đà) in the third century B.C., the scholars of this time produced works which brought a Sinic order to the mythic past of Vietnam and which extended this indigenous history back to a time comparable with the distant Chinese past, forming a link with Shen Nung, the Chinese god of agriculture. In the process, they appear to have drawn on T'ang period materials from China to give birth to the eighteen Hùng kings of the Hồng-bàng dynasty and their extensive land of Văn-lang. The resulting works, Đại Việt Sử Lược [Short history of Đại Việt], Trần Thế Pháp's Lĩnh Nam Trích Quái [The extraordinary beings of Ling-nan, south of the passes], and Hồ Tông Thốc's Việt Nam Thế Chí [A record of the generations of Vietnam] used both Chinese and nôm in their bestowal of a legitimate past on their country. In addition, Tông Thốc wrote a work titled Việt Sử Cương Mục [Text and commentaries of Vietnamese history], undoubtedly modeled after Chu Hsi's moralistic Kang Mu whence it took its name.[37] Gradually the regional élite cultures, as represented by Tông Thốc of Thanh-hóa and Thế Pháp of Sơn-tây, were becoming fused.

Interestingly, a rapprochement occurring with China simultaneously with these literati developments was due to the quality of Vietnamese Buddhism. Two eunuchs, Nguyễn Tông Đạo and Nguyễn Toán, were sent to Nanking where the Ming Hung-wu Emperor made them imperial attendants. First Tông Đạo told the emperor that the monks of the south were better at explicating religious ritual than their northern brethren, perhaps in response to an inquiry on his own name ("Revere the Way"). Consequently, the Chinese sent a mission to Đại Việt in 1385 seeking twenty more monks. Tông Đạo had also boasted in China that the fruits of the south were much more delicious and of a far greater variety. Thus, in 1386, another mission came to Vietnam seeking

these fabled southern fruits. Cuttings were sent, but they
could not survive the cold on the return trip and died. This
renewed interest in the south was, in reality, due to the Ming
conquest of Yünnan. In 1384, the Chinese requested rice to
support their campaign there, and in 1386 they petitioned for
access to the roads to Champa, a force of fifty elephants,
and the permission to establish stations from Nghệ-an to transport the supply of rice to Yünnan.[38]

Nothing seems to have come of the situation, however, as
the Vietnamese remained absorbed in internal politics. In March
of 1387, Nghệ-tông returned to the capital from his retreat
in the Bảo-hòa Palace at Phật-tích. The following month, Quý
Ly was appointed chief minister (**đồng-bình-chưởng-sự**) and given
a sword and a banner respectively inscribed with the phrases
"Perfect Talent in Military and Civil Affairs" and "Sovereign
and Servant Together in Virtue". Quý Ly wrote a poem in **nôm**
to thank the retired ruler. Now enjoying a secure base of support, Quý Ly finally began to bring his lieutenants into positions of power. In 1388, his stepson Trần Đỗ became chief of
the palace, and his younger brother Quý Tỳ seems to have emerged
as a key figure in the diffuse administrative apparatus. Other
supporters took posts in the palace and the administration.[39]

By September, as a comet was recorded in the west, anti-
Quý Ly intrigue began to surface in the court. The unyielding
Prince Ngạc joined forces with the young ruler Phế-đế to make
charges of strong favoritism on the part of Nghệ-tông for his
maternal kinsman Quý Ly and reckless use of Quý Ly in public
office. The two members of the royal family felt that matters
might soon be getting out of hand. Lê Á Phu, a legal official,
had warned Ngạc about Quý Ly and sent a secret memorial to
Phế-đế seeking Quý Ly's death. The young ruler's tutor, son
of a recently removed Counsellor, managed to leak the conspira-
cy; Quý Ly found out about it and, on the urging of Nguyễn
Đa Phương, was about to go to Mount Đại-lại in northern Thanh-
hóa (site of his future capital) to wait matters out. Caught
off guard, he thought it best to seek refuge in the area of
his greatest strength, but Phạm Cự Luận advised against such
flight ("Once out of the capital, you'll lose touch!") and
urged a concerted effort to bring Nghệ-tông to their side in
the strife, thus "turning calamity into blessing". Quý Ly agreed

and set out to destroy Phế-đế.[40]

Following Cự Luận's advice, Quý Ly began by working on Nghệ-tông's strong feelings over the execution of his favorite son, Prince Húc, for aiding the Chams seven years before.[41] Nghệ-tông's hatred was directed towards his nephew Phế-đế, and the two rulers did not get along well. By humbly seeking advice from Nghệ-tông, Quý Ly exploited the differences which separated the two and urged the old ruler to rid himself of Phế-đế and to place his own youngest son, Prince Ngung, on the throne. Four months later, Nghệ-tông feigned to be leaving for a visit to the royal tombs at Yên-sinh early one morning, when he order-ed courtiers to summon the young ruler for a conference on state affairs. The king rose immediately and proceeded to the conference without eating. On his arrival, Nghệ-tông declared, "The royal prince (đại-vương) comes!", purposefully not address-ing him by his kingly title, and sent him to confinement in a Buddhist temple. In a palace announcement, the reason given was that "officials" controlled the Throne and Phế-đế's virtue was inconsistent. "Petty men" like the cousins Lê Á Phu and Lê Dữ Nghi were alleged to have influenced him against meritori-ous officials and had thus shaken the foundations of the state. Phế-đế was demoted to prince and, through Quý Ly's machinations, Prince Ngung was chosen to succeed him. Nghệ-tông had apparently wanted his elder son, Prince Ngạc, to take the throne, but Quý Ly, while publicly praising Ngạc, managed to sow doubt in the old king's mind and maneuvered for Ngạc to turn down the position. At once, five generals, among whom were three who grew up with Phế-đế and were appointed to their posts by him, prepared to strike in his defense, but the dethroned king merely said, "Disband the troops." Unable to rebel against his uncle, Phế-đế led his supporters to their deaths. He himself was taken to his palace and strangled. The generals and some officials, including Lê Á Phu, were executed.[42]

In the following months, the ten-year-old Prince Ngung became the ruler later known as Thuận-tông (1388-98), taking the same year as the first of his reign in the usual non-Confucian way. Prince Ngạc, having been outmaneuvered for the throne, became a royal prince (đại-vương) on Quý Ly's urging. Ming envoys arrived with recognition from Nanking at a moment of pique with Champa, only to find Phế-đế dead. Quý Ly promptly married his eldest daughter to the new ruler and sent his brother Quý Tỳ to bury Phế-đế. Moreover, the powerful minister continued to place his own men in high civil and military posts, specifically moving to take over the Secret Council by placing Phạm Cự Luận on it and by following Cự Luận's advice on who else should be appointed to the same. The latter included Cự Luận's younger brother and seven others, two of whom were also appointed generals.[43] Quý Ly thus began to gain control of the aristocratic structure restored in the coup of 1370.

By the middle of 1389, however, the series of revolts and invasions began again. In the fall, a Thanh-hóa man declared himself to be the Linh Đức Prince (Phế-đế's final title) and gained a great response from the local population before government troops forced him to flee. The following month, another Thanh-hóa man, farther south, gathered a band of raiders and took the classical Chinese name of Điền Ky, Prince of Lỗ (T'ien Chi, a general of Ch'i in the Warring States period). In all likelihood taking advantage of the resulting chaos, the Chams struck north into Thanh-hóa a month later. Quý Ly moved against them, again fell into a trap, and was badly defeated. He quickly returned to the capital for aid, leaving Phạm Khả Vĩnh and Nguyễn Đa Phương to hold the invaders. Đa Phương and Khả Vĩnh devised a ruse of their own to get the Vietnamese troops out of the trap, abandoning their heavy equipment. Meanwhile, Quý Ly asked Nghệ-tông for the royal warships, but Nghệ-tông said no, undoubtedly because he preferred to keep them in defense of the capital. Quý Ly thereupon asked to be relieved of his command. Chế Bồng Nga was once more heading for the capital and panic reigned among the Vietnamese. All seemed lost and it appeared only a matter of time before the Chams reoccupied the country. At this point, political discord led to the familiar pattern of defection from the Vietnamese ranks. A younger brother of the late Phế-đế went over to the Chams with all his men in order to avenge his brother's death. Immediately thereafter other members of the royal clan were promoted to high positions, perhaps to keep them from leaving as well.

Nguyễn Đa Phương then returned from the south, singing his own praises and Quý Ly's faults. Quý Ly responded in kind, blaming the entire debacle on Đa Phương and seeking his dismissal. Nghệ-tông tended to take the charge lightly in this hour

of crisis, but Quý Ly, no doubt badly stung by his former protégé's attack, charged that Đa Phương might easily go over to
the Chams or the Chinese ("to release a tiger brings disaster")
and asked for the death penalty. An unchastened Đa Phương replied, "My talent has led to honor and now leads to death;
I only regret that I did not die in battle," and disappeared
from the scene.[44]

As disaffection reigned in the capital, disintegration continued in the countryside. In the last month of the year, a
Buddhist monk rose in revolt in Sơn-tây province just west
of Thăng-long, gathered many around him with his preaching
and proclaimed himself king. His Counsellors (**Hành-khiển**) were
two other men from Sơn-tây, just beyond the West Lake (Tây-
hồ) on the outskirts of the capital. Bringing together their
"vagabond" (unregistered) followers, they formed three armies
and attacked the capital. The two monarchs, Nghệ-tông and the
young Thuận-tông, once more fled across the river into Kinh-
bắc, leaving the city to the monk and his forces who occupied
it for three days before returning to camp in Sơn-tây. A general
from Thanh-hóa who had been fighting the troops of the Cham
general La Ngai to the south withdrew, making his way through
the dried-up winter streambeds of northwest Sơn-nam by digging
canals for his warships, and smashed the rebellion, killing
its leaders and dispersing their followers. During this episode
the Cham forces maintained themselves on the Hoàng River on
the southern edge of the delta.

Finally, the Vietnamese, with great luck, were able to in-
flict a heavy defeat on the Chams in February 1390. The fortune
came in the shape of a disaffected Cham officer of low rank
who joined the Vietnamese and pointed out Chế Bồng Nga's ship.
When the Chams and Vietnamese rebels began a probe in force,
the great Cham king was killed and his troops fell back in
disarray. The rebel Vietnamese prince saw that all was lost
and, taking the Cham ruler's head, fled back to his countrymen,
only to be killed. The head and the news were promptly sent
to the fearful septuagenarian Nghệ-tông who was overjoyed to
look upon the countenance of his adversary of two decades and
capped the occasion with a classical Chinese allusion. La Ngai
retreated to the main force, cremated his ruler's body, and
returned directly to the Cham capital, Vijaya, by forced march,

using his elephant units as a rear guard. Upon reaching Vijaya, he proclaimed himself king. Chế Bồng Nga's two sons fled north to join the Vietnamese.[45]

The disappearance of the Cham threat brought to the fore the task of reestablishing royal power throughout the realm. The southern provinces in particular, with their rebellions and support for the Chams, had fallen away from the capital. Thuận-hóa and Tân-bình, closest to Cham territory, had seen many of their people actively aid the Cham efforts; the men of Nghệ-an farther north held a double allegiance; and Thanh-hóa, a no-man's-land between the two contending forces, had been the scene of numerous revolts against Thắng-long. Even the hill peoples were restive and could not be controlled. Though the court appointed a pacifier for the two southernmost provinces, it decided that rule from a distance would not be effective and designated two local leaders ("bravos"), Phan Mãnh and Phạm Căng, to bring the local populace under Vietnamese control. Mãnh in particular was very familiar with the Cham situation (probably having served with the Chams before) and had helped rout them in their flight. Nghệ-tông appointed him to an army post, promoted him rapidly, and eventually gave him command of the Vietnamese border troops in Tân-bình and Thuận-hóa. Over the following two years, officials, including the successful examination candidate La Tu, were appointed prefects (**tri-phủ**) in Nghệ-an and Thanh-hóa, La Tu going to the latter, his home province. For the first time since the Mongol wars over a century earlier, officials of the central administration were serving at a local level in an ordinary capacity.[46]

With peace finally brought to his realm, Nghệ-tông set out to put affairs in order. The month after the great victory, the young king Thuận-tông led a royal tour to the tombs of his ancestors in Sơn-nam and Hải-dương and performed ceremonies there, no doubt to report the favorable events and to settle the tombs following the removal of the tablets almost nine years before. Two months later, more forbidden names were declared for earlier kings and queens, and local spirits were given their formal titles. Thus the state of Đại Việt regained its spatial and temporal order. Later, however, when officials attempted to dig up the treasures buried for safekeeping at

Mount Thiên-kiện in 1379, they found the entrances blocked
by cave-ins and had to abandon them. Two military heroes, Trần
Khát Chân and Phạm Khả Vĩnh, were honored and brought into
the aristocracy as marquis (hầu), while the two officers who
had presented Chế Bồng Nga's head were rewarded together with
others who had served meritoriously. One of the late rebel
prince's younger brothers was given a high counsellor post
because he was "not at peace with himself", presumably for
fear that he too might go over to the Chams.[47]

During the early 1390s, both the Chams and the Vietnamese
worked to assure control in their own territories, and a new
balance remained to be struck on the east coast of the Southeast
Asian mainland. The Chams, due to their usurpation, lost the
favor they had held with the Ming court and the Hung-wu Emperor.
When La Ngai sought recognition in 1391, the Chinese refused
his tribute and accused him of "assassinating his ruler". The
Vietnamese, however, do not appear to have gained by the Cham
loss of favor. A Vietnamese mission was rejected in 1390 and
would be again in 1394. The old Chinese emperor seems to have
become weary of dealing with the troublesome barbarians of
the south and generally cut off their tribute missions. Some
consideration was given in the Vietnamese court to changing
its foreign policy also. Nghệ-tông had taken to visiting the
elderly and ill Counsellor Trần Nguyên Đán in his retreat and
asking about both his health and his views on what policy to
follow in the future. Nguyên Đán, avoiding the internal situation and the question of Quý Ly, took up the call for a Sinic-
style pattern of foreign relations: "[I] wish the Throne to
pay reverence to Ming China as a father and to love Champa
as a son, then our country will have no trouble." He died before
the end of the year, leaving the aged Nghệ-tông to adopt a
policy denounced twenty years earlier. Quý Ly, however, was
in charge and the old Vietnamese policy towards Champa continued. Moral denunciation by the Vietnamese of the Cham usurpation
was nowhere apparent. The two Cham refugee princes were well
received and taken into the aristocracy as nobles, and the
fear persisted that Vietnamese nobles would flee to Champa.
The two courts were thus equals, neither viewing the other
as culturally inferior. Politics was another question, and
in 1391 Quý Ly led troops to reconnoiter the border of Hóa-

châu, establish military units, and repair the fortifications
there. He sent Thanh-hóa troops to probe into Cham territory.
The Chams ambushed and destroyed the force, capturing the commander, though he later escaped. Quý Ly executed thirty of
the officers responsible, but spared the commander on his return
before leading the army back to the north.[48]

The powerful minister had business in the capital. The forces
opposing him were growing weak and could be destroyed. Soon
after the victory over the Chams, six members of the aristocracy
had already been removed. Most of them were in the royal clan,
including three who were promoted immediately after the rebel
prince's flight to the Chams. Two of these men drowned attempting to escape, while one, Nguyễn Khang, fled to China, later
claiming to be the Trần ruler Thiên Bình. Others were spared.
The month after Quý Ly's return from the south, the royal prince
Ngạc, driven to distraction, fled the capital, going east first
by land, then by ship, to an outpost near the coast in An-quảng
province. The people there, however, refused him aid. The prince
was captured by a pursuing general and killed on secret orders
from Quý Ly. On his return to the court, the general told Nghệ-
tông that his son had been killed, because of his cruelty,
by the very people from whom he had sought refuge. Later, the
old king, feeling remorseful, began to ask who had been responsible. The general panicked and committed suicide.

Some months afterward a discussion about the overall situation took place among the generals on the southern border in
Hóa-châu. One of them, the ex-local "bravo" Phan Mãnh, stated:
"Heaven cannot have two suns; the people cannot have two rulers
[the true king Nghệ-tông and the false power holder Quý Ly]."
Another officer concurred, complaining about the fear people
had of speaking out. A number of officers, including Đặng Tất
of Nghệ-an and Hoàng Hối Khanh of Thanh-hóa (the latter a degree
holder), secretly informed Quý Ly of the conversation. The
powerful minister arbitrarily executed the two officers for
subversion and promoted Tất and Hối Khanh. A censor, appointed
while Quý Ly was in power, had not reported the matter and
was chided by Quý Ly in verse for his lapse. The year 1392
brought the removal of another member of the royal clan, Trần
Nhật Chương, for plotting to kill Quý Ly. This time Nghệ-tông
ordered the execution, for reasons of "perverse thinking".

Two months later, one official, on hearing Nghệ-tông's plea
for "straight words" during a major drought, seized the opportunity to point out the extent of Quý Ly's power and what the
people were saying about him. Nghệ-tông merely handed the memorial over to Quý Ly and the official disappeared. Meanwhile
Quý Ly continued to promote his control of the government.
Phạm Cự Luận became head of the Secret Council, and two other
lieutenants, Hà Đức Lân and Lê Cảnh Kỳ, were named Counsellors.[49]

Having established his personal power, Quý Ly slowly began
to concentrate on the development of a more tightly run state.
At the end of 1392, the Throne set up river and patrol stations
in all regions, with three, four, or five officers in each
depending on the locality's strategic importance, in order
to control bandits and invaders. The Throne also ordered that
all soldiers and civilians who shirked their obligations were
to be fined and branded, with the headman in the locality losing
his head and his land.[50] For the first time in Vietnamese history
we see a strong attempt being made to counter the ebb and flow
of a naturally fluid society. The Chinese method of tying village residents down to their localities and of holding their
village chiefs responsible for them thus appeared on the Vietnamese scene.

At this point, Quý Ly also composed a fourteen-section statement titled "Enlightening the Way" (**Minh Đạo**) in which he brought
his own brand of classical Chinese learning to the Vietnamese
state. The Duke of Chou, himself responsible for aiding a young
ruler and establishing a strong state in Chinese antiquity,
held the primary place among the sainted ones of Quý Ly's cult,
and Confucius was honored as the foremost teacher of this philosophy. **The Analects** by Confucius, however, was declared to
have "four dubious places": one when the Master visited the
lewd wife of the Duke of Wei; another when the state of Ch'en
(Trần) ran out of provisions; and twice when the rebels Kung-
shan Fu-jao and Pi Hsi summoned the Master and he was willing
to go. The ninth-century Chinese scholar Han Yü was declared
to have "plundered the learning" (**đạo nho**), a T'ang term for
the act of achieving the wisdom of the former kings, while
seven later scholars were accused of laxity in their official
service and constant plagiarism in their work, despite the
breadth of their knowledge. The great Chu Hsi was listed last

here. Quý Ly thus disposed of all post-T'ang Chinese thought
and the Neo-Confucian orthodoxy then beginning to reign in
China. Moreover, by installing the Duke of Chou in the primary
position, facing south, with Confucius to his left, facing
west, Quý Ly was placing the man of action over the man of
thought. Nghệ-tông praised the composition and had it promulgated throughout the realm. On the other hand, two of the top
Vietnamese scholars, Đào Sư Tích (first in the examination
of 1374) and Đoàn Xuân Lôi (first in that of 1384), objected
to the new ideology. Though Sư Tích was a Counsellor and had
helped Nghệ-tông in the compilation of his thoughts and Xuân
Lôi was a member of the National College, the latter was exiled
and the former demoted.[51]

Given his old patron's support, Quý Ly was not deterred
by this response and held examinations for both classical scholars and low officials at the start of the following year (1393).
We may presume that the new doctrine was adopted throughout.
Later Nghệ-tông ordered the painting of portraits showing the
great ministers of Chinese and Vietnamese history and the monarchs they served—for example, the Duke of Chou aiding King
Wen[52]—and presented them to Quý Ly to inspire the administration
of the state. No doubt the old ruler meant to flatter his powerful minister by implying that Quý Ly too (not to mention himself) belonged in such company. Yet soon thereafter Nghệ-tông
saw his deceased brother Duệ-tông in a dream leading his troops
back from Champa and wrote a song about it in which he explicitly mentioned Quý Ly in a none too favorable light: "Inside,
there is only the Red Monkey Marquis [Quý Ly]./ Diligently,
he slanders the White Cock Tower [Nghệ-tông]./ The mouth of
the king [these two characters combined make the Chinese charac-
ter for "state"] has already determined the gains and losses
of the matter, which are no [longer] before but behind [i.e.,
in the past]."[53] Nghệ-tông himself elucidated the subtle meaning
and thereby made known the remorse he was beginning to feel
over the loss of his power. Yet, following the administration
of the blood oath on the fourth day of the fourth month, Nghệ-
tông summoned his cousin Quý Ly to the palace and calmly expressed his confidence in him: "The chief minister's own clan
and the affairs of the state have become one in order [for
it] to be in charge of them. Now the power of the state is

in decline [and] I am a very old man. After [I] die, [if you] can aid the officials, then aid them; [if matters] of public service are obscure, then [you yourself should] approve them."[54] Eight months later, in January 1395, the old monarch passed away at the age of seventy-three and was buried in the royal tombs of Yên-sinh.

III. QUÝ LY IN POWER

Having thus received the old ruler's benediction, Quý Ly thanked
him with tears in his eyes and swore to heaven and earth that
if he were unable to achieve what Nghệ-tông asked, let heaven
resist him. But again he justified the execution of Phế-đế
and, after the funeral, Quý Ly set his campaign in full swing
to transform the Vietnamese state. Through 1393, there had
been a series of natural catastrophes—drought, a violent storm
of wind and rain, an earthquake and flood, and finally a plague
of insects—yet there was no sign of any social unrest in the
countryside. Quý Ly was able not only to build his political
support well, moving his supporters into positions of power
and disposing of his enemies, but also began to control the
outlying area as well as the capital. The basis of his political
support was essentially unique in Vietnamese history up until
this time. Though consisting of anyone who offered his loyalty,
Quý Ly's strength was based in the south, the region whence
his family had arrived in the capital. While the old aristocracy
came from the capital region and the area north and west of
it, and the Trần family rose in Hải-dương and Sơn-nam with
many of its members now opposing Quý Ly, for the first time
Thanh-hóa and Nghệ-an men were coming to power through political
maneuvers. A special case in point was the naming of Hồ Cương,
a native of Diễn-châu, as commander of an army in January 1393.
The **History** states: "Quý Ly furtively sought out the descendants
of the Hồ family [and] thought about taking back the old name
of his family" as he was later to do. As early as 1372, men
from the south bearing the Hồ surname gained positions, perhaps

37

a result of Quý Ly's effort to renew his knowledge of his family's heritage on his trips into the south. Men like Hồ Cường
became intimate associates of the powerful minister.[1]

Quý Ly received his start from his cousin's coup of 1370;
he married into the royal family; one of his female cousins
married another cousin, Duệ-tông; and his eldest daughter married a third cousin, Thuận-tông. His step-children also served
his purposes. One step-son, Trần Đỗ, was an official in the
palace and a step-daughter helped to form an alliance with
the old but powerful Trần Nguyên Đán by marrying his son and
binding his family into the new political developments. (Another
link was the official Nguyễn Phi Khanh, who was also married
to a child of Nguyễn Đán, and his famous son Nguyễn Trãi).
In addition, both Quý Ly's old and new families gave support,
the former coming from his younger brother Quý Tỳ and his eldest
sons Nguyên Trừng and Hán Thương; the latter from the family
ground of Diễn-châu noted above. By drawing on this southern
branch, Quý Ly no doubt derived support from the discontent
smoldering there due to the disruptions of the Cham wars and
central government activities. No longer would men like Hồ
Thuật of Diễn-châu have to follow the Chams; instead the service
of Quý Ly offered them opportunity. Eventually the powerful
minister would develop northwestern Thanh-hóa as his base.

Quý Ly's chief lieutenants, however, were those men who
had joined him early in the capital, especially the son of
his old teacher, Nguyễn Đa Phương, and the Hải-dương native
Phạm Cự Luận. Though Đa Phương's greater military ability led
him to break with his patron and be destroyed, Cự Luận continued
as Quý Ly's chief advisor through the 1390s. On his counsel,
Quý Ly brought Cự Luận's younger brother Phiếm, Đỗ Mẫn, Nguyễn
Cảnh Chân, and five others onto the Secret Council, presumably
using it as a base of operations. Other officials performed
services for, and eventually joined, Quý Ly's developing political force. These included the graduate and official from Thanh-
hóa, Hoàng Hối Khanh, and the southerner Đặng Tất. Others,
such as the generals Trần Khát Chân of Thanh-hóa and Phạm Khả
Vĩnh of southern Sơn-nam, did not mind receiving Quý Ly's favor
as long as he was loyal to the Throne. Similarly, good officials
like Hà Đức Lân and Lương Nguyên Bưu could be trusted to help
Quý Ly in the development of a strong state under Trần rule.

In the year following Nghệ-tông's death, these supporters began to move higher in the state structure. The loyal Hoàng Hối Khanh was first placed in charge of the region to the west of the capital, no doubt in order to control this strategic location during the change of power, before being brought back into the capital. Quý Ly established the Thượng-lâm Court (tự) and gave his eldest son, Nguyên Trừng, the chief position therein. Phạm Cự Luận took on military duties as well as being head of the Secret Council. Hà Đức Lân, already a Counsellor, received the full title of **Nhập-nội Hành-khiển** and took a post in the Chancellery (**Môn-hạ-sảnh**), while Lương Nguyên Bửu of Tuyên-quang province in the northern mountains (descendant of a Lý prince and married to a Trần) also became a Counsellor and was placed in control of the royal clan (as **đồng-tri đại-tông-chính**), thus revoking the clan's autonomy.[2]

Quý Ly went beyond merely relying upon direct control by his kin and his lieutenants. With the late Nghệ-tông's help, he drew up the image of himself as a Duke of Chou, first serving his royal kin as a dedicated and loyal caretaker of the state, then guiding the state as regent during the infancy of the young ruler following the death of the old king. Even though he faced internal opposition and jealousy, Quý Ly, like the Duke of Chou, was determined to carry out the wishes of the old king and to put the state in order. Indeed, **The Book of History (Shu Ching)** states regarding the young king, "Let him not slight the aged and experienced, for it may be said of them that they have studied the virtuous conduct of our ancient worthies, and still more, that they have matured their plans in the light of Heaven", and the Duke of Chou himself told the young king, "If you sincerely and fully carry out the course of your correct father, and follow exactly my example, there will be no venturing to disregard your orders." Thus entrenched in the old testament of the Chinese Classics, whereby the Duke of Chou stressed the need for paying attention to faithful ministers, Quý Ly utilized the ancient Chinese pattern to justify his control. Moreover, the Duke of Chou had built a new royal city as Quý Ly himself was soon to do.[3]

Meanwhile, shortly after the old king's death, Quý Ly struck at his immediate enemies. In the first month of 1395, he executed a general and Prince Sư Hiền's son, both members of the royal clan, for constantly speaking, during the mourning period for Nghệ-tông, of Trần Nhật Chương's plot to kill the powerful minister three years before. Sử Hiền himself escaped death by claiming to be deaf. As the old law of the dynasty required, the general's surname (and presumably that of his descendants) became Mai. At least one official fell victim to the situation as well.[4]

Throughout 1395, Quý Ly continued to rise to even greater heights, officially becoming the central figure in the government.[5] A royal proclamation appeared ordering Quý Ly to move into a residence to the right of the Secretariat and the Censorate. From his position within the court supervising his cousin, the seventeen-year-old Thuận-tông, Quý Ly began to bring the Vietnamese state in the direction he wished—a direction seemingly determined by the weakness of the state under the Cham pressures of the 1380s and by the new intellectual pattern (an amalgamation of indigenous and classical Chinese thought) of that decade. His first move was to have a chapter from **The Book of History** translated into nôm (or as the Vietnamese **History** puts it, **quốc-ngữ**, the "national language") so as "to teach the officials" as well as the young king. Titled "Against Luxurious Ease", the text tells how the famed Duke of Chou (Quý Ly) instructed the young ruler on the diligence required to run a state.[6] Implied here was again the idea that, by following the counsel of such a minister, a long rule would result; to quote the Duke of Chou:

> Oh! I have heard it said that, in the case of the ancients, [their ministers discharged their functions] in warning and admonishing them, in protecting and [loving] them, in teaching and instructing them... If you will not listen to this [and profit by it], your ministers will imitate you, and so the correct laws of the former kings, both small and great, will be changed and disordered.

The young ruler was to be "grave, humble, reverential, and fearful," a passive example for his people to follow. The text of this chapter ended in the Duke's words, "Oh! you king who have succeeded to the throne, make a study of these things."[7]

At the same time that Quý Ly was stepping into the ancient role of the Duke of Chou, he was fending off military and cultural requests from the China of his own day. Ming forces were pressing to gain control over tribal groups on the southern frontier of their domain (specifically in Kuangsi), and they sought aid to the extent of fifty thousand men, fifty elephants, and half a million piculs of rice from the Vietnamese. The Vietnamese court, however, was secretly told by the Chinese envoy that, while the rice was badly needed, the Chinese intended to seize any envoys sent. Therefore, no men or elephants were granted and only a bit of rice was deposited at the border. Soon after this mission, another appeared which again sought Buddhist monks and, in addition, masseuses and eunuchs. Only a few were sent. Interestingly, as the Vietnamese élite was becoming more and more conversant with classical Chinese thought, China was drawing upon older, more indigenous aspects of Vietnamese culture. In doing so, the Chinese maintained a strong sense of ambiguity regarding Vietnamese cultural identity and the relationship of Vietnam to the East Asian cultural sphere.[8]

In 1395 Quý Ly consolidated his power and hold on the government following the death of his patron, and in the years thereafter began his effort to restructure the state. In his guise as the Duke of Chou, he first concentrated on the general pattern of the state; later would come the implementation of his plans. His approach seems to have been one of a classic Chinese scholar, putting aside more recent Neo-Confucian developments. He had twice (in 1392 and 1395) stressed the Five Classics over the Four Books and had a tendency to downgrade post-T'ang learning. Indeed, by the end of 1396, he had composed a work in **nôm** titled "The Meaning of the **Shih Ching** (Book of Poetry)" in which, to quote the Vietnamese **History**, "[he] did not follow the collected writings of Chu Hsi" but rather his own inclinations, and he ordered Buddhist nuns to instruct the men and women of the palace in his teachings.[9]

In reordering and setting right the state, Quý Ly wished to demarcate the categories in the social order and to maintain these categories as his cousin had done two decades before. Already in 1395, he forbade officials to wear broad-sleeved garments, allowing only narrow sleeves. A year later, he set out the entire pattern of the state by means of dress regulations. Military and civil ranks one to four had their own colors —purple, dark red, "fish" red, and green respectively; ranks

five to seven wore blue; eight and nine, black; and those with
no rank, white. Civil officials, the royal clan, military officers, the aristocracy, and the Censorate were all set apart
by different types of cloth. The common people were not to
use utensils which were gilded or painted vermilion, nor were
they to spend time on ritual. Quý Ly also ordered an examination
of army ranks and the purification of Buddhist doctrine. All
monks not yet fifty had to return to regular life, while civilians who possessed a thorough understanding of the doctrine
were to become officials in the Buddhist hierarchy (head of
the church, palace officer, Taoist temple officer, and Buddhist
temple officer). The remainder of the monks were to be temple
servants.[10] Thus Quý Ly acted to control the younger elements
of the Buddhist world and the Buddhist structure itself.

Quý Ly also reinstituted the classical examinations, establishing a fixed pattern for them, in what appears to have been
a more complete rendition than ever before attempted in Vietnam.
First he put aside the initial test of dictation in the old
Chinese style (ku-wen); whether he utilized nôm and the Vietnamese intellectual style developed in the previous decade is
difficult to say. Provincial examinations (hương-thí) were
to be held one year with the capital examination (hội-thí)
the following year. District and other examinations were probably considered unnecessary, and yearly intervals were not dis-
closed. The pattern of these Vietnamese examinations differed
from that set up by the Hung-wu Emperor in China first in 1370,
and finally in 1384. Where the Yüan and Ming had three fields
in their examinations, the Vietnamese had four. Both the Chinese
and the Vietnamese examinations started with the explication
of philosophical writings, but where the Ming had a large section on the Four Books and stressed the Neo-Confucian commentaries of Chu Hsi and the Ch'eng brothers, it appears that
Quý Ly was concerned only with the Five Classics since no mention was made of the Four Books. In the second field, the Vietnamese scholars were to write poetry, both T'ang fu and the
old style, while their Chinese counterparts composed, in addition to poetry, various types of edicts and orders (this the
Vietnamese did in their third field using Han and T'ang styles).
The final field for each was an extended essay on a particular
situation slected from the Classics or the Histories. The suc-

cessful Vietnamese scholars then had a final practical essay
to determine their rank in the ultimate results.[11] Quý Ly's
style of examination, though not actually put into effect for
another four years, did reflect the inclusion of poetry (the
major Vietnamese literary vehicle) and an emphasis on the Five
Classics rather than on the Four Books of the Neo-Confucians.

The classical orientation of the new regime did not, however,
put aside the basic approach of the Vietnamese court to its
neighbors, that of cultural relativism and forced political
submission. In September 1396 Quý Ly, still striving to defeat
the Chams, sent the general Trần Tùng to attack Champa. Before
returning Tùng was able to capture one of the Cham generals,
Bố Đông. Back at Thăng-long, Bố Đông was generously received,
given a Vietnamese name, and appointed general in the Vietnamese
forces. A year later, another Cham general and his younger
brother fled to Vietnam with their entire families and were
also renamed and given military commands. The latter two were
sent back to the southern border territory of Hóa-châu "to
resist Champa"[12] and later became bulwarks of the Vietnamese
defense in the south. Quý Ly's classical learning was thus
meant essentially for internal development, being in accord
with neither the Neo-Confucianism of Ming China nor with the
foreign relations arguments of earlier Vietnamese literati.
Vietnam, though it had begun to integrate Chinese classical
learning into its own patterns, was still far from being a
"little China".

For Lê Quý Ly, 1396 was the year in which he operated within
the capital and established the patterns for his state. Only
in the following years would these patterns be implemented
in the countryside. An example of this may be seen in the single
economic act taken by him before mid-1397—the order for a
system of paper currency in seven denominations. This act,
apparently borrowed from China, could be undertaken in Thăng-
long. It required the people to exchange their metal cash for
the new money and charged that counterfeiters would be put
to death and their property confiscated by the state. The exchange was to be prompted by offering a profit of twenty per
cent for those who would make the exchange, while the splitting
up or private hoarding of strings of cash was forbidden. All
cash was to be collected within the capital or at the regional

administrative offices.[13] What Quý Ly had in mind is hard to say. There is no evidence of any reserve being maintained to stabilize the new currency (unless the collected cash acted in such a capacity), nor are the full results of the attempt known. Perhaps this act marks the moment when Quý Ly began to undercut the autonomy and economic clout of the rich local powers of the Red River Delta. By insisting on the use of paper currency and on the exchange of all metal cash, Quý Ly could gain knowledge of their wealth as well as some measure of control over it.

Finally, during the first months of 1397, Quý Ly was ready to act more fully in this direction, moving away from mere pronouncements in the capital to ensure their implementation in the countryside. Though his supporters were undecided and his chief Counsellor, Phạm Cự Luận, argued against it, Quý Ly had already made up his mind to begin the construction of his own base of power, placing it in Thanh-hóa, a location farther south than at any other time in Vietnamese history. One member of the Secret Council made an earnest plea against the project, stating:

> In olden times, [when] the Chou and the Wei [in China] moved their capitals, it was seen as having been unfortunate. Today the land of Long-đỗ ["Dragon's Belly", meaning the Đại-la or Thăng-long area], [with] Mount Tản-viên standing high and the Lô and Nhị rivers running deep, lies flat and spacious. Since the kings and princes of old opened up their domain and established the state, there has never been a case of one who did not take [this land] as [the place where] his roots lay, deep and firm. Let us be in accord with the earlier situations. [We] have humbled and killed the Mongols; [we] have taken the heads of the Cham invaders. Think on these a moment [and] consider the indestructible [literally, 'hard as rock'] nature of [our] country. The borderlands of An-tôn [in northwest Thanh-hóa], [on the contrary], are closed in and miserable, [lying as they do] at the end of the rivers and the beginning of the mountains. It is a rebellious area, unable to be ruled, whose men may be trusted to be dangerous. There is an old saying which states, "Live in virtue; do not live in danger."

Quý Ly refused to listen to this paean of faith in the Red River Delta, a plea which in all probability reflected the basic feeling of the old Vietnamese aristocracy for their home-land and their distrust of the outer areas. Later, on coming across the official's name and recalling the old saying, Quý Ly put him aside and refused to use him.[14]

By building his citadel in northwestern Thanh-hóa, Quý Ly moved away from the Trần aristocratic center in the Red River Delta and toward as close a regional base as he possessed-- the southern territory of his ancestors, a territory still in the process of being populated. He had already sent his loyal follower Hồ Cường of Diễn-châu out as provincial officer (đai-tri-châu) in the latter's home territory. Now Quý Ly dele-gated the president of the Ministry of Civil Service to go to Thanh-hóa to examine the site for the fortress and to build it. The official was also to dig a moat, to establish a shrine (miếu) and an altar to the local spirits (xã), and to open up the local roads. This place up in the hills was to be the new capital. The work was completed by April in the general Vietnamese tradition of such construction; to quote Louis Beza-cier, "... the plan of the principal work always takes the form of a regular quadrangle with neither bastions nor corner salients, in front of which there was always raised, at a great-er or lesser distance, a first line of defense whose outline was generally very irregular." Laid out in a huge square, five hundred meters on a side, and oriented almost north-south, the walls of the citadel consisted of thick earthen ramparts covered with freestone. At the base of the walls was a strong double foundation, each about a meter thick, made of local rock. Much of the earth for the walls was probably dug out of the wide and deep moat surrounding the citadel. About a kilometer away lay the irregular outer citadel.[15]

The massiveness of the construction seems to reflect the degree to which Quý Ly was attempting to thrust central power and control throughout Vietnamese territory. Each wall had a great gate built in stone masonry, with the southern wall having a huge triple gate, its central vault slightly higher than those of the other two. Some of the blocks in these gates weighed about sixteen tons, being no less than seven meters in length and one to one and a half meters thick. With their slight overhang and heavy wooden doors, the massive gates stood over the roads which were paved with flagstone. On the terraces topping the gates were Chinese-style pavilions for the soldiers on guard. Directly south of the southern gate, seventeen kilometers away, stood a hill four hundred and fifty feet in height, serving as an outer guard in both military and geomantic terms. Also to the south stood an entrenched camp close to the quarry whence the well-hewed limestone blocks for the walls and gates had come; semicircular in form, this camp too had a rock-faced earthen wall with a small triple gate. Quý Ly's stronghold sat in a defensible position: several kilometers to the north lay a range of hills; to the west was the Mã River; and to the south and east, facing the plain, were the outer earthen wall, the hill, and the fortified camp.

The citadel had become the Western Capital (Tây-đô) by the end of the year when Quý Ly brought Thuận-tông from Thăng-long, now the Eastern Capital (Đông-đô). What undoubtedly was on the powerful minister's mind in these times was the statement from **The Book of History,** by a minister to the Duke of Chou concerning the young king:

> Dwelling in the new city, let the king now sedulously cultivate the virtue of reverence. When he is all-devoted to this virtue, he may pray to Heaven for a long-abiding decree in his favor.[16]

The royal party had first taken a visit to the Trần family tombs at Yên-sinh in northern Hải-dương, only to be detoured and taken south to Thanh-hóa. Some of the royal party (two palace women and the director of the ancestral temple, together with a local chief) attempted to warn the young ruler and were executed. Quý Ly also sent the Counsellor Lương Nguyên Bửu, who had been placed in charge of the royal clan, to tear down the palaces around the old capital and ship all the remaining brick and tile to the new capital. This was accomplished, though half of the materials was lost in a storm. Quý Ly's hurry led to the moving of the materials during the northeast monsoon season and hence a greater risk of loss, which in fact occurred. This same haste, presumably intended to keep the old aristocracy off balance, also led to the construction of the majestic citadel (the only Vietnamese fortress before 1800 to make such a massive use of stone) in only three months. The result was that major repairs were required within four years.[17]

Externally and in its layout, the new capital had a strong Sinic pattern to it. The triple gate of the south, with its central gate presumably for the use of the ruler only, demonstrates this fact. The rectangular pattern of east-west and north-south streets, paved with marble, further brings out the Chinese influence. The main palace, built of wood, sat on the axis between the northern and southern gates in true Chinese fashion. Yet, as with his intellectual patterns, Quý Ly placed indigenous substance within the Sinic outline. The entrance of the main palace is still marked by two balustrades shaped in the form of dragons. On the bodies of the dragons are beautifully sketched little flowers each with four petals which, in Louis Bezacier's eyes, recall the Ðại-la style of three centuries earlier, though the mane of the dragon has definitely evolved since that time. The same can be seen at the Hồ-công temple within the wall of the small encampment to the south. Located there is a nicely sculpted kneeling elephant with the same small flowers etched on it. A sculpted lion also exists there with the four-petaled flowers on its torso in the shape of the Buddhist swastika, recalling those to be seen on Lokapala.[18] It is clear, then, that under Quý Ly's encouragement there was a continuation of the development of indigenous patterns, even while they came to exist within a Sinic framework. Quý Ly was using this framework to restructure and rebuild the state after the near-catastrophe of the 1380s, not to change Vietnamese society itself.

Having laid down his base, Quý Ly moved immediately to impose his new structure on the countryside beyond the capital. In April of 1397, he first changed the names of the eight outer provinces, those in the mountains and to the south, making, for example, Thanh-hóa Thanh-đô since it now held the capital. He also rearranged the local offices "in accordance with the old structure", presumably bringing them more directly under central control. Then he established his own set of regulations for external ("outer") administration of the above eight provinces: in each province (lộ), there would be a pacifier or defender (an-phủ-sứ) and an assistant (phó); in each prefecture (phủ), a governor (trấn-phủ-sứ) and an assistant; in each subprefecture (châu), an assistant prefect (thông-phán) and a secretary (thiêm-phán); in each district (huyện), an officer (lệnh-úy) and a registrar (chủ-bạ); each intended to "oversee" (quan) his own particular administrative unit. Quý Ly's main purpose in tying down these outer areas was the penetration of central authority to the local level, as he made clear in his order: the district would be under the direction of the subprefecture; the subprefecture, of the prefecture; and the prefecture, of the province. No longer would the capital have at best only an indirect hold over its outlying territories.

All the local household registers, records of wealth, and legal decisions were to be recorded in the provincial registers, and at the end of each year reports would go from the province to the secretariat (sảnh) for examination. Having set up the regional structure, Quý Ly next turned to the central area of the Red River Delta surrounding the old capital, now called Đông-đô (the Eastern Capital), and established a new administrative pattern there. The province around Đông-đô was called the protectorate (đô-hộ-phủ) and was governed by a protector-general (đô-hộ) in the old T'ang style. Here Quý Ly placed his second son, Hán Thương, to "govern" (lĩnh). Next in importance stood the two provinces to the north and west of the old capital, each entitled government general (đô-thống-phủ) and "governed" by governors-general (đô-thống). In the north, the royal counsellor Trần Hãng filled this position, and in the west it was the young Trần Nguyên Hãn, a descendant of Trần Nguyên Đán. Both were members of the royal family. Hence Quý Ly and his son controlled the two capitals, while loyal members of the old aristocracy governed the key delta provinces, the ancient center of Vietnamese civilization. The two lesser delta provinces, to the east and south, were merely called major provinces (phủ-lộ), the former being "administered" (tri) by a prefect (thái-thú), the Counsellor Hà Đức Lân, and the latter by an administrator (quân-dân-sự), the royal counsellor Vương Như Chu, both men being officials faithful to the new regime. In addition, all provinces received instructors (giáo-thụ) and archivists (giám-thư-khố).[19] Quý Ly's strategy appears to have been first to construct his own base outside the central region, then to gain administrative control over the less entrenched "outer territories" before gingerly approaching the established structure of the central region. He would eventually attack the latter in a much more fundamental way than merely through administrative reorganization.

At the same time Quý Ly was acting to spread his ideology throughout the state. In June of 1397, an edict was promulgated by the Throne for the spread of education. It stated:

> In olden times [in China], the state had colleges, social groups (đảng) had halls, [and] everyone had public schools with the result that [they] clarified the civilizing [mission] [and] firmed up custom. In our view, this is most desirable. Today, [however], while the [educational] system in the capital is quite sufficient, [that in] the subprefectures and districts is still lacking. How then can [we] spread widely the Way of civilizing the people?

Then various prefectures, curiously only in territory immediately north, east, and south of Đông-đô, were ordered to appoint an education official (học-quan) and award him the fruit of a certain amount of public land depending on the size of the prefecture in which he was serving. This produce was to be used to support the official's instruction, one third of the amount each going for the ancestral offering on the first of every month, for the school, and for books and materials. Besides the education official, provincial officials and examiners were also to take part in the instruction of the students "in order to develop [their] abilities and talents". At the end of the year, the best students were to be "presented" (cống) to the court where the king himself was to test them and assign them to government positions.[20] The content of the teaching was undoubtedly meant to be that variant of classic learning adopted by Quý Ly which emphasized the position of the Duke of Chou and the Classics while generally ignoring the Neo-Confucians. In this way the powerful minister would, on the one hand, have spread a state ideology supporting his activism, while on the other have gained new recruits for his expanding state structure.

The ultimate aim of this activity was apparently an attack on the regional social and economic structure of the Red River Delta which had encouraged the growth of local and private autonomy and had forced the decline of central power over the previous century. Beginning a month after the edict on education

and apparently continuing through 1398, Quý Ly acted to undercut
the economic base of the delta élite by restricting its landholdings. In July of 1397, an edict was promulgated limiting
family land. Only the families of the royal princes and princesses, generally cousins of the king, were allowed an unlimited
amount (presumably to keep the senior members of the royal
family on Quý Ly's side), while common families could have
no more than ten mẫu. Any of the latter who possessed a fair
amount of land were allowed, according to their own convenience,
to pay a fee and redeem their land; if they were unable to
do this, they would lose their excess property which would
then become state land. Anyone debased or dismissed from office
automatically fell into this category. Presumably those lying
between the mass of the common people and the major royal figures—essentially those in public office—were left at the
mercy and favor of Quý Ly in terms of their landholdings. If
he wished, the powerful minister could theoretically deprive
an official in one move of both his position and his land.
Quý Ly was also able to contain the expansion of landholding
by families within the royal clan who had been using their
followers to carve out land deep in the Red River Delta, on
the edge of the sea. The followers of these families would
build dikes and keep the water out. After two or three years,
they would clear the new land and develop it. Since many of
these royal families intermarried and lived on the new lands,
large private estates came to be formed. This is precisely
what Quý Ly wished to cut short. Having moved against the bulk
of the royal clan and the mass of local interests, he sought,
in the following year, to force all landowners to report the
amount of property held and mark their lands with posts bearing
their names. The local officials from province to district
were jointly responsible for checking and registering all land
within five years. Any land left unclaimed, unmarked, or unregistered would become state land.[21]

As Quý Ly acted to overcome local autonomy and to expand
the central power of the state, there was surprisingly little
sign of opposition to his rule, either at home or abroad. At
a time when the Ming court in Nanking was expending much effort
on military activity along the northern border and was weary
of the squabbling barbarians of Southeast Asia, the aging Hung-

Wu Emperor grudgingly acquiesced in the Vietnamese attempt
to consolidate their hold on a disputed border region against
the wishes of a local Thai chieftain. Though an embassy from
Nanking was sent with all the requisite materials to prove
the Chinese case, Quý Ly apparently paid no attention to its
claims and even expanded his control on the northern border
a few years later.[22] Within the country, the powerful minister
presumably received the support of those interested in reviving
the power of the badly weakened Vietnamese state. What he had
achieved so far in his actions against elements of the royal
clan and local powers was probably seen by many of the élite
as necessary for strengthening the state. Only when Quý Ly
decided to have everyone declare their landholdings did any
opposition emerge. The Counsellor Hà Đức Lân complained privately that if the regulation were established it would lead to
the confiscation of people's land. When this remark reached
the ears of Quý Ly, he removed Đức Lân from the inner circle
and placed him in a strictly administrative position (president
of the Ministry of Finance). While in 1397 Quý Ly began to
reestablish the central power of the state, the following year
was marked by a degree of nervousness, even among those who
had supported him thus far. Đức Lân's comment may well have
been symptomatic of this feeling—were Quý Ly and his family
acting more for their own power than for the proper development
of the state (under Trần rule)?

In early 1398, Quý Ly manipulated the twenty-year-old Thuận-
tông, Nghệ-tông's last son, into abdicating, ostensibly in
the old Trần pattern, for his eldest son, a little over two
years old and the grandson of both Quý Ly and Nghệ-tông. Apparently reluctant to break his word to Nghệ-tông of support for
the young king, Quý Ly is said to have used a Taoist monk to
plant the seed of abdication in the mind of the susceptible
young ruler by pointing out that his forefathers had all cast
aside the problems of the world to follow the spiritual way
of Buddhism; yet while none of them had ever found true immor-
tality, he, Thuận-tông, definitely had the chance. The young
king took the monk's advice and stepped aside as Quý Ly generously provided him with a palace in the mountains for his con-
templation. The abdication edict stressed the young ruler's
love for the spiritual life and his inability to handle the

throne. As he stated, "[My] word stands as a barrier [to my deciding against this], and heaven and earth, the ghosts and spirits have all heard." The Heir Apparent Prince An took the throne and was known as Thiếu-đế (1398-1400), while "the pillar of the state (phụ-chính), the grand tutor (thái-sư) Lê Quý Ly, is to be taken as the ancestor of the realm (quốc-tổ) [being An's grandfather] and as the regent (nhiếp-chính)." Interestingly, the year of the abdication also became the first year of the new king's reign (appropriately entitled Tiến-tân or "Establish the New") as the Vietnamese continued to ignore the proper Confucian pattern of waiting until the following year. Quý Ly's daughter was honored as the Queen Mother (Hoàng-Thái-Hậu) as Quý Ly directed the ceremony and took the title of royal prince (đại-vương), officially heading the administration (as president of the Secretariat) and serving as tutor to the infant king.[23]

On the day of Thiếu-đế's accession, the new capital was officially completed as the construction of the royal palace and the proper ceremonies for it were finished. Quý Ly held a banquet for all officials of the fifth rank and above, and allowed men and women to watch the celebration from the southern gate of the citadel as it lasted through the night. The following year (1399), however, Quý Ly moved the abdicated Thuận-tông to a more isolated contemplative life, separated from his family, at a Taoist temple in northern Hải-dương. He also planted a scholar with the royal entourage as an informer. The minister, according to the Vietnamese History, then sent the latter a message in verse stating, "[If] the senior ruler (nguyên-quân) does not die, you will die with him!", and at the same time sent a poem to Thuận-tông with the message, "In the past, [we] had [two] rulers without much intelligence or ability, Hôn Đức and Linh Đức [Nhật Lễ and Phế-đế]. Why didn't [we] achieve peace and order earlier? [Because] commoners were used to keep people employed [and no one was capable of thinking]." Again we have the justifying theme of bringing order and power back to the state, reinforcing Quý Ly's position therewith. What followed was a tragicomedy of errors. The scholar first tried poisoned medicine on the young king and then cut off his food, allowing him only coconut milk, until the general Phạm Khả Vĩnh ultimately strangled him.[24]

This act, in particular, and Quý Ly's manipulation of the Throne, in general, seem to have set off the revolt that followed. Many of the powerful minister's major supporters in his efforts to strengthen the state broke with him, apparently over the issue of his own personal power. Leading the new opposition were the royal counsellor Trần Hãng of the royal clan and the Thanh-hóa general Trần Khát Chân who planned to kill Quý Ly after he had taken the blood oath (presumably on the fourth day of the fourth lunar month) at Mount Đốn near the Western Capital. Quý Ly had paid a visit to Khát Chân's home in a rather regal manner, "following the rules for the emperor's (**thiên-tử**) visit to the ancestral temple or arrival at a Buddhist temple". Two nephews of Phạm Khả Vĩnh, one a Counsellor, seized swords and attempted to enter, but were seen by Khát Chân and stopped. Quý Ly caught on, however, and began to leave with his guard; thereupon the Counsellor Phạm Ngưu Tất threw his sword on the ground, exclaiming, "We're all dead!", and the plot was discovered. All those implicated died, over three hundred and seventy, including participants and colleagues; their possessions and families were seized with the women becoming slaves and the males, from babies on up, either buried alive or thrown into the water. As with the recent Hu Wei-yung affair in China, the search for the guilty dragged on for years. According to the Vietnamese **History,** those who shared any knowledge of the affair could only acknowledge each other by eye, not daring to speak. No one would take a traveler into his home overnight without first calling a neighboring family and together going over the man's papers and baggage. Each village set up an inspection office, open day and night, to keep watch.[25] If the extent of terror outlined in the **History** is to be believed, the attempted coup and its repercussions throughout the country undoubtedly came as Quý Ly used the opportunity to rid himself of all opposition, actual and potential, from his base in Thanh-hóa.

A number of Quý Ly's supporters for his new directions passed from the scene at this time. His chief aide, the Counsellor Phạm Cự Luận, had already been killed on a pacification campaign against red-clothed (**hồng-y**) bandits in the northern mountain province of Tuyên-quang two years earlier, and the Counsellor Đỗ Mẫn had taken his place there.[26] Though Cự Luận was dead, his lieutenants, like Mẫn and other early followers, stuck with Quý Ly and continued to be the core of his support. None of them are known to have been implicated in the coup attempt. The officials like Nguyễn Phi Khanh, Đặng Tất, and especially Hoàng Hối Khanh of Thanh-hóa, still served the new state. However, the two southern generals, Trần Khát Chân and Phạm Khả Vĩnh (probably implicated by his nephews), were executed, as were Trần Hãng and Trần Nhật Đôn of the royal clan and the Counsellors Hà Đức Lân, Lương Nguyên Bửu, Phạm Ông Thiện, and Khả Vĩnh's nephew Phạm Ngưu Tất. Now the shaky elements of Quý Ly's coalition—varied members of the old structure based on the royal family and its aristocratic supporters who were not personally and directly loyal to Quý Ly and his beliefs[27] —were gone. The Trần royal clan itself, however, was not annihilated and most likely continued in succeeding years as a subsidiary part of the new royal clan of the Hồ, being linked to it by marriage. Quý Ly and his family tolerated the presence of their Trần kin in the government, even employing the former prince Trần Sư Hiền (whose son Quý Ly had killed in 1395) as chief of the Secretariat. The officials serving the Hồ, on the other hand, sought harsher acts against the Trần, and in 1401 such men as Hoàng Hối Khanh were to urge that the remaining members of the Trần be killed. This did not occur since Sư Hiền and other members of the Trần family survived under the Hồ regime until its end in 1407.[28]

Now firmly in power, Quý Ly's own political organization, consisting of a mixed group of loyal followers with the Counsellors Hoàng Hối Khanh and Đỗ Mẫn as its chief figures, was solid and could not be shaken internally. Indeed, Quý Ly did away with the traditional ceremony of the blood oath.[29] Having survived the eruption of the attempted coup and the resulting purge, his organization was undoubtedly strong enough to do without it. At the same time, the founding emperor of the Ming dynasty had died and his realm was edging toward civil war under the rule of his grandson. China did not appear as an immediate threat to Quý Ly's plans.

This strength can be seen in the minister's own acts. Soon after the purge began, Quý Ly, still acting in his Duke of Chou image, publicly proclaimed himself the "designated regent, ancestor of the country, and illustrious supporter of the throne

(phụng-nhiếp-chính   quốc-tổ   chưởng-hoàng)". Simultaneously,
he took the royal yellow as the color for his own garments
and began to live in the central palace and to follow the regulations for the emperor (thiên-tử) in his arrivals and depar-
tures, using twelve royal yellow parasols (nine was the standard
number for the Southeast Asian ruler), though he did not dare
to use the royal "We" (trẫm) and continued to employ the lesser
"I" (dư). His eldest son, Nguyên Trừng, was made chancellor
(tư-đồ), and his second son, Hán Thương, his chosen successor,
was proclaimed vice-regent (nhiếp) and grand tutor (thái-phó)
as well as being given a palace to the right of the central
palace.[30]

Almost immediately, however, doubts appeared concerning
these practices. A man from east-central Thanh-hóa presented
a memorial in which he asked, "What [kind of a] title is chưởng-
hoàng? What [kind of a] color is the yellow [you are using]?
As to observing and extending [the traditions of] the former
rulers [of the Trần dynasty], what [is going on]?" The man,
no   doubt   from   the   same   tradition   as the Thanh-hóa
scholars before him, was first jailed before being spared by
Quý Ly. Soon after came a stiffer challenge. A bandit engaged
in counterfeiting paper money had taken refuge on Mount Thiết
[Iron Mountain] in the northern hills and, when he heard of
Thuận-tông's death and the judgment on Trần Khát Chân, called
on the people to revolt, quickly raising a large force ("over
ten thousand"). With these troops, he raided northern and central Sơn-tây to the west of Đông-đô, indiscriminately striking
and looting for several months. He continued to disrupt the
local administration until the pacifier of the Eastern Capital
region put down the rebellion.[31]

Meanwhile Quý Ly was again strengthening his base in Thanh-
hóa. First he moved a colony of prisoners from just west of
the old capital down to Thanh-hóa; then he ordered one of his
early supporters to organize the people of Thanh-hóa and erect
a wall of sharpened bamboo spikes all along the western edge
of the citadel region from north to south, apparently completing
the irregular outer wall. Anyone who stole bamboo from the
fence would be executed. Next came projects to clear the forests
and build resthouses in order to ease travel and to establish
an inspection station on a river in northern Thanh-hóa, whereby

a big, strong rope was stretched across the river in order to force the boats to come in. Finally, Quý Ly ordered the digging of canals all the way down to a harbor in southern Nghệ-an (using exiled criminals as labor) to facilitate boat traffic.[32] From the citadel, he was gradually opening the country of Đại-Việt to the extension of central government control and easing the effort needed to keep in contact with the local regions. Matters were going well.

With the New Year (1400), the time was ripe for the final extension of his power: the acquisition of the throne for his family. Facing the key problem of any new dynasty, that of transition from the founder to his chosen successor, Quý Ly began in the first month of the new year by firmly establishing his second son, Hán Thương, the grandson of Trần Minh-tông, as his heir. At first unsure as to whether he should act, he picked up the latter's inkstone and declared, "This piece of magic stone—there are times when [it] is [like] the clouds and the rains, enriching the well-being of the people." Thus he sounded out his eldest son, Nguyên Trừng, concerning the latter's feelings on the matter. Nguyên Trừng self-deprecatingly replied, "This small three-inch piece of pine, in other days, would have been the ridgepole of a house or the lintel over a door so as to uphold the national altars." In so speaking, Nguyên Trừng acquiesced in his younger brother's accession to the throne as pine symbolized steadfastness and perseverance. Later, their father would warn the two sons in a poem: "[As] heaven protects and earth sustains, the older and younger brothers—how can they not love each other? Alas! How sad! Why sing so dolorously?" With the dynastic succession secure, Quý Ly made up his mind to act. In March, he had the infant king abdicate, later demoting him to royal prince (đại-vương) and, because he was his own grandson, sparing his life. Quý Ly then forced a final humiliation on the aristocratic remnants of the old rule, compelling them thrice to present him with a request urging him to take the throne while he continued to state ("falsely" as the **History** puts it), "On earth, [one] only has a certain term [he was sixty-four at the time]. In the future upon what countenance will [you] look [when] the first emperor (tiên-đế) is beneath the ground?" Ultimately, of course, Quý Ly took the throne upon their "insistence", and at the

end of the year he himself abdicated for his Heir Apparent,
Hán Thương, taking the traditional title of Supreme Ruler (**Thái-
thượng-hoàng**). Jointly father and son ruled the state. Hán
Thương's wife of the Trần family became the queen.[33]

IV. THE HỒ REGIME

Quý Ly, now the ruler of Vietnam, immediately began to fit the form as well as the structure of the state to his own conceptions. He established his own reign period "Sacred Beginning" (Thánh-nguyên), changed the name of the state from Đại Việt to Đại Ngu, and officially took back his old family name of Hồ, discarding that of Lê. By so doing, he kept in step with the intellectual trends of his time in Vietnam, that is, the merging of the indigenous and classical patterns of thought. The legendary Chinese emperors Yao and Shun appear frequently in the poetry of these years, and Quý Ly claimed an unknown Man, Duke of Hu (Hồ-công), as a distant ancestor, through him linking the Hồ clan to Man's supposed grandfather, Shun, and his dynasty of Yü (Ngu). Thus Quý Ly abandoned his now restrictive Duke of Chou role and sacrificed to the great Shun as the primary ancestor of his family, forging a specific link between his regime and the old testament of the Chinese Classics. Where, in the intellectual sphere, Hồ Tông Thốc had pushed Vietnamese history back to compare with that of China, Quý Ly did the same in terms of political legitimacy.[1]

In the process of these activities, Quý Ly had both his paternal (nội) and maternal (ngoại) genealogies compiled, the first presumably going back to his distant Chinese ancestor, the second including his maternal grandmother of the Chu family and his own mother of the Phạm family. At the end of the year (early 1401), the new ruler sent an embassy to China stating that the Trần line had died out and that Hán Thương, as the grandson of the former king, Trần Minh-tông, by way of his daughter, Princess Huy Ninh, had taken charge of state affairs. Shortly thereafter, the Trần "Conforming to the Universal Regulations" calendar was changed to the Hồ "Conforming to Heaven" calendar. Everything seemed to be going quite smoothly, and the Hồ regime appeared well on its way. The people of Sơn-tây to the west of the old capital presented a black bird with a red bill that could imitate the human voice, and people inside the citadel presented a white bird.[2] Were these episodes meant to bode good or ill for the new dynasty?

Quý Ly sat high and dignified in power, as Confucius in **The Analects** stated about the adopted ancestor of the Hồ: "May not Shun be instanced as having governed efficiently without exertion? What did he do? He did nothing but gravely and reverently occupy his royal seat." Quý Ly had initially cast himself in the image of the Duke of Chou; now he took for himself that of the great Emperor Shun of whom Confucius had also said in **The Doctrine of the Mean:**

> How greatly filial was Shun! His virtue was that of a sage; his dignity was the throne; his riches were all within the four seas. He offered his sacrifices in his ancestral temple, and his descendants preserved the sacrifices to himself.
>
> Therefore, having such great virtue, it could not but be that he should obtain the throne, that he should obtain these riches, that he should obtain his fame, that he should attain to his long life.
>
> Thus it is that Heaven, in the production of things, is sure to be bountiful to them, according to their qualities. Hence the tree that is flourishing, it nourishes, while that which is ready to fall, it overthrows.
>
> In **The Book of Poetry,** it is said, "The admirable, amiable prince displayed conspicuously his excelling virtue, adjusting people, and adjusting his officers. [Therefore], he received from Heaven the emoluments of dignity. It protected him, assisted him, decreed him the throne; sending from Heaven these favors [as it were] repeatedly."
>
> [We may say] therefore that he who is greatly virtuous will be sure to receive the appointment of Heaven.[3]

This is the sort of propaganda, undoubtedly known to him, for

which Quý Ly would have linked his name directly to that of
Shun, thus justifying his claim to the throne and, hopefully,
strengthening his hold upon it. In this way did a new style
of claim to the throne enter the Vietnamese system.

While Quý Ly ruled, seemingly in the image of Shun ("pro-
found, wise, accomplished, and intelligent,... mild and respectful, and entirely sincere"),[4] his son Hán Thương reigned, first
with the title "Continuing to Perfect" (**Thiệu-thành**), then
in 1403 "Opening of Greatness" (**Khai-đại**). As king, Hán Thương
presided over and took part in the ceremonies of the court.
Having abolished the blood oath, the Hồ regime established,
in September 1402, the first sacrifice to Heaven (later called
the **Nam-giao**) and built an altar, presumably circular, for
the sacrifice on Mount Đốn. In accord with the Sinic pattern,
there were three types of ceremony, great, medium, and small,
held every third, every second, and every year respectively.
Thus, in the third year of Hồ rule, Hán Thương performed the
great sacrifice and proclaimed a general amnesty. Proceeding
from the southern gate of the capital in his "Cloud-Dragon"
(**Vân-long**) palanquin and escorted by a crowd of men and women
from the court in their proper order and dress (wives, unless
royal, being one degree below that of their husbands), he went
to the altar and made the offering there, but his hand trembled
so much, we are told by the **History,** that he spilled the wine
on the ground.[5] In the following year, Hán Thương also established temples (**tấm-miếu**) at the tombs of his ancestors in
Thanh-hóa and Diễn-châu, making offerings to his immediate
paternal ancestors at the former (morning and evening) and
to his distant ancestors at the latter. Furthermore, he set
up within the capital an Eastern Royal Temple (**Đông Thái-miếu**)
for the Hồ family ancestors and a Western Royal Temple (**Tây
Minh-đế**) for his maternal ancestors Trần Minh-tông and Trần
Nghệ-tông.[6]

It is difficult to know what Hán Thương's role was beyond
the ceremonial. All official pronouncements came out in his
name, as was to be expected, and any symbolic action required
his presence, yet undoubtedly Quý Ly made all the political
decisions. At one point, as the threat from China mounted in
1405, the two rulers together toured the provinces and examined
the terrain and harbors in order to know first-hand the danger

points. In all probability, Quý Ly wished to make the observa-
tions and took his son with him to ensure that Hán Thương ac-
quired the same knowledge. Whenever a critical event occurred,
Quý Ly dealt with it. He handled foreign relations and responded
to memorials from officials, asked questions and moved quickly
when any special problem arose. Internally, Quý Ly seems to
have maintained a firm control. If there were any situations
that got out of hand within the state they were not documented,
except perhaps as described symbolically in the **History**; for
example, in 1401 two instances of thunderstorms striking the
capital (with three killed) are recorded, and in 1405 the thunderstorms recurred again killing several palace servants. Were
these coup attempts? Interestingly, two of the storms (1401,
1405) hit the Eastern Palace, the residence of the Heir Apparent, and when in 1402 a scholar presented a memorial directly
suggesting that Quý Ly ought to retire to the mountains, that
Hán Thương ought to become Supreme Ruler, and that the Heir
Apparent Prince Nhuế ought to take the throne, Quý Ly was furious. Claiming that the scholar was condemning the regime in
dangerous times, he had him executed. The surviving opposition
may well have wished to gain control via the Heir Apparent
who was the son of a Trần woman. In another instance in 1405,
Quý Ly punished a number of scholars, putting two of them to
death and exiling others for being involved in the leak of
a royal poem (that cited above which Quý Ly had written to
his sons warning them of falling out with each other).[7] Though
having little trouble with internal control, Quý Ly evidently
felt himself in no position to let down his guard.

The core of the Hồ regime was basically quite similar to
that of the previous dynasty and its reliance on the royal
clan. The major difference lay in the fact that, by the second
half of the fourteenth century, the sons of the Trần clan generally lacked the capability to direct the state, while the Hồ
clan in the first years of the fifteenth century still enjoyed
the momentum of its initial success. Though he turned seventy
in 1406, Quý Ly appears to have retained his aptitude for handling political power. The king Hán Thương and his son Nhuế,
the Heir Apparent, do not seem to have figured in the actions
of the state. On the other hand, Quý Ly's eldest son, Nguyên
Trừng, and his brother Quý Tỳ served as his major lieutenants

in their positions as left and right ministers of the state (tả, hữu tướng-quốc) with Nguyễn Trừng in particular becoming the prime executor of his father's orders.[8] Beneath these two chief ministers came the varied members of the royal clan, Quý Ly's two other sons, Triệt and Uông, his other grandsons and their children, and his six nephews. In addition, there were those like Trần Tùng, Trần Vấn, and Phạm Xạ who were awarded the Hồ name and became attached to the clan, while on the periphery were undoubtedly the members of the Trần clan related by marriage. At least one of Quý Ly's mother's relatives, Phạm Nguyễn Khôi, received a high position. The most important of these men served as generals, while all members of the clan, not to mention palace servants, were forbidden to arrogate titles of nobility to themselves.[9] Thus, the central strength of the regime lay, like that of the Trần in the thirteenth century and the Lý before them, in direct personal loyalty, whether by blood or by service. In 1401, a countrywide census was ordered, one of its purposes expressly being "to record [those belonging to] the two branches of the Hồ family in Thanh-hóa and Diễn-châu", though we have no record of the actual result. The physical base for this kin-oriented oligarchy naturally lay in the provinces of Thanh-hóa and Diễn-châu around Quý Ly's capital of Tây-đô. In 1403, this home territory was reorganized and taken under the direct control of the Throne, being formed into the Four Pillars of the Capital (**Kinh-kỳ Tứ-phụ**) and used presumably to tighten and to buttress the defense of the new capital. We know, for example, that a separate Three Pillars Army (the **Tam-phụ Quân**) existed for the Thanh-hóa area.[10]

As in the Trần government of the fourteenth century, a group of Counsellors (**Hành-khiển**) existed within the framework of the Hồ government subordinate to the royal clan but above the administrative apparatus. With the vigor of the Hồ family itself, these Counsellors were nowhere nearly as important in running the state as their predecessors had been. In this type of state, a vigorous group of those directly and personally loyal to the Throne had a distinct advantage over the regular officials of however great an ability. It has already been demonstrated that Quý Ly would brook neither suggestion or act against his interests by such officials. The role of the

Counsellors, instead of being essential for the administration of the state, now faded into insignificance. A case in point is Lê Cảnh Kỳ who received a Counsellor position in 1392 and held it when taken to China in 1407, but is nowhere mentioned in between. The only persons of any identifiable significance known to have held the position were, as we have already noted, Đỗ Mẫn and Hoàng Hối Khanh, but the former was usually involved in military campaigns and the latter was generally not referred to by the title of Counsellor.[11]

Yet, despite the strong position of the royal clan and the unimportance of the top administrative positions, a group of civilian officials appears to have had a major impact on state policy through their memorials, advice, and pressure. Led by Hoàng Hối Khanh, Nguyễn Hy Chu, and Đồng Thức, all graduates of the examinations in the 1380s and 1390s, this group was educated, in favor with the Hồ family, and actively against recalcitrant Trần officials. Thức, for example, was honored for his service with the surname Nguy (a T'ang reference) by Hán Thương in 1402 and strove to drive officials loyal to the Trần out of high office. With an "innumerable" backing, this group tried to eliminate the weaknesses which had sapped the previous dynasty, particularly the locally autonomous class with its land and followers. These officials urged that all the Trần be put to death and that all who privately controlled land and manpower be limited "in order to suppress their power". Though the motives of these officials have been disparaged by later historians who stated that they "were greedy for wealth and power [and] toadied to the wishes of the Hồ clan", a strong sincerity of purpose existed here which led these men to join Quý Ly in the first place and to stick with him to the end. They, like him, wished a strong state, but they wanted more extreme measures and undoubtedly led the new regime to be more radical and less traditional than it had intended.[12]

Paradoxically, then, Hoàng Hối Khanh's role in the Hồ state may have been more effective than that of his more active predecessor as Counsellor in the first half of the fourteenth century, Nguyễn Trung Ngạn. Where the latter sought to establish a more efficient government and had little success while serving the Trần in many capacities, Hối Khanh played a less important role administratively but experienced greater success in having his ideas accepted. In his capacities as a member of the Secret Council and prefect of the Eastern Capital Region as well as that of Counsellor, Hối Khanh was the author of the plan to conduct the countrywide census which directly furthered his other political goals. While, like Nguyễn Trung Ngạn, Hối Khanh also carried out a variety of tasks—serving as Quý Ly's envoy on a matter dealing with the northern border and being sent by Hán Thương to build a citadel in Sơn-tây—the main significance of him and his followers was that their ideas were accepted by the Throne and consequently had a greater impact on Vietnamese society, helping to break up the **ancien régime.** In all probability, men of this persuasion occupied posts scattered throughout the central administration, though this is difficult to chronicle.

As reflected in the **History,** the central administration of this time does not seem particularly different from that of earlier years. Once more we are shown a variety of positions with no clearly discernable pattern of organization, though we know that Hán Thương "set" the administrative system and the pattern of law for the state of Đại Ngu towards the end of 1401. The Secret Council still existed, as did the Secretariat (**Trung-thư-sảnh**) and the Chancellery (**Môn-hạ-sảnh**), and the records show the names of five Ministries, those of Rites, Punishment, War, Finance, and Civil Service, with only that of Public Works missing. Yet no mention is made of the Six Ministries per se, and only the Ministry of Rites is shown in action, conducting the examinations. It would also appear that there was a chief administrator (**thượng-thư-lệnh hữu-tham-tri-chính-sự**) who supervised this segment of the government.[13] At the same time, little pattern emerges in the use of men and the administrative positions they held during the peaceful years of Hồ rule (1400-1405). Officials who had served the Trần without being in Quý Ly's service were vulnerable, particularly as the purge continued and the new political goals were pushed forward. No doubt many were under suspicion for recalcitrance, and two cases are documented in which officials were demoted to lowly clerical jobs.[14] Otherwise, it would appear that anyone considered appropriate for a task, whatever his background, was used.

While the pattern of recruiting for government service under the Hồ remained fixed depending primarily upon loyalty and performance regardless of the manner in which a man might have come to the attention of the powerful,[15] the examination system was fully resurrected by Quý Ly. This was done not so much to staff his administration as to serve a cultural function, that of helping to establish the brand of classical learning that had grown through the last quarter of the fourteenth century. The scholars who succeeded in these examinations, particularly that of 1400, were the last generation infused with the teaching of the classical texts before the flood of Neo-Confucianism entered Vietnam with the Ming. The influence of these literati was to last into the middle of the century and proved instrumental in establishing the style of Vietnamese state which immediately followed the Ming occupation. These men represent the culmination of the intellectual development of the 1380s and of Quý Ly's own peculiar brand of classical thought. The first major examination (for the thái-học-sinh degree) was held in 1400 (presumably following the rules established four years earlier) and produced twenty successful scholars including Nguyễn Trãi (son of the official Nguyễn Phi Khanh and grandson of Trần Nguyên Đán), Lý Tử Tấn, and Vũ Mộng Nguyên.

A more complete examination process was established in 1404. First there was the provincial examination (hương-thí) which seems to have been held in September of that year. Soldiers, actors, and criminals were barred from participation. Those successful at this level were exempted from corvée labor. A year later (September 1405), a new examination was introduced at the Ministry of Rites to select those eligible (the cử-nhân) for the capital examination (hội-thí); the one hundred seventy successful scholars appear to have been withheld from those selected for administrative posts. In October, immediately after this selection, another test was held, apparently for those who had not passed the cử-nhân examination, to make a selection of low-level officials and clerks. The capital examination was scheduled for the year after, in the fall of 1406, with the whole cycle starting again in 1407, but the chaos of the Chinese invasion put an end to it. Those who would have passed this final examination were to be appointed royal scholars (thái-học-sinh). In these examinations, the Vietnamese borrowed three fields from the four in the Yüan system and

split them into four fields, adding a fifth on calligraphy
and arithmetic. The only subject matter still known from the
examinations of the Hồ period is the topic given the candidates
of 1400 for the phú poem in the second field. This topic was
"The Golden Storehouse of the Spirits", a reference to the
place holding the sword of the founder of the Han dynasty in
China. It apparently confused the candidates and they sought
an explanation. In response, they were asked if there was any
precedent for such an explanation. One candidate, a forty-nine-
year old former officeholder for the Trần, quickly cited a
precedent from Sung times concerning a sentence from the works
of Chuang-tzu, the early Taoist philosopher, and the explanation
was consequently given.[16]

When the schedule for the examinations was announced in
1404, "the scholars (sĩ-nhân) devoted themselves wholeheartedly
[to their studies], strongly desirous of attaining an official
post".[17] The positions for which the examinations were held
were scholarly rather than administrative. Nguyễn Phi Khanh
had already become a scholar in the Hàn-lâm Academy. Of the
twenty thái-học-sinh from the 1400 examination, it would appear
that a number of them went into the National College, though
Nguyễn Trãi did take a position in the Censorate; certainly,
for the cử-nhân examination of 1405, two of the one hundred
seventy did so well that they became thái-học-sinh on the spot
and six others were made scholars of the Tư-thiện Palace (originally, under the Trần, the name of the school for the Heir
Apparent). Other scholars are mentioned as having been given
positions in Nguyễn Trừng's palace and used by Quý Ly to investigate local officials in 1400. On the other hand, there is
little evidence of graduates assuming administrative positions,
whether in the agencies of the capital or the local offices
in the countryside.

These scholars, emerging during a generation in which classical Chinese learning was on the rise, similar to those of
1304, were, however, from a broader geographical range than
their predecessors. Where the early fourteenth-century literati
were concentrated in the east (Hải-dương) and south (Sơn-nam,
Thanh-hóa), the early fifteenth century had a better balance
of north (Kinh-bắc) and west (Sơn-tây) as well as south (Sơn-
nam, Thanh-hóa) and east (Hải-dương). The most important of

these scholars, Nguyễn Trãi, Vũ Mộng Nguyên, and Lý Tử Tấn,
were in their early twenties.[18] Prime examples of their generation of scholars, they had a broad knowledge of Chinese philosophical and historical materials. Their verse is clustered
with Sinic allusions. For example, a poem of Lý Tử Tấn's spoke
of specific scholars and warriors of the Confucian period in
China and of particular women from the distant Chinese and
Vietnamese pasts, all in contrasting pairs. Tử Tấn also wrote
this poem: "[I] follow the path of Chou Tun-i [and] inquire
of Chu Hsi,/ in order to discuss the 'stone drum' texts and
examine the 'clear thinking'./ [By] the flame of the lamp [I]
study zealously through the night, only to be exhausted like
Han Yü./ [I] follow the Classics of Poetry and of Rites [and]
look towards Mr. Li's courtyard." The end of the poem also
made reference to being totally absorbed in the Six Classics
(the Five plus the **Yüeh Chi**). Lý Tử Cấu, apparently also a
laureate from the examination of 1400, wrote in a poem to
his fellow candidate and scholar Vũ Mộng Nguyên on the successful candidate becoming an old minister whose belly contains
ten thousand books.[19] Nguyễn Trãi was said to have memorized
the whole of the Classics and the Histories.[20] These scholars
and their protégés, as Lê Quý Dôn would state centuries later,
were to "bring together again the culture [of Vietnam] and
gather the remaining texts" after the catastrophe of the Ming
occupation. Indeed, to quote Ngô Thì Sĩ, also of the eighteenth
century: "Looking at those who passed the examinations at the
end of the Trần dynasty [and under the Hồ], Nguyễn Trãi was
the first [among them]; his literary wisdom and resourcefulness
heldped the Lê dynasty first establish its state. Moreover,
[other scholars], like Lý Tử Tấn, Vũ Mộng Nguyên, Phan Phu
Tiên, and Nguyễn Thiên Túng, were all renowned for their literary abilities."[21]

Despite the significance of these young scholars for later
decades, within the Hồ regime they were a mere appendage to
Quý Ly's personal interest in the Classics. In many ways, their
situation was much more similar to that of their fellow literati
thriving under the princely patronage of a century before than
to the existence of those who would follow them and help found
the Chinese model of government in Vietnam. Indeed, none
of the elements of the Hồ regime described above may be said

to represent any great difference from the pattern of Trần rule throughout the fourteenth century. As the early nineteenth-century scholar Phan Huy Chú noted,[22] the basic pattern of administration under Quý Ly represented a fundamental continuity from the previous dynasty. A royal clan and aristocracy which patronized Confucian studies, among others, and selected its favorites and its most trustworthy servants to run the state essentially marked both dynasties. Classical Chinese learning had grown in influence to the point where the head of the state made use of it in a rather eccentric way for his own purposes, but Vietnam had not become a Confucian state. Rather, it continued to exist within its traditional ruling framework.

Nevertheless, a major difference did exist between Quý Ly's government and the one in which he had first risen thirty years before. This difference lay in the contact of the central administration with, and its control over, the outlying areas. A continuing question in the history of the Southeast Asian state has been the extent of control of the capital region over the territory stretching away from it. The Vietnamese state, with the exception of the mid-thirteenth century, governed this territory with royal kin or others directly loyal to the ruler. As the fourteenth century progressed, this meant an increasing local autonomy with almost no responsiveness to the center. Quý Ly intended to break this pattern. The role in which he must be seen is neither that of evil usurper nor that of people's hero; rather, his chief aim was to rebuild the central power of the Vietnamese state. The best way for him to do this was by being in complete control himself and by abolishing the great degree of local autonomy. Where Nghệ-tông had wielded a minimum of direct control throughout the countryside, Quý Ly was determined to establish his government in the provinces.

The first administrative action he took upon his ascension to the throne was to send a group of lower officials from the Three Agencies as well as men from the palace and palace scholars out to all the provinces. Secretly investigating the local scene, these men were to designate which officials and clerks were doing a good job and which were not. No doubt political considerations and support for the new dynasty were involved, but beyond this was the question of controlling the local manpower and resources. A major change in provincial personnel

seems to have subsequently occurred as officials were promoted
and demoted. Moreover, this type of investigation appears to
have become a regular feature of the Hồ regime. It is hard
to say what sort of men did fill the regional posts under the
Hồ, particularly below the provincial level. Only two of them
are known to have passed the examinations (both in the late
Trần period); another such scholar had been selected by Phạm
Cự Luận for the Secret Council in 1389. All the others merely
existed in their positions with no distinguishing characteris-
tics. There is no sense of a bureaucratic grouping of these
men; rather, it appears that they served the particular interests of the men at the top. Rarely is there a passage in the
History referring to them as a class. When the pattern of court
music was established in 1402, the sons of civil officials
and the sons of military officers were separated to practice
civil and military dances respectively, a rare separation in
a state where men shifted back and forth so easily. Only in
one other instance do we have the civil officialdom addressed
as a whole, and that took place in 1404 when its members were
forbidden to wear Chinese-style shoes, though past precedent
had allowed those of rank six senior and above to do so. The
officials were only allowed to have rough hemp sandals.[23]

Having already put down a deeper administrative structure
(1397) than had hitherto existed and having checked it with
an investigation, Quý Ly was prepared to continue his confrontation with the autonomous local powers. He had put a limit on
excessive landholding, as encouraged by his officials, and
now he approached a more fundamental issue, that of manpower.
Probably in the second half of 1400, the Throne, on the advice
of Hoàng Hối Khanh, ordered the compilation of the countrywide
census. While rooting out all members of the two branches of
the Hồ family, as noted earlier, the primary task was to bring
all the manpower of the state under central control, particularly for military purposes. All persons from one year on up were
recorded, and that number was the figure used for computation
purposes. No persons were allowed to wander indiscriminately
while seeming to be on the rolls. Placards scattered throughout
the provinces proclaimed that all lowlanders (Vietnamese) temporarily in residence in the border territories had to return
to their places of origin and be recorded. The task was complet-

ed in May of 1401, and the names of all males aged fourteen to fifty-nine (fifteen to sixty in the Sinic way of counting years) were marked for military duty. The figures achieved were compared with previous figures and almost immediately, in response to the urging of Hoàng Hối Khanh and his group, the Hồ government placed a limit on the number of men controlled by private families. This ruling applied only to native Vietnamese, not to foreigners. It was not an act of emancipation; its goal was to concentrate the control of manpower in the hands of the regime, not to free it. As in the case of excessive landholdings, those released from their private owners came under state control with the families being compensated for their losses in paper money. All those allowed to have followers—the number depending on their official rank—had to produce documents on the followers covering three generations. The followers were tattooed on the forehead, each in a different manner depending on whether they belonged to the state ("fiery pearl") (some instead went into the palace guard), to a princess ("poplar and ash"), to a prince ("vermilion circle"), to an official of the first or second rank (one "black circle"), or to an official of the third rank or below (two "black circles").[24]

The thrust of the Hồ regime was to concentrate the control of the state's resources in its own hands. Followers now served the state instead of private individuals. In 1402 a new schedule of taxation was put into effect. The taxes on paddy fields jumped two thirds (five **thăng** of rice per **mẫu** as opposed to three), while those on fields of mulberry trees dropped from seven or nine strings of cash (**quan**) to five for the best fields, four for medium fields, and three for the worst fields, all payable in paper money. Where the yearly head tax for males had been three **quan** per person regardless of the circumstances, it now depended upon the amount of land each person held, ranging from five **mạch** (half a **quan**) of paper money for five **sào** (half a **mẫu**) of paddy fields to three **quan** for any holdings over two and a half **mẫu** with four classes in between. A greater flexibility was thus added to the system as the Hồ lowered the head tax for those with two and a half **mẫu** and under as well as the mulberry tax for all concerned. Undoubtedly no money was lost to the capital due to the greater efficiency

of the recent census. Moreover, the fiscal base of the regime
would have been the paddy fields and the tax increase per acre
which most likely brought in a good amount. For those without
land, together with orphans and widows even though they had
land, no taxes were required.[25]

The regime had other plans for the landless. In 1402, following the compilation of the census, the poor were organized
into labor battalions to support the regular army units. There
followed not a distribution of excess land (this all went to
the state), but forced movement to new lands which would benefit
the state even more. At the beginning of 1403, not too long
after the setup of the new tax schedule, the Throne sent men
who were without land but had possessions of their own (presumably household implements, seed, and buffaloes) to an area
newly seized from the Chams (Thăng-hoa). There they built their
homes again and were transformed into military units, being
tattooed on both forearms with the name of the territory they
were in. Only in the following year could their wives and children follow and many were lost in a storm at sea, leaving much
bitterness. That same year (1404), the support battalions made
up of the poor were transformed into regular army units, and
an order went out for all the remaining landless on the provincial records to form a Brigade of the Paupers.[26]

With its apparently strong presence throughout the countryside, the Hồ government did not have the problems of the Trần
regime forty years earlier. When an emergency led to a need
for foodstuffs, the Hồ did not merely request the rich to give,
they ordered it, though they seem to have avoided this direct
technique if they could. When "ever normal" granaries were
ordered to be set up in 1401, paper money was sent to all the
provinces to be exchanged for rice at the local price, thus
keeping the price true (though due to the administrative changes
taking place at all levels at that time, nothing came of this).
A year later, an official presented a memorial suggesting that
Han and T'ang dynasty patterns be followed in requesting people
to give rice in exchange for either gaining titles or escaping
punishment so as to establish granaries in the border regions.
Quý Ly merely gave the caustic comment, "[You] know a few characters [and you feel you] can speak of the affairs of Han and
T'ang. [If] such were the case, the mute could talk. [You]

will only be ridiculed." Nevertheless, in 1403 when the landless
had been sent south, the Throne did not hesitate to ask people
to provide cattle for them in exchange for titles, and during
a famine in 1405 the Throne ordered all officials from province
to district to mark the rich families in the population records,
depending on how much rice they had, and to subsidize the purchase of rice for the people.[27]

While the welfare of the people was being maintained through
the distribution of rice, as well as via the upkeep of the
dikes (in a somewhat local fashion), the Hồ administration
moved to develop and control the commercial sector, especially
by encouraging the use of paper currency already introduced.
As we have seen, in their concerted effort to establish paper
money as the currency of the realm, the Hồ made payments and
demanded payments in the paper money for nearly every transac-
tion in which the state was involved—reimbursements for followers who came under public control, the purchase of rice for
setting up the "ever normal" granaries, and payment of the
head and mulberry field taxes. In 1400, a tax had been levied
on three classes of merchant and passenger ships—five **quan**
for large vessels, four for medium ones, and three for small,
in cash, though presumably this was because foreign ships were
involved. Thus the Hồ gained some control over international
and interregional trade. Three years later, the Hồ government
tightened its control on internal commerce. The post of market
inspector was established, weights and measures promulgated,
and prices fixed in paper money. Due to the dislike of many
merchants in handling the new currency, a law was drawn up
forbidding any refusal to deal in it along with any attempts
to inflate prices, to close one's shop, or to band together
in collusion.[28]

Concurrently with its attempt to extend central power into
the provinces, the Hồ regime was also continuing its efforts
to expand its territory to the south. Quý Ly had already sent
one attack against Champa when La Ngai, the old general who
had taken Chế Bồng Nga's place on the throne as Jaya Simhavar-
man, died in 1400 and was succeeded by his son Ba Đích Lại
(Ngauk Klaung Vijaya). As the Vietnamese internal situation
came under control, Quý Ly launched one attack per year for
a period of four years against the new king. Meanwhile, the

strength of the army was increased in 1402 following the census
and a review of the military organization. Moreover, as the
campaigns went on, facilities for communication and transporta-
tion were repaired and developed. In early 1402, the road from
the Western Capital south to Hóa-châu was ordered repaired,
rest stations were set up, and a book titled **The Road of One
Thousand Lý** was compiled. However, in 1404, the Vietnamese
tried unsuccessfully to clear Liên Harbor from Tân-bình to
the border of Thuận-hóa, first being stopped by the sand and
mud, and then encountering broken dikes at the Eo rivermouth
farther south in Hóa-châu which required troops from the capital
for their repair. Perhaps these physical problems, together
with pressure from the Chinese, were what brought an end to
the southern campaigns in 1404.

Yet, while Champa itself was not conquered, the campaigns
as a whole were successful. Specific ones, like those of 1401
and 1403, failed because of individuals, but the Vietnamese
were able to drive the Chams back from their northern borders
and gain control over more territory. The armies of each of
the four campaigns, apparently leaving in the latter half of
each year from 1400 to 1403, seem to have been organized differently. The first, for which no specific result is mentioned,
had the Counsellor Đỗ Mãn in charge of the maritime forces
and a general of the Long-tiệp [Dragon Victory] Army, Trần
Tùng, in charge of the land forces, with a general from the
Left Thánh-dực [Sacred Wing] Army assisting each. For the second, led by Trần Tùng, the officers are not mentioned. This
campaign failed because Tùng separated the land and maritime
forces and could not coordinate them during a storm, forcing
the land units to boil leather for food and eventually to return. In 1402, with the army reorganized, the Vietnamese made
a massive effort, with Đỗ Mãn in charge of the campaign and
two civilian officials as his coordinating officers. This force
crossed into Champa and defeated the army sent against it,
striking fear into the Cham king and forcing him to make a
peace offering of two elephants (one of them white), local
goods, and more land. The last campaign, which attempted to
utilize small boats (apparently for better penetration inland),
failed due to the incompetence of Phạm Nguyên Khôi, a general
in the Dragon Victory Army and related to the Hồ through Quý

Ly's mother's family. He had been placed in charge of the maritime forces, assisted by Trần Vấn, and had final say over the
operations of the entire army, while Đỗ Mãn and another general
commanded the land forces. The army, despite strong discipline
(loss of life, family, and property being the price for coward-
ice on the battlefield) and a lengthy siege of Vijaya, the
Cham capital, ran out of supplies just as the Chams were about
to surrender and was forced to return, meeting on the way a
Ming fleet sent to intervene.[29]

The only campaign that made any specific gains was that
of 1402 when the Cham king sent his uncle to offer the northern
territory of Indrapura, the ancient capital (called by the
Vietnamese Chiêm-động [Cavern of the Chams]), in exchange for
peace. Quý Ly promptly pressured the envoy into adding the
Cavern of Cổ-lũy (the Old Fortress), thereby bringing all of
the old northern Cham territory of Amaravati to the Vietnamese.
No longer did the Chams control their old sacred centers of
My-sơn and Đồng-dưỡng. Having lost the provinces of the north,
Champa was reduced to less than half of the territory held
under Chế Bồng Nga only twelve years earlier and much of the
remainder lay in the poor mountain regions. Quý Ly divided
the new territory into four subprefectures (châu)—Thăng, Hoa,
Tư, and Nghĩa—and shifted the Thuận-hóa pacifier, Nguyễn Cảnh
Chân, south to hold the same position in the new province of
Thăng-hoa "in order to govern it". The upriver regions were
brought together as Tân-ninh trấn.

In the border territory farther to the south, the refugee
son of Chế Bồng Nga, Chế Ma Nô Đà Nan, was put in charge of
the two châu of Tư and Nghĩa with the purpose of "appealing
to the mass of those belonging to Champa so as to keep [them
in Vietnamese territory]". But the Chams had already refused
to give up this Southeast Asian competition over manpower and
had pulled all those countrymen who were "close and convenient"
to the Vietnamese back into their own territory, leaving only
soldiers on the border. Then, as in 1403, Quý Ly sent the landless south to populate Thăng-hoa, tattooed them, and staffed
the army and civilian posts down to the district levels. Requi-
sitioned cattle and, later, cooked rice were sent to aid the
area. Next, before the final campaign, the Vietnamese organized
the territory from Tư and Nghĩa south to "Siam" (Xiêm-la) into

subprefectures and districts.[30] In the autumn of 1405, as the pressures from the north were building up, Quý Ly sent the palace official Nguyễn Ngạn Quang as a special administrator to take charge of Thăng-hoa and Tân-ninh over Nguyễn Cảnh Chân. On Ngạn Quang's departure, Quý Ly presented him with this poem:

> The borderlord [who] has received an official charge [must] support [us] with great determination;
> [for] a courageous control of the borderlands is a good tactic.
> [Like] a green pine, protect yourself in [these] wintry times.
> [Then, with] white hair and a calm heart, I [can] look towards the west [and its] troubles.
> Instruct the soldiers and the farmers diligently [so that they] will all progress and fit in.
> Pulling out the border soldiers, what kind of a harvest is that?
> [With] hard labor [yet] nothing said, there will be no one who knows [what you are doing].
> [But my] four eyes examine [and you] will not be hidden in [your] ceremonial garb.[31]

The aggressiveness of the Vietnamese in seizing land under the Hồ regime would seem to indicate that a change was taking place in the relations between Vietnam and its Southeast Asian neighbors. For the first time the Vietnamese made a specific attempt to carve out new territory and fill it with their own people, yet their underlying approach (one that was still culturally relative and designed mainly to gain hegemony rather than absolute control) remained the same. The border territories had to be bound more tightly to the capital than they had been in the past, since, as Chế Bồng Nga had demonstrated, the former state of loose control could be overthrown at any time. Thus, while Quý Ly strengthened his border policies in the same way that he strengthened his state, he retained the basic approach of his predecessors. There was no Confucian condemnation of the Chams as barbarians; indeed Quý Ly welcomed them into his service. As noted above, one of Chế Bồng Nga's sons became the chief of the former Cham territory on the new southern frontier. Another Cham, once a general in his home country, had taken a Vietnamese name, Đinh Đại Trung, and served as prefect of Hóa-châu. There he was on the front lines of the fighting against his former countrymen. Trần Tùng conferred with him during the campaign of 1401, and the following year Đại Trung led the decisive attack on horseback against a Cham general. Nor did disgruntled Vietnamese shrink from serving the Chams if it served their purposes. Trần Tùng, who had been cashiered for his poor performance in the 1401 campaign, plotted with the other refugee son of Chế Bồng Nga, Chế Sơn Nô, to contact the Chams secretly and communicate beneficial information to them.[32]

The Vietnamese state under the Hồ regime continued to exist within the framework of the Vietnamese state of the prior four centuries. The clash for the hegemony of the eastern coast of the Southeast Asian mainland had reached a peak of intensity in the second half of the fourteenth century and, in the process, had exposed desperate weaknesses in the Trần state. Acting to remedy these weaknesses, Quý Ly moved to take power himself and to strengthen the state against both the powers of local autonomy within and the Cham threat without. In so doing, he brought changes to Vietnam that reflected the increasingly integrated intellectual world of Vietnam from the 1380s, the merger of indigenous thought and the Vietnamese brand of Chinese classical learning, encouraged under the traditional rule of the Hồ clan. Quý Ly also seems to have followed certain practices of the founder of the Ming dynasty. In these terms, Quý Ly's efforts appear to have been a success, yet as he achieved these goals the Vietnamese state came to be exposed to pressures from the north that swiftly destroyed his regime. The dispossession of the Trần family, the attacks on the Chams, and the dispute over borderlands with China would all leave openings for the newly expanding power of the Yung-lo Emperor in Nanking.

V. DESTRUCTION OF THE VIETNAMESE STATE

Perhaps the decisive event for the future of Vietnam was the seizure of the Dragon Throne by Chu Ti, Prince of Yen, and the rise to full power of Ming China under his rule, though Tamerlane's death far to the west had its effect too. Following the demise of the Hung-wu Emperor, Ming T'ai-tsu, in 1398, the young successor (a grandson) tried to undercut the power of his uncles. These princes were enfeoffed with principalities in which they independently built up their own personal forces. In response to his nephew's threat, Chu Ti, strongest of the princes and therefore the major target of the young ruler, rebelled in mid-1399 and began a drive on the capital at Nanking from his own base at what is now known as Peking. Three years of heavy fighting took place before he was successful and able to take the throne.[1]

During this time of internal struggle, little interest was taken in relations with the countries to the south. In his Ancestral Instructions of 1395, termed by Charles Hucker as "a kind of dynastic constitution",[2] the Hung-wu Emperor had reaffirmed his pacific intent of 1371 and listed fifteen states, including Vietnam, which China would not invade. Besides the moral framework imposed, Lo Jung-p'ang would argue, this list of states may also have been an effort to calm the southern and eastern countries at a time when Tamerlane's conquests in western Asia were perceived as the threat of a new Mongol empire. The civil strife, then, compounded this freedom of action allowed the Southeast Asian states, and when Chu Ti reached the throne in mid-1402, order, in the Chinese view, had to be established externally as well as internally.[3]

From the beginning, the Yung-lo Emperor took it upon himself to continue what his father had bequeathed, while arguing that the reign of his nephew had distorted this legacy due to bad advisors around the Throne. Almost immediately, six weeks after taking the throne, he followed his father's precedent and began to send missions out to the surrounding countries to inform them of his accession and to welcome their missions and trade. In his own terms, "now that the Four Seas are one family, it is the time to show no outer-separation". Within nine months missions were dispatched to all countries, both overland and overseas, which were seen as significant at the close of his father's reign. Thus, the first years of his reign (1402-1405) were ones in which the patterns of administration and foreign relations were reaffirmed and the necessary reconstruction took place. Externally, there was still alarm over the threat of Tamerlane, particularly at this time of national weakness, and an attempt was made to maintain the northern border by diplomatic means.[4]

It is no surprise that the pacific intentions of the Chinese empire towards the smaller states of the south and east, which the Hung-wu Emperor had pronounced in 1371 and 1395, were again voiced by the Yung-lo Emperor. Where the father had damned the vain seeking of conquest by Sui Yang-ti, the son disclaimed, to quote his own words, the "militaristic policy and warlike activities" of Han Wu-ti.[5] Such arbitrary conquest was to be abjured. However, where the Ming founder had backed off from a strict implementation of impartiality and fairness due to the barbarian complexities of the south, his son was fully prepared to enforce the moral world order as he perceived it —to quote Wang Gungwu, "the newly defined ideology of impartiality and no-separation towards all countries, big or small, old or new."[6] This meant maintenance of the status quo, antipathy towards any action upsetting it as being immoral, and desire for recognition of the new order by the countries themselves; in a word, no country was to separate itself from the moral order as defined by Nanking.

The disclaimers of the goals of Han Wu-ti and Sui Yang-ti must have calmed any initial fears the Hồ may have felt, as the former had conquered Vietnam in 111 B.C. and the latter

had put down an attempt at autonomy in A.D. 605. The fate of
the Vietnamese embassy sent out in 1400 to seek recognition
for the new ruler is unknown. Delayed or forced back by the
turmoil, this (or another) embassy arrived at the Ming capital
in Nanking in April 1403. There the Vietnamese envoys presented
the case for recognition of the new ruler and the new dynasty:
no Trần survivors existed; Hán Thương was a maternal cousin
of the Trần and grandson of the late king Trần Minh-tông, and
he had been elected by the ministers of the court. Meanwhile,
the Yung-lo Emperor had already sent envoys to proclaim his
accession in Vietnam the previous October at the same time
as embassies had been dispatched to other eastern and southern
countries, including Champa. This embassy had been received
by the Vietnamese in 1403, according to their records which
apparently indicate a knowledge of what had been going on in
China.[7]

Having received the Vietnamese embassy, the Chinese emperor
ordered a delegation from his Board of Rites to investigate
the new situation in Vietnam regarding its legitimacy and to
make a recommendation to him. The commission of inquiry left
for Vietnam at the beginning of May and was probably the same
mission which arrived in Vietnam that fall, having traveled
straight through by road. Some members of the mission had come
to find out what was going on, while others sought to reprimand
the Vietnamese rulers. Hán Thương, however, ordered men who
were adaptable, sharp, and courteous to receive the commission
and the mission which returned at the end of the year carried
documentation supporting the Hồ claims. The court in Nanking
thereupon agreed to grant the title An-nan Kuo-wang [King of
Annan] and the camel seal to the new regime with the stipulation
that the Vietnamese maintain their borders, cease their warfare,
keep their people calm, and continue to seek good relations
with China. In return, the Vietnamese rulers agreed to restrain
their efforts towards Champa (which had probably been stalled
already) and presented to the Chinese the pair of elephants
(one white, one black) which had originally been a Cham tribute
to the Hồ in 1402.[8] Matters appeared to be developing well
for the Vietnamese as they voluntarily took part in the Ming
world order.

Yet the seeds of aggravation were well established, particu-

larly considering the passion of the Yung-lo Emperor for order.
The Cham ruler, on receiving the Chinese mission of October
1402, had without doubt complained bitterly of the Vietnamese
conquest of his northern territories that same year. The return
mission from the Chams arrived at the beginning of August 1403
and, according to Vietnamese records, a Ming embassy with a
fleet of nine ships appeared just following the cessation of
the Vietnamese attack on Champa that year. The Ming officers
challenged the Vietnamese commander, Phạm Nguyên Khôi, with
these words: "[You] can consider [the situation] and bring
[your] troops back, [but you] cannot take a long time [to make
up your mind]." On Nguyên Khôi's return, Quý Ly rebuked his
maternal cousin for not having annihilated the Ming forces.
Quý Ly apparently had long figured that he and the Chinese
would eventually clash. The first note of this came in late
1400 or early 1401 when the reason given for the census was
the question put to his ministers by Quý Ly: "How can [we]
get a million troops in order to resist the northern bandits?"
The Vietnamese case in the matter, perhaps ex post facto, was
that the Chinese in general and the Yung-lo Emperor in particular had been out to get them from the beginning. In their terms,

> First Ming T'ai-tsu [the Hung-wu Emperor] sought eunuchs,
> Buddhist monks, and masseuses, [and] we accommodated
> him. Several years [later], [we] allowed the Buddhist
> monks and the women to return, but the eunuchs stayed
> behind and took positions as inner palace officials (nội-
> quan). When Ch'eng-tsu [the Yung-lo Emperor] took the
> throne, he had ambitions of invading the South and sent
> [the Vietnamese eunuchs] Nguyễn Toán, Từ Cá, Nguyễn Tông
> Đạo, and Ngô Tín as envoys [probably on the mission of
> inquiry] to interrogate [their] relatives and to tell
> them in secret, "If northern soldiers come, raise a yellow
> banner marked with one of our names and [you], [our] re-
> lations, will certainly come to no harm."

When this was discovered, Hán Thưởng is said to have put the
relatives of these eunuchs to death.[9]

The Chinese too had a potential case against the Vietnamese,
specifically the dispute over border territory in Kuangsi,
which merely awaited the moment when Nanking wished to confront
its southern neighbor directly. Tension seems to have built

up through the spring of 1404 following the investiture. The Vietnamese continued to develop their military forces in defense against the Chinese, and built "iron-bolted ships" disguised as rice transports.[10] At the end of July, the Board of Rites in Nanking was ordered to present a memorandum on the Kuangsi border dispute to the Vietnamese ambassador and to charge him with instructing his ruler that, if he wished a long and peaceful reign, he should give up any claim to the land and live in peace with China. A month or so later, an envoy arrived in Nanking with a letter from the Cham king which again pressed the earlier charges of Vietnamese aggression and interference. Wisely the Chams played a humble role and offered complete obeisance to China in return for protection. Immediately, a Chinese envoy left for Vietnam to accuse the Vietnamese of committing a breach of faith in their relations with the Chams, and to demand in more forceful terms the return of the disputed Kuangsi border regions. A warning against further intransigence was attached and, in a return note to the Cham king, the Yung-lo Emperor stated that, if the Vietnamese ruler "should be unenlightened and intransigent, the blame lies with him, and this Imperial Court has ways of coping with him."[11]

The major issue which the Chinese would seize upon, however, was neither the border problem nor the Cham complaints; it was the more fundamental question of the rightful ruler of Vietnam. Three days after the Chinese mission left for Vietnam, on September 10, 1404, Bùi Bá Kỳ, a supporter of the late Thanh-hóa general Trần Khát Chân from western Hải-dương who had survived the purges, arrived at the Ming court to tell all on his enemies, the Hồ. Having been encouraged by a good friend of the same province, Lê Cảnh Tuân, Bá Kỳ proclaimed himself a loyal subject of the southern court and described the oppression of the new regime, swearing that "the people are as opposed to them as water is to fire. They long for the return of the Trần rulers and they look to China to deliver them from their suffering. Send an army down to save the people and punish the guilty."[12] The man Bá Kỳ had in mind for the throne of Vietnam was another political refugee named Trần Thiên Bình who, the Chinese records say, arrived in Nanking from Lao territory on October 2 and claimed descent from the Trần kings. The Vietnamese records, on the other hand, assert that Thiên Bình was an impostor, whose true identity was Nguyễn Khang, a trusted retainer (**gia-thần**) or follower (**gia-nô**) in the household of a member of the Trần royal clan, and one who fled Vietnam when Quý Ly cracked down on opposition within the Trần family in 1390. Indeed, Yamamoto Tatsuro has pointed out how jumbled the Trần genealogy given to the Ming was and has noted that a number of the complaints which the Trần pretender claimed to have made were entirely Chinese problems (like the Kuangsi border dispute). He therefore concluded that the entire case had been made up by the Chinese.[13]

Whatever the truth, by the end of 1404 the Yung-lo Emperor seems to have been ready to move against the Vietnamese. Where the father had been content to use threats in the attempt to maintain the world order in the south, the son was prepared to take action for this end. Over the first decade of his reign, the Yung-lo Emperor felt, to quote Wang Gungwu, "the need to show majesty (**wei**) to ensure the status quo", and nowhere was the act quite so necessary as in Vietnam. A usurping house, the attempted conquest of a neighbor, and border troubles with China, all violated the pattern the Chinese emperor wished to establish in the world order, and he meant to act by reconstructing the old and proper order. Perhaps the events as described in the Chinese **Veritable Records** (**Ming Shih Lu**) merely reflect a doctored ex post facto justification for the Ming maneuvers, a manipulation of documents much less serious than the censoring of the records concerning the late emperor Hui-ti then going on.[14] In any case, the decision to put pressure on the Hồ came with the improvement of the situation in China after two and a half years of consolidation under the strong hand of the new ruler, as Chinese interest in Southeast Asia and its own maritime influence developed and as the threat of Tamerlane disappeared with his death in 1405.

The Ming court started to force the pace by putting on a show for the Vietnamese embassy which had come to honor the emperor at the New Year of 1405. Dramatically confronted by Trần Thiên Bình, the Vietnamese envoys supposedly fell to their knees before the pretender and were lectured by Bùi Bá Kỳ and the emperor himself on the duties of a subject towards his proper ruler. The chief Vietnamese envoy subsequently stayed in China (in Vietnamese terms, he was "kept" there), and the

second in command was summarily executed when the act was discovered by the Hồ in 1406.[15] Thus, at the beginning of 1405,
the scenario had been established by the Ming, no doubt with
the help of Bùi Bá Kỳ and "Trần Thiêm Bình" (or Nguyễn Khang):
the Ming, by all propriety, had to correct the situation in
Vietnam where an oppressive usurping family committed aggression
against its southern neighbors as well as harassed and disputed
the Chinese on their own common border.

Twenty-two days after the confrontation of pretender and
envoys, the Yung-lo Emperor dispatched a message to the Hồ
in which he threw down the gauntlet: "Your guilt is manifest:
your crimes reach to heaven!" The envoy carrying this harsh
message was the censor Li I who, according to the Vietnamese
annals, set an extremely fast pace in delivering it. Obstinately
driving his mission on, he lashed the servants and officials
who accompanied him and took no account of the distance already
traveled. Where the trip from the Eastern Capital to the Western
Capital normally took twelve days, Li and his mission made
it in eight. Having delivered the message, they examined the
local situation thoroughly and left, accompanied by the Vietnamese envoy Nguyễn Cảnh Chân. As Quý Ly was quite nervous over
the behavior of the mission and afraid of what it might have
learned, he sent one of his supporters to follow Li and kill
him. But the assassin was unable to catch up with the mission
before it crossed the border at Lạng-sơn, and Li was able to
report to his ruler that the Hồ had taken for themselves the
imperial title **Ti (Đế)**. Meanwhile, the Ming court hurled another
(possibly contrived) charge at the Hồ: the seizure of seven
villages in Yünnan.[16] Quý Ly, already edgy over Li I's mission,
also seems to have worried about relations between his two
eldest sons as the Ming pressure grew; it was at this point
that he wrote the poem encouraging them to stick together,
and later executed several officials who leaked the poem.

When the Chinese mission carrying the warning about the
border dispute arrived, Quý Ly sent Hoàng Hối Khanh to take
charge of accommodating the Chinese in the cession of the disputed land. Hối Khanh consequently turned over some fifty-nine
villages to the Chinese. Quý Ly, however, scolded him severely
for having given up too much and then secretly sent a local
man to poison the indigenous chiefs set up by the Chinese.

Yet the Hồ were basically taking a submissive stance, at least in any direct dealings with Nanking. In their reply to the Chinese court carried by Nguyễn Cảnh Chân, the Vietnamese rulers humbly conceded all charges, though they continued to insist that no paternal descendants of the Trần still existed and that Hán Thương was a maternal nephew to that line. Indeed, they said in effect, if you have found a true descendant of the Trần, send him here and we will willingly serve him. The Ming distrusted what they saw as a sudden turnabout and in another message warned against the "fickleness and deceit" they had grown to expect from the Vietnamese. Yet, they said to the Hồ, if you are sincere, we shall establish you in your own fief to the south (the territory of Thuận-hóa).[17]

The second half of 1405 and the beginning of 1406 passed amicably enough. The Vietnamese received the eunuch turncoat Nguyễn Tông Đạo once again as a Ming envoy and sent Nguyễn Cảnh Chân to bestow New Year's greetings upon the Yung-lo Emperor. Cảnh Chân bore a message swearing the good faith of the Vietnamese ("We dare not bear two hearts") and promising to welcome the Trần ruler. By the end of January 1406, the Ming were ready to move into Vietnam and place the pretender on the throne.[18]

The Vietnamese continued to prepare for trouble. First, the areas upstream from the Red River Delta were ordered to provide big wooden stakes to be placed in all harbors and strategic riverine and maritime points for defense against the growing Chinese fleets. Then came the drought, the requisitioning of rice from the rich, and an amnesty following some trouble in the palace of the Heir Apparent. At this point, in mid-year, Hán Thương decided to dismantle the remainder of the palaces in the Eastern Capital and to remove them to a nearby grotto, ostensibly to calm the people. The project for abandoning the city, however, was not carried out. In August and September, Hán Thương and his father toured the countryside to examine the strategic points and display their confidence before the people. Gradually, the military forces were made ready. Four arsenals were set up where skilled artisans, both civilian and military, turned out needed weapons. Then the army was reorganized with the establishment of north and south special armies of twelve battalions (vệ) and east and west

rear palace armies of eight battalions. Generals, usually members or close supporters of the Hồ clan, commanded the major
units.[19]

Quý Ly bravely put on the great celebration for his seventieth year and then sent Hoàng Hối Khanh to direct the labor
in building the stronghold of Đa-bang. Located to the west,
upriver from the Eastern Capital, Đa-bang lay near Bạch-hạc
at the confluence of the rivers which flowed from the western
mountains, and thus across the route of any troops coming from
Yünnan to the northwest. Ever careful, Hối Khanh rebuilt the
shrine of a local spirit which he had been forced to remove
for the construction. The army from the Eastern Capital was
also dispatched to install the wooden stakes in the crucial
Bạch-hạc river mouth and to block any Chinese advance through
the mountains of Kuangsi and Tuyên-quang from the north. At
about this time, the population of all the provinces north
of the Red River received orders to remove all the rice from
the path of the Chinese troops. This was done and the territory
stripped bare of food resources.

Having sealed off the edges of the Red River Delta, all
the provincial pacifiers were called to the Western Capital
and there, together with the officials of the capital, they
discussed the situation: peace or war. Some excitedly called
for war with little heed for the misfortunes of other days.
The pacifier of Kinh-bắc, on the other hand, urged patience
and the seeking of peaceful ways, as the Chinese wished, thus
slowing down their advance. But the left prime minister Hồ
Nguyên Trừng declared: "[You] ministers need not fear war;
instead fear only [whether] the hearts of the people will follow
[or] oppose [you]." Quý Ly then gave his son a gold betel box
and war it was. Nguyên Trừng took command of the armies for
the resistance while his younger brother, the king, looked
after the needs of the state, banning the finest alcohol in
order to save rice.[20]

In the first week of the New Year, 1406, responding to Hồ
Quý Ly's statement that "your minister [Hán Thương] will lead
his countrymen to meet [Trần Thiên Bình] at the border", the
Yung-lo Emperor called the pretender before him and announced
that he was returning him to Vietnam with an escort of troops.
The Hồ regime was to retire to the southern territories of

Thuận and Hóa. The "escort", said by the Chinese to have been five thousand soldiers (though the Vietnamese claimed it to be one hundred thousand men from Kuangsi) and led by the "Attack the South" general Han Kuan, gradually worked its way south through Kuangsi, reaching Vietnam by early April.[21] Han set up camp at the border and halted, perhaps expecting the official Vietnamese party to appear. If this were the case, then Han probably waited a bit before sending his second-in-command, Huang Chung, to explore the situation, apparently taking Thiên Bình with him. With his troops strung out along the road, Huang walked into an ambush laid in a mountain pass four days north of the Eastern Capital. There, crack Vietnamese troops, reinforced by ships and elephants and under the command of Nguyễn Trừng, struck the Chinese column.

The Vietnamese victory was complete, destroying the Chinese forces and seizing the pretender. However, it was also costly as Phạm Nguyên Khôi, Quý Ly's maternal kin, and three other generals were killed. Nguyễn Trừng himself was almost captured in the heavy fighting and was saved only by the quick action of his men. The Chinese commander Huang Chung, seeing the disaster, broke off the fighting and fled in the middle of the night. Reaching Chi-lăng Pass, which the Vietnamese general Phạm Xạ had been ordered to block, the Chinese presented a letter saying that they had accomplished their task by delivering Thiên Bình (it being obvious that the people did not support him) and were on their way back to report the fact. Xạ let them through, much to the chagrin of the Hồ.[22]

The Vietnamese, having captured Thiên Bình, asked him directly to which branch of the former royal family he belonged. Reportedly, he was unable to tell them. They then offered a reward for any who could identify him. In the words of the History, "None dared recognize [him]." Thiên Bình was then tortured and killed for his crime. The military prisoners of war were sent south to till the fields of Nghệ-an, and the captured Chinese officials and clerks were kept in the capital to be used as servants in aristocratic homes. One of them told Hán Thương about the Vietnamese envoy who had saluted the pretender in Nanking, and Hán Thương promptly executed the former envoy. Then the Throne rewarded the valorous action of the campaign, promoting each person three ranks. Only Phạm Xạ and his officers received less (promotion of two ranks) due to their having fallen for the Chinese ruse which allowed Huang Chung to slip away.

Yet the Vietnamese Throne was not prepared to rest on its laurels. When the officials presented him with a message of congratulations, Hán Thương refused it and began to work towards the next attack, which he knew would come. The pacifier of Sơn-tây, perhaps a member of the former royal family, and two other officials, including a graduate of 1393, were sent to China to seek peace and to attempt to explain the Thiên Bình incident. According to the Vietnamese source, the Minh retained the envoys, allowing their return only when Quý Ly and Hán Thương were captured. Meanwhile the Hồ were reorganizing their government for the expected attack. As 1406 wore on, a number of key personnel changes were made. A favorite of Quý Ly's, Nguyễn Ngạn Quang, was brought back to the court from Thăng-hoa in the south as director of the Grand Court of Revision (Đai-lý-chính) and replaced by a southern official. Moreover, Hoàng Hối Khanh went south to take charge of the border area from the base in Thăng-hoa where he was assisted by the scholar-official Đặng Tất. Quý Ly's long-time ally Đỗ Mãn was shifted from his chief administrative duties to become a Counsellor again as well as president of the Ministry of War and one of the top generals. His son, Đỗ Nhân Giám, took his father's old place commanding the Heavenly Iron Army (Thiên-cương Quân). The eunuch Ngô Miễn was made a Counsellor and took over Mãn's chief administrative duties as well as the task of overseeing the Hồ royal tombs in Thanh-hóa. The Counsellor and Chancellery officer Trần Ngạn Chiêu was demoted to president of the Ministry of Finance and replaced with another longtime servant of the Hồ and member of the Secret Council, the scholar Nguyễn Cẩn.[23]

Thus, it would appear that Quý Ly was making final adjustments before the expected onslaught, adjustments which placed trusted lieutenants in major positions of authority. Moreover, the Throne seems to have suspended the capital examinations and summoned former officials (probably those who had been purged) to be ready to serve when needed. Local forces were strengthened, noblemen put in charge of them, and an appeal was made for those who "had fled the [king's] mandate" to form a special élite corps, "resolute and courageous". All provinces

along the southern bank of the Red River, from the fortified
position at Đa-bang on the west to Hải-dương east of the Eastern
Capital, as well as those provinces along the river from Lang-
sơn on the northern border deep into the Red River Delta, received orders to erect wooden barricades along the stream banks
for defense. The people in the northern and western parts of
the delta (Kinh-bắc and Sơn-tây) were also to accumulate stocks
of grain in isolated places along the streams and to set up
shelters in which to hide when the invasion came. The man in
charge of preparing the Đa-bang fortification, the Cham general
Bố Đông (Kim Trung Liệt), proposed that he lead troops to the
border to attack the Chinese as they sought to enter the country. Though his men were willing and the way was clear, the
other generals did not agree, preferring to play their usual
waiting game.[24]

The wait was not long. The Yung-lo Emperor was furious when
he heard of the defeat, of the shattering of his pacific attempt
to restore harmony between China and that part of the world
and to bring Vietnam back into the fold. Now, the disrespectful,
insincere, and unreliable Hồ had to be crushed; to use the
emperor's words: "The guilt of those shameful little wretches
reaches up to the sky... If we do not destroy them, what are
our armies for?"[25] Impartiality was no longer to be considered;
the Hồ had, by their acts, removed Vietnam from the ranks of
the favored states. The list of "twenty crimes" drawn up by
the Ming as justification for the subsequent invasion reflects
the extent to which they saw Vietnam as standing outside their
world order. Primarily, the Hồ, father and son, had violated
virtue by ignoring the Chinese calendar, by falsely adopting
the classical Chinese name of Ta-yü (Đại Ngu) for their state,
by distorting the sacred patterns, by attempting to deceive
Nanking, and by changing their family name, as well as by mur-
dering the Trần and oppressing the people in their efforts
to centralize the state (crimes 1-8). In Ming terms, such acts
"were contrary to heaven and diminished the natural order (li)".
Secondly, the Hồ had violated Chinese security by disruption,
seizure, and murder in the border territories (crimes 9-13).
Thirdly, they had continued to attack and forcefully subdue
Champa, though the latter was also a vassal of China (crimes
14-18). Lastly, they had directly insulted the Ming in the

question of envoys (crimes 19-20).[26]

Thus, where the morality of "no-separation" and maintenance of the status quo was threatened, the Yung-lo Emperor was fully prepared to use force to rectify the situation, as his threats to Siam and the West King of Java in 1407 would also indicate. In each of these latter cases, the chief crime was aggression by one vassal of China against another, and the threat was made in terms of the recent crushing defeat of the Hồ. Vietnam did not stand alone before the Chinese colossus, for, in the Ming emperor's words to Siam, "you all receive our recognition and stand equally [before us]... Mind your own affairs, be friendly to your neighbors and preserve your own lands..." Siam and Java acquiesced, but Vietnam did not. Yet the Yung-lo Emperor, according to Vietnamese records at least, reiterated his intention to reestablish the Trần family on the throne of Vietnam and made Bùi Bá Kỳ the main prop upon which this restoration would take place, sending him south with the army as a censor to deliver this charge.[27]

First, however, came the attack. By May 11, twelve days after news of the defeat had reached Nanking, plans for a major invasion were laid out, though the invasion itself was not to occur for another six months. The preparations which took place during this time brought together over two hundred fifteen thousand men in two locations; one hundred thirty-five thousand (from the five provinces of southeastern China) gathered in Kuangsi, and the remainder (from the three provinces of the southwest) assembled in Yünnan. This two-pronged attack was the first major campaign of the Yung-lo period, quite comparable to the five great campaigns that were to come on the northern border. A third, though minor, adjunct of the campaign existed in the south where the Ming hoped to receive aid from the Chams. The Cham mission of 1406 was given the Chinese request for aid, and six hundred men from Kuangtung were sent south as a naval unit to expedite matters.[28] Many of the twenty-five generals in charge of the massive expedition were personal favorites of the emperor, having served him loyally in his conquest of the throne, and those who survived would later serve on the northern expeditions. Chu Neng, commander of the expedition, had been, to quote Wang Gungwu, "one of Chu Ti's most trusted generals", but he died at the beginning of the campaign and was succeeded by his deputy commander Chang Fu. The latter's father had abandoned the Mongol cause only in 1385, but had then joined Chu Ti in Peking, and both father and son had fought well for their prince in the succession dispute. Indeed, Chang Fu's sister had entered the palace as one of the emperor's concubines.[29]

In the second half of November, with a specific strategy laid out by the emperor, Chang Fu led the eastern forces of the "Force the Barbarians to Submit" Army into Vietnam, quickly defeated a Vietnamese force at Chi-lăng Pass and, with the aid of pontoons, set up a base midway to the Eastern Capital. As the Vietnamese fell back, a Chinese reconnaissance force penetrated the lowlands to Gia-lâm, directly across the river from the Eastern Capital. According to the Vietnamese description, the Chinese troops shuttled ahead with one group resting, the other on the move, each helping the other. Meanwhile, Mu Sheng and his western army were cutting a path down the Clear River from Yünnan toward the fortified position at Đa-bang. A message was sent to the Hồ in one last effort to allow them to conform to the dictates of the Ming. The Vietnamese rulers would have to submit, to offer an apology for the violence they had done to the Ming pattern, and to make restitution of fifty thousand ounces of gold and one hundred elephants, the same as the Ming would request from the Javanese a year later. Quý Ly again refused.[30]

The Ming offensive pushed on, stripping the land as it went. The eastern troops moved by way of Kinh-bắc toward the Bạch-hạc river junction to join Mu Sheng's western force. In mid-December, the Chinese armies set up camp there on the north bank of the Red River as far as the Chú River and built boats and pontoons. The Hồ forces continued to hold their positions along the southern and western banks of the river system. The two capitals formed the core of the defense line which ran from Mount Tản-viên in the west, directly opposite Bạch-hạc, to western Hải-dương, east of the Eastern Capital, with the northern line, of little consequence, going northeast up the Thái-bình River into southern Lạng-sơn. Nguyễn Trừng commanded the troops along the Red River with Quý Ly's stepson Hồ Đỗ taking charge of those along the Chú. In front of the lines warships were linked together, while on the bank Vietnamese troops and elephants stood facing the Chinese position but did not offer battle.

During this lull, according to the Vietnamese account, Chang Fu and Mu Sheng floated many wooden placards down river carrying a message that detailed the crimes of the Hồ and an appeal for the restoration of the Trần (a message originally prepared by Chu Neng in Kuangsi). The demoralized Vietnamese troops are said to have taken the words to heart, though this is probably the interpretation of later, anti-Hồ Vietnamese historians.[31] Yet significant defections had begun to take place, particularly in the areas of northwest Hải-dương and Sơn-tây, northeast and west of the Eastern Capital. Three descendants of a major literati minister of the early fourteenth century, Mạc Đỉnh Chi, never accepted the Hồ regime. They now took the opportunity to go over to the Ming, as did others who likewise brought their followers. Chang Fu was having trouble with the terrain in planning his attack, but Mạc Thúy and a local Sơn-tây district magistrate aided him and led the Chinese troops across the river.[32]

This act paved the way for the Chinese attack in mid-January 1407. Mu Sheng moved against Đa-bang, Chang Fu swept the river clean, and another officer made a diversionary move downriver toward Gia-lâm. The Vietnamese split their forces, sending ships downriver toward Gia-lâm, and the Chinese attacked upriver. The Bạch-hạc area fell quickly with the unfortunate Phạm Xạ retreating to the south. The Ming forces pushed on and, though momentarily defeated by Xạ's deputy, caught a Vietnamese commander in a moment of dalliance, crushed his forces, and stormed the Red River on pontoon bridges. Đa-bang fell in bitter fighting, attacked from both north and east by Mu Sheng's and Chang Fu's armies. The Vietnamese troops along the river disintegrated and, within a week, the Eastern Capital collapsed while the Hồ abandoned the Western Capital, putting it to the torch, as the Chinese rapidly moved in their direction.

With the dawning of the New Year (February 8, 1407), the Vietnamese withdrew to the coast, apparently hoping to draw the Chinese into battle during the summer heat (in the same way that they had previously taken advantage of the Mongols). The Yung-lo Emperor worried about that very problem and, fearing the possible damage of malaria to his men, ordered them to slow down. The Chinese had the momentum, however, and continued to push their takeover of the Red River Delta, moving east into Hải-dương and south through Sơn-nam. At the same time, they began to take the Vietnamese population in hand. Officials and people were brought together and encouraged to support the Ming. On the other hand, the Vietnamese records charge that the Chinese immediately seized women, children, and property, collected and tabulated the grain supplies, designated local officials for specific tasks, gathered the scattered people, and made plans for a long stay. Certainly, all the Vietnamese were marked so as to link them to a specific location, while many boys were sent north to China to serve as eunuchs. Artisans and copper cash were likewise sent to Nanking.[33]

Regardless of their acts, the Chinese did get a major response from the people around the Eastern Capital for, as even the **History** states, "many in the capital region followed the bandits and went into revolt [against the Vietnamese state]". Meanwhile the Chinese were, in all probability, widely publicizing the crimes of the Hồ. In the coming months, the Yung-lo Emperor continued to stress these themes: "The Annamite bandit chief Lê [Quý Ly] has killed his king and taken his kingdom, has arbitrarily taken a name for his state and a name for his reign period, and has shown himself to be violent, inhuman, destructive of his state, and aggressive towards his neighbors; he has resisted the orders of the court and has been remiss in his tributary duties. I must, in spite of myself, give you the order to chastise him for his crimes." Certainly those Vietnamese who hated the Hồ took the opportunity to serve the Ming on such grounds. Already during the initial campaign, Vietnamese had joined Chang Fu. Now members of the old royal family went over to the Chinese, particularly Trần Nguyên Chỉ and Prince Trần Sư Hiền. Nguyên Chỉ and Sư Hiền, who had served the Hồ in central administrative capacities, fled with their respective entourages. In another case, a group of men deep in the Red River Delta killed their provincial official and went over to the invaders.[34]

During the first months of the new year, the Hồ were attempting to regroup and to strike back at the Chinese forces. The Vietnamese army under Nguyễn Trừng, based in the southeastern

section of the Red River Delta, twice attempted to move toward
the capital and was turned back. In desperation, the Hồ offered
to reward any who gave support with titles, marriage into the
royal clan, and ten mẫu of land. Meanwhile, the Ming pressures
were building on the Vietnamese forces despite the heat and
growing illness. Due to the swampy nature of the terrain, however, the Chinese pulled back to Hàm-tử Wharf, southeast of
the capital, and built their defenses there. Quý Ly and Hán
Thương then came up from Thanh-hóa as the Vietnamese army prepared a major attack. According to the Vietnamese records,
those around the capital were already grating under the conquer-
or's heel and were flocking to join the Hồ. In the beginning
of May, the Vietnamese generals, Nguyên Trừng, Hồ Đỗ, Trần
Vấn, Phạm Xạ, Đỗ Mẫn, and Đỗ Nhân Giám—all members of the
Hồ aristocracy—led the offensive up both the banks of the
river toward the Chinese position in one final effort. The
Ming shattered the thrust, and Quý Ly fled to the coast of
Thanh-hóa. Hotly pursued by the Chinese, the Hồ forces began
to fall apart. Quý Ly and Hán Thương desperately sought to
escape and, when the radical official Đồng Thức flatly stated
that the two rulers should immolate themselves in order not
to die at the hands of the enemy, Quý Ly, in a fury, had him
beheaded.[35]

   In full retreat and severely pressed by the Chinese, Quý
Ly sent orders to Hoàng Hối Khanh on the southern border to
select one out of every three of the Vietnamese male migrants
for the army and to send them north "to give their all in serving the king" (cần vương). The southern area was then ostensibly
made an autonomous fief under Chế Bồng Nga's son, the Cham
prince Chế Ma Nô Đà Nan, who received the title of Thăng-hoa
Border Prince (Quân-vương) "in order to keep the multitudes
of Champa peaceful". Though Hối Khanh kept the news as quiet
as possible, the Cham ruler, having sent rich tribute to China,
ordered his troops to retake the old northern territory. The
Vietnamese migrants took fright and scattered, while Hối Khanh
moved north, abandoning the border area and leaving the Cham
prince alone to face his countrymen. Caught like a fox, Chế
Ma Nô Đà Nan stood and fought to the end for the Vietnamese
cause, dying in the effort. Meanwhile the Vietnamese forces
moving north began to fight among themselves (with the loser

fleeing to Champa where he became a major minister), and the Chams moved farther north into Hóa-châu.[36]

The southern troops would most likely have made little difference to the Hồ cause. The Chinese, guided by Mạc Thúy and a former official of the Hồ, had already pressed south into Nghệ-an and captured Quý Tỳ, his son, Quý Ly, and Nguyên Trừng near the Kỳ-la river mouth. Thúy then helped seize Hán Thương and his heir, Nhuế, in the mountains. Of the survivors of the Hồ cause, some were caught, others surrendered, and a few committed suicide, repaying the "kingly beneficence" (**quân-ân**) they had received.[37] The core of the Hồ state was sent north to Nanking in cages, together with the official seals. There the Yung-lo Emperor charged them with the question, "Is this the way of a subject?", and, refusing their pleas of ignorance, jailed all but Nguyên Trừng, the Heir Apparent Nhuế, and some lesser figures who supposedly (according to the Vietnamese records) were put into official positions.[38]

While he was pushing the campaign against the Hồ, Chang Fu issued a proclamation seeking out the descendants of the Trần and gained the allegiance of many of the former officials of that family. Yet, despite the fact that some members of the Trần clan, such as Prince Sư Hiền, defected to the Chinese, and at least one (Trần Thúc Dao, the son of Nguyên Đán) served the Ming as an administrator while others later rebelled against the occupation, the only result of the search became manifest a few months later, when the Chinese gave posthumous titles to seven members of the Trần clan.[39] Instead of recognizing any Trần prince, Chang promptly sent a memorial to Nanking stating that over eleven hundred of the Vietnamese élite had first, declared the former royal clan to have been wiped out by the Hồ and second, asked that, due to the circumstances, Vietnam revert to its former status as the colony of Chiao-chih.

Since it is difficult to see the Yung-lo Emperor arbitrarily putting aside the pattern of world order which he was in the process of establishing, it may have been the hardened general (and later historiographer) Chang Fu who believed that Vietnam should not be given up after the costly campaign, and that the Ming should duplicate the efforts of Han and T'ang in making it a part of their empire. Certainly, two years later, Chang interpreted his role to be one of pacification, not of restoration. Meanwhile, Bùi Bá Kỳ, apparently told by the Chinese Throne that he would be the major prop of the new state, was merely made a local prefecture official in his home area and only allowed to keep up the Trần temple. However the approach to Vietnam may have changed, the Yung-lo Emperor accepted Chang Fu's memorial immediately after receiving news of the Hồ capture, and in early June he proclaimed the existence of Chiao-chih as a part of the Ming empire.[40]

Thus the state of Đại Ngu came to an end. As Nguyễn Trừng would note three decades later, "time flies, things change, almost nothing leaves a trace."[41] The Hồ clan and its immediate supporters had either been killed in battle or lay in the prisons of Nanking. The major radical officials, those staunch advocates of a revitalized Vietnam, were dead: Nguyễn Hy Chu was captured and then executed for reviling Chang Fu as a brutal bandit; Đồng Thức was killed for having advocated self-immolation to Quý Ly; and Hoàng Hối Khanh committed suicide in the south rather than join his assistant Đặng Tất in serving the Ming, however temporarily. The senior scholars, such as Nguyễn Phi Khanh, were probably taken to China, while the younger ones, graduates of 1400 and 1405 like Nguyễn Trãi, Lý Tử Tấn, and Vũ Mộng Nguyên, remained in Vietnam and lay low (Trãi with a death sentence commuted to restriction within the capital). The eunuchs, particularly Ngô Miễn, committed suicide, and the refugee Chams fell in battle. A number of Quý Ly's enemies actively went over to the Ming during the campaign; most of the rest seem to have accepted Chinese rule passively.[42]

When the Hồ regime fell to the Ming incursion, it had not completed its work, and it is thus difficult to estimate what its final pattern might have become. Yet we may say that, while Quý Ly's actions would not determine the precise nature of Vietnam's future, they did set the framework for this future. His behavior did not accord with Confucian theory, nor was it meant to, and the interpretations of his successors generally overlooked his situation and his goals. His significance lies in his efforts and their consequences, rather than in any specific success or failure he may have experienced.

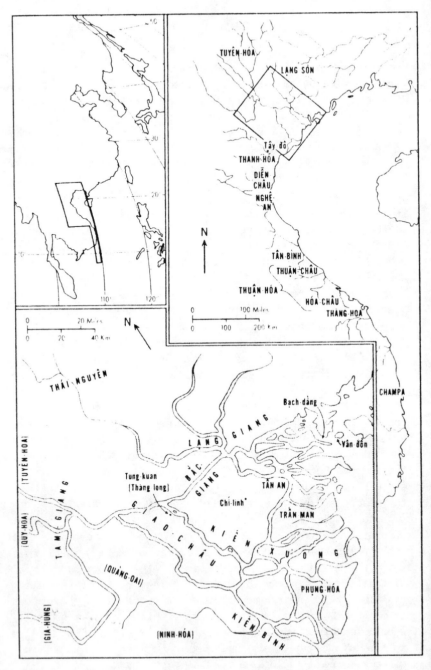

VIETNAM AT THE TIME OF THE MING OCCUPATION

VI. CHIAO-CHIH AND MING COLONIALISM

The Yung-lo Emperor was at this time also disseminating his
notion of world order farther to the south (Malacca and later
Brunei) and to the east (Japan). This we can see in three inscriptions composed personally by him. Unlike the Vietnamese,
these peoples fitted the pattern toward which the Chinese Throne
was working, responsive as they were to the Chinese will and
thus fulfilling the "no-separation" sought by the Ming. Malacca
was the first distant state to seek the aid and protection
of China, while the Japanese ruler had performed a service
by destroying two nests of Wako pirates. The latter was praised
highly for his respect, his sincerity, and his reliability.
As the message to Brunei was to declare in 1408, there was
"no separating into inner and outer, all beings seen as one
whole", a whole which followed the moral dictates of the Ming.[1]

On this basis, the Yung-lo Emperor moved not only to correct
the Vietnamese behavior but also to contact more foreign peoples
and countries than at any other time in China's imperial history.
In mid-1405, he had given the order for his eunuch Cheng Ho
to visit and display the power of China to the maritime states
of the "Western Ocean" (the Indian Ocean) in the first of the
great overseas expeditions.[2] Notions of morality and world
order underlay all these actions.

Yet, as the Chinese juggernaut crushed the local resistance
with aid from Vietnamese like Mạc Thúy, the change took place
in the Ming aim. This change undoubtedly occurred on the battlefield as the veteran Chang Fu refused to give up his hard-earned
conquest. Even though members of the Trần royal family joined

him against Hồ Quý Ly, Chang apparently engineered a request
from some of the indigenous élite for Vietnam to become once
more a part of China, since, they allegedly reported, the Trần
family no longer existed. The old aggressive acts of the Han
and T'ang dynasties became once again the reality under the
Ming, despite its moral proclamations. The Yung-lo Emperor
accepted Chang Fu's report and made Vietnam, now Chiao-chih,
a province of his empire. He was determined to bring the Vietnamese fully into the orthodox Chinese world.

The formal establishment of Chiao-chih in July 1407 brought
an official province administration to Vietnam. Lu I and Huang
Chung, veterans in the campaign, took charge of the Military
Office (**Tu-ssu**), staffed mainly with other veterans. A former
minister of the ill-fated Hui-ti, Huang Fu, had been sent south
in a sort of exile as coordinator of supplies during the campaign and now received the appointment, not without protest,
to head the offices of both administration and surveillance
(**pu-cheng-ssu** and **an-cha-ssu** respectively). These offices were
based in the capital of Tung-kuan, the former Vietnamese capital
of Thăng-long (now Hanoi). Below the provincial level, the
standard civil and military organizations were set up with
prefectures (**fu**), subprefectures (**chou**), and districts (**hsien**)
for the former and the **wei-so** system for the latter. In the
first year or so of their occupation, the Chinese organized
all the territory under their control, mainly the Red River
Delta and the northern mountains, into fifteen prefectures,
forty-one subprefectures, and 210 districts. The Vietnamese
provinces became Chinese prefectures as the upper administrative
levels were reduced by one level (province to prefecture, prefecture to subprefecture), and many of the Vietnamese names
were changed in the process. Militarily, there were at first
ten guard units (**wei**) and two battalions (**so**), mainly centered
around the capital, and twelve citadels.[3]

Despite the establishment of a civil administration in Vietnam, the military, particularly Chang Fu, continued to be in
control of affairs in the new province. Many of the civil offices seem to have remained unfilled, and thus existed only
on paper, for the first eight years (to 1415) as the major
problem confronting the Ming continued to be that of pacification. Not until this problem was sufficiently in hand would

the Chinese really begin their attempt to transform Vietnamese society. Meanwhile, as Chang Fu and the other officers pursued their efforts against the Vietnamese resistance, Huang Fu strove to feed and maintain the required forces, at the same time trying to cope with local security problems, the development of agriculture, the collection of taxes (imposed lightly for the first few years), control of sub-officials, and the maintenance of proper land and population records. Vietnam never was able to supply enough food for the occupying army and officials; every year a huge amount of rice (in 1422, ca. 700,000 piculs) was brought south and even that amount was not adequate. Various devices, such as the introduction of the military colony system (**t'un-t'ien**), were attempted, but the Chinese were unable to solve the problem. The persisting instability constantly prevented them from maintaining the solid grip necessary for turning Vietnam into a prosperous colony.[4]

To a great extent the problem lay with the lower officials (**t'u-kuan**) who were mainly Vietnamese and whose allegiance and obedience were needed not so much to maintain control as to gain the support of the population at large.[5] Although we have little specific information about the great number of Vietnamese recruited for the Chinese service in the first years of the occupation, many were undoubtedly opportunistic and most probably came from the area around the capital. By 1410 and 1411, as Huang Fu was attempting to put the tax system in order, the lack of skilled local officials became keenly felt. In one stroke with a triple purpose Huang gave open public land with tenants to farm it to local officials so as to enable them to support themselves, to save the imported grain for military use, and to further develop the economic base of the colony. He also began his attempts to upgrade educational facilities for potential Vietnamese officials. Yet the problem of indigenous officials remained throughout the period of occupation, becoming acute as scattered resistance movements put pressure on them. In the beginning there were men like Nguyễn Đại who, having helped in the capture of the Hồ, had received a military position, only to be executed soon after by Chang Fu for arrogance, illegal activities and riotous living, not to mention a tendency towards rebellion.[6]

This was a major problem for the Chinese—how to know which

Vietnamese to trust. Not long after the collapse of the Hồ, when the Ming attempt to occupy Vietnam had become quite clear, resistance began with the explicit aim of assassinating collaborators. "If [you want] to live, take refuge in the forests and the mountains; if [you want] to die, [become] a local official for the Ngô (in Chinese **Wu**, implying Ming) dynasty" was a popular saying supposed to have been current at the time. As the **History** states, "False officials with evil reputations were to be completely exterminated."[7] Officials opposed to the Ming had already begun to challenge those who had chosen to serve the Chinese.

Through the last months of 1407 and the first of 1408, uprisings broke out across Vietnam. People in Diễn-châu to the far south killed their district officials and burned the jails. On the far northern border tribal groups made the Ming pay a price before going down to defeat. Around the Hồ capital of Tây-đô in western Thanh-hóa, west of Tung-kuan itself in Tam-giang, to the east in Tân-an, to the south in Kiến-bình, and to the north in Bắc-giang and Lạng-giang, in all these areas rebels appeared and the Ming continued to crush them.[8] Historically, the most serious revolt was that involving Trần Ngỗi, said to have been a younger son of the former Trần ruler Nghệ-tông, who went into resistance on November 1, 1407, and proclaimed himself Giản-định-đế (the Discern and Establish Emperor). Taking the reign title Hưng-khánh (Restore Felicity), he set himself up in the northern part of Thanh-hóa, just south of the Red River Delta. Here he had secretly moved with some close followers after almost giving himself up to Chang Fu's search for the members of his family. Using the old rites, the pretender took the throne and proclaimed the state of Đại Việt. He began to build up his forces, being joined by a probable kinsman from the ancestral home of the Trần family slightly to the north in the Red River Delta. Almost immediately, however, a Ming patrol probed the area and the Trần forces, fearing their own weakness, fell back to the hills of Nghệ-an. At this time Đặng Tất, who had taken the position of chief administrator on the southern border for the Ming, heard of the pretender and killed the local Chinese official, bringing his Thuận-hóa followers to Trần Ngỗi's camp. There Tất, who gave his daughter to serve the king and received the title of duke (**quốc-công**), became the backbone of the resistance. The two men proceeded to plan for the restoration of the Vietnamese state.[9]

Gathering the remnants of other anti-Ming groups, the Trần forces slowly mustered strength and began to focus their efforts on the collaborators who served as local officials under the Chinese. They assassinated some six hundred "false officials" (ngụy-quan), including two prominent Vietnamese aristocrats who had taken Chinese positions in the south and refused to join the resistance. For the next three years, to 1410, the resistance efforts continued amidst a series of environmental calamities. Though Chang Fu and his Vietnamese supporter Mạc Thủy inflicted defeat on the Trần, the Chinese troops were not able to crush their opponents and soon began to feel a counterpressure. Chang, back in Nanking, had to return as the Trần forces moved into the Red River Delta in 1408 and revolts broke out close to Tung-kuan on the south, east, and west.[10]

Frightened by this rebel progress, the Chinese brought Mu Sheng with an army of 40,000 men down from Yünnan to join the local forces and block the Trần entrance into the Red River Delta. First, however, they offered an hereditary position to any Vietnamese who surrendered, but none accepted. Trần Ngỗi and Đặng Tất shattered the new Chinese force in the southern Delta at the end of December, killing among others the president of the Board of War, Liu Chun, and the military commissioner of Chiao-chih, Lu I. Trần Ngỗi urged his troops on toward the capital, but Tất ordered them to wipe out the remainder of the Chinese forces, thus losing the opportunity for a quick advance. The engagement ended in a stalemate as Mu Sheng and his soldiers retreated to Tung-kuan while Tất deployed his troops to surround the various citadels lying before him and called on all the Vietnamese localities to send more men.[11]

The Chinese were desperately trying to stabilize the situation so as to be able to go about their business. The Yung-lo Emperor had already sent out an edict informing the Vietnamese that China would be compassionate, pardon all crimes, help civilize Vietnam, and be unstinting in its care for the Vietnamese people. In his words, "I shall lead [them] to humaneness (jen)."[12] Yet what weakened the Trần threat was not Ming policy but internal factionalism. The Vietnamese resistance split as Trần Ngỗi executed Đặng Tất and another powerful minister, whereupon sons and associates of these ministers swung their support behind Trần Ngỗi's nephew Trần Quý Khoáng. This group prevailed and, adopting the old Trần pattern, made Ngỗi the abdicated monarch (thượng-hoàng) with Quý Khoáng the actual ruler.[13]

Chang Fu had returned from China by August 1409 with a new army of 47,000 men from south China, and the Ming forces began again to press the Vietnamese. The two Trần rulers had already moved their troops, this time deep into the eastern Delta to take advantage of what seems to have been a rather loose Chinese hold on the swampy region. After a period of training for his new troops north of Tung-kuan, Chang cleared the capital area of rebels, shattering one base to the west, and in the autumn began to move east. The Vietnamese forces showed strength at first, defeating a Ming probe, but their campaign soon came apart as the Trần units lost all coordination. Chang struck and pushed the Vietnamese back south. Trần Ngỗi tried to escape to the west but was captured, taken to Nanking, and executed.

The Chinese promptly set out to make sure that such a threat would not arise again. Chang killed two envoys sent by Quý Khoáng seeking enfiefment as a descendant of the Trần, cleared the rivers of the stakes and defenses put up by the resistance, and spread a wave of terror across the land with a variety of excruciating and grisly executions. In the capital region, as the local areas gave up one after another, rebels were made slaves and sold in all directions. Local men who had not resisted or who had killed or captured any of the rebels became local officials. Having bloodily finished his task, Chang Fu returned north to serve with his Emperor on the first of the great northern campaigns which would eventually turn Ming attention away from Vietnam. Still well established south of Thanh-hóa, the Trần in mid-1410 again raided the eastern Delta, gained support from various local chiefs, and wreaked scattered havoc, in some instances fairly close to the capital. Yet Quý Khoáng could not bring the many local forces together, even those of the eastern Delta.[14]

Consequently, the Vietnamese pretender again attempted to make diplomatic contact with the Ming. Towards the end of 1410, he sent the Counsellor Hồ Ngạn Thần, top scholar in the examination of 1405, to seek recognition with local products and two

images "in place of myself", one in gold, the other in silver.[15]
Though the Yung-lo Emperor had in a fury ordered the execution
of the two earlier envoys, he now, at a time of problems on
the northern border, confronted the Vietnamese with the captive
Hồ Nguyên Trừng, eldest son of Hồ Quý Ly, who was "to [express]
the kindness [he had received]" and to sound them out on the
situation of the country. Ngạn Thần responded fully, for which
he was offered the post of prefect of Nghệ-an, appointment
for his ruler as administrative commissioner in Chiao-chih
(Huang Fu's job?), and positions for other Trần followers.
On the return of this mission, Quý Khoáng executed the scholar
and turned his back on the offer, though he would try again
to win recognition for his dynasty in 1413 with an equal lack
of success.[16]

The Yung-lo Emperor continued to adopt a lenient attitude
towards his new and unruly subjects of the south. Another amnesty was proclaimed in March of 1411 with a three-year moratorium
on some lesser taxes,[17] and two other imperial edicts quickly
followed. The main points of these edicts were that the Chinese
emperor was striving mightily to include Vietnam in the broad
pattern of "no outer separation"—"The men of Chiao-chih are
all Heaven's people" and "Our children"—and that the local
Vietnamese officials had to be encouraged to bring peace to
their land.[18] The "bandit" minority still existed in the mountains and along the coast and "coerced" the people into supplying them with food and participating in their acts: "they do
not go of their own free will." To solve this difficulty, the
Chinese Throne first praised and rewarded the local officials,
like Mạc Thúy and his brothers, for what they had already done
and then called on them to wipe out the rebels. In the process,
the emperor also appealed to any who "dared" deal with the
officials to lead the rebels back into the fold. High offices
and noble titles awaited those who did. Once such men achieved
"self-renewal", the Yung-lo Emperor foresaw no problems in
widespread acceptance of his "reform". The somewhat sarcastic
comment of the **History** is: "Thus [the Ming] ordered that all
the people be saturated with virtue and kindness."[19]

With little response from the Vietnamese to these conciliato-
ry gestures and the first northern campaign successfully over,
Chang Fu once more swept into Vietnam in mid-1411, defeated

the Trần forces in Thanh-hóa, and chased Quý Khoáng briefly all the way south to Thuận-hóa. Thereafter the resistance remained strictly in a guerrilla stance, troublesome to the Ming, but not threatening to any degree. Though local uprisings would continue to swirl around the capital area and across the northern mountains, no coordination could be achieved either among them or with the Trần in the far south, and they were mercilessly crushed by Chang Fu or dissipated through internal strife. Quý Khoáng, executing another t'u-kuan, struggled to keep his movement alive in Nghệ-an, but all that was left to the Trần were desperate maneuvers to dodge and escape the advancing Ming forces.

By the early months of 1412, the capital region was firmly allied with the Chinese, and the people served as runners, supplied their rice, and were generally obedient to the colonizers. The Vietnamese officials built boats, developed military colonies around the capital and up in the mountains, and helped handle the harvests of Thái-nguyên, Tuyên-hóa, and Tam-giang prefectures. The military also traded salt for rice in the mountain areas. All these activities helped supply the occupying army. Huang Fu had already set about re-establishing the disrupted bureaucratic structure, at least from Thanh-hóa north, as Chang Fu staffed the lower civil and military positions with Vietnamese who had resisted the insurgents. It was at this time that Huang suggested providing land and local labor to the indigenous officials for their support, the amount depending on their rank. The Chinese officials (liu-kuan) also received agricultural labor from the military forces.[20]

Only in Diễn-châu and the far south was there no Chinese-enforced stability, and in these areas agriculture was disrupted. Here the Trần remnants were attempting to regroup, reinforced by those from the capital who could evade the Chinese hold. Raids into Nghệ-an by Chang Fu and Mu Sheng kept them off balance, consolidated the Chinese hold on Thanh-hóa and Diễn-châu and, in accord with the emperor's instructions, gained turncoat Vietnamese for official positions. The final two Trần raids to the north, one in early 1412, the other a year later, struck along the coast in search of supplies, but both failed, despite continued revolts in the Red River Delta that tended to distract Chang Fu. Thereafter, the Vietnamese resistance began to melt into the hinterlands under Chang's constant pressure. By April 1413, only 30 to 40 percent of Quý Khoáng's forces remained, and Chang soon forced him to leave Nghệ-an again for Hóa-châu on the southern border, where his supporters' greatest strength lay. There a last stand collapsed as turncoats gave vital information to the Chinese. The survivors scattered, some going up into the Lao hills, others to Champa, many taking their families with them. Though defiant to the end, Quý Khoáng and his major followers had all fallen into Chinese hands by May 1414. With their capture ended the Trần attempt to reconstitute the Vietnamese state. In the words of the Vietnamese **History**, "from this time, the people of our state were totally the subjects and handmaids of the Ming personnel."[21]

As the last rebels were being taken, Chang Fu was tightening the Ming grip in the newly-won southern territories. The people of Hóa-châu had surrendered, and demoted "local officials" were sent south to fill the newly created administrative offices, take a census, and draw up a household register. Farther south, in the Thăng-hoa region, problems with the Chams cropped up as the latter's officials had already gained a hold on the territory. Here the Ming seem to have backed off and taken possession in name only, while making threatening gestures. Chang Fu set up the military **wei-so** system in the south (Diễn-châu, Nghệ-an, Tân-bình, and Thuận-hóa, but not Thăng-hoa) with special control over four distant barbarian prefectures which directly joined Lao, Cham, or Thai territory. Vietnamese troops and officials were placed in these strategic locations. Chang also broadcast a warning that all military families which seized servants or women and moved to another place should be dragged back to his own office, whereupon indigenous officials grabbed many people who were poor or vagrant and sent them to Chang, fulfilling his wish.[22]

Yet not all Vietnamese became so subservient. Quý Khoáng and his loyal lieutenants left a vivid memory of their sacrifice, particularly since it was said that that the pretender and a chief lieutenant had leapt to their deaths in the ocean from the same ship that was carrying the elaborate gifts of the Vietnamese collaborators to the Yung-lo Emperor. However the Vietnamese **History** might insist that "the state, from this time, was completely subject to the Ming", the spirit of resistance remained among the Vietnamese.[23]

A. THE STRUCTURE OF THE PROVINCE

Wang Gungwu has observed that it took much longer to quell the rebellion than to conquer Vietnam. Even though Chang Fu would stay the good part of another three years in the south, the Chinese task was now mainly in the hands of his civil compatriot, Huang Fu.[24] This task entailed not only breaking down any situation of outer-separation, but also "civilizing", i.e. Sinicizing, the controlled population. Towards this end, the Ming had one major fact on their side: their political and administrative control spread far wider over Vietnamese society than that of any previous regime, Vietnamese or Chinese. The Hồ in their reforms had broken down the local concentrations of land and manpower and established a greater administrative structure than had theretofore existed. The Chinese occupiers now went much further in their attempt to bring the pattern of the Ming state to this new territory. At the peak in mid-1419, there would be over one thousand major and minor civil, censorial, and military offices (ya-men) established to control, administer, and transform Vietnam, more than double the 472 initially set up by July 1408.[25]

The Vietnam into which this administrative structure penetrated had had a "pacified" population in 1408 of over three million, mainly located in the Red River Delta, with some two million "captive barbarians" presumably living on the fringes of the lowlands.[26] The area under control at that time produced 13.6 million piculs of rice, had almost a quarter of a million draft animals (elephants, horses, and cattle), over 8,500 boats, and two and a half million weapons, all by official Chinese count.[27] A Chinese text from a decade later shows the bulk of of this controlled population to have been spread across the Red River Delta. The prevalent type of community was the peasant village (xã), supported for the most part by wet rice agriculture or fishing, and governed by its elders, headman, and local gentry. The only major urban area was the capital, now Tung-kuan, located in Giao-châu, the Chinese prefecture which also had the greatest number of markets (thị), thirty-eight. Tam-giang prefecture to the west with twelve markets and Kiến-bình to the south with ten probably fed in a desultory fashion into

those of Giao-châu, as did those of other southern Delta prefectures (Kiên-xương, Trân-man, Phụng-hóa). Thanh-hóa was the
single center of local commerce farther south. Curiously, the
rather heavily settled eastern portion of the Red River Delta,
Tân-an prefecture, seems not to have been commercialized in
a local manner, having only one market, though the major port
of Vân-đôn led to much commercial activity in one portion of
the prefecture. The main commercial route seems to have gone
north and east from Giao-châu through Bắc-giang and Lạng-giang
prefectures, with nineteen and eleven markets respectively,
and on to the Chinese border via Tuyên-hóa. Away from the lowlands, a variety of different types of settlements existed,
many areas having their own unique styles of life if the differ-
entiation of terms may be taken seriously. In the northern
mountains (Thái-nguyên, Tuyên-hóa, and Lạng-sơn), there were
communities called **trang** or **thôn,** while the mountains to the
south and west (Thanh-hóa, Nghệ-an, and the various autonomous
subprefectures) also had **sách.** Such terms perhaps reflect ethnic
differences. Overall, the Ming counted more than 3,300 communities of varying sorts throughout the length and breadth of
Vietnam, some 2,500 of them xã.[28]

The administrative office for this new territory was located
in the same place as had that of the T'ang protectorate centuries before, what had become in the interim the Vietnamese
capital of Thăng-long and was now Tung-kuan. It lay in the
midst of the flat, fertile, "fiery" delta, completely encircled
by the many streams and beyond by the mountains. Access lay
open to it from all directions. Huang Fu's office was within
the Giao-châu citadel, initially to the west of the drum tower.
With the end of pacification in 1415, Chang Fu took this location for the military office as the administrators moved to
the southern section of the eastern quarter and started building
a new office. Finally, in April 1419, after two and a half
years' work, they had an office which "met official specifica-
tions [and] was just like the former one".[29] From this location
Huang controlled the administrative structure of the province.

To the west of the drum tower, but in the northern quarter,
was the provincial surveillance office, the local branch of
China's censorial system, which was also under Huang Fu's command. From this position Huang could bypass the administrative

chain and procedures and go directly to the emperor with his memorials. Under him were four circuit branch offices (tao-fen-ssu), one each apparently south (Shan-nan), north (Shan-pei), and east (Hai-tung) of the capital with one for the southern prefecture (Hai-hsi). In total, there were fifteen local surveillance offices with differing civil and military responsibilities scattered throughout the province. This office was, to quote Charles Hucker, "required to maintain surveillance over all local government personnel, taking whatever disciplinary action was called for to uphold government morale and to relieve the people of bureaucratic corruption and oppression."[30] It was supposed to keep a particular eye on judicial proceedings, and its reports and memorials covered both civil and military matters. In addition, there also existed in the northern quarter from the middle of 1417 the office of a regional inspector, a direct representative of the Censorate at Nanking, who appears to have been independent of Huang Fu. His responsibility was to cross-check all aspects of local government.[31]

One report from a Chiao-chih assistant surveillance commissioner in March 1408 had complained that in the Vietnamese administrative system the subprefectural (chou) offices had not been close enough to the people and it was the district (hsien) offices which governed local affairs. Instead, he believed, the new administration should "use the subprefectures to govern the people and do away with all the districts"; the emperor concurred.[32] Basically, in the Chinese mind, there were too many districts for too few people, and the Ming worked to consolidate the local jurisdictions. In July of the same year, there existed fifteen prefectures, forty-one subprefectures, and 210 districts.[33] Four months later the consolidation process began as eighteen districts in six central prefectures were absorbed into their subprefectures, one for each of the latter.[34] The following seven years brought little change as the revolts kept the Chinese preoccupied, only nine districts in Lạng-sơn, Thanh-hóa, and Tân-an being merged with their subprefectures or with other districts.[35] Apparently, the Chinese were being cautious in their administrative manipulations so long as the fighting continued.

Only in September 1415 did major changes occur. By this

time other subprefectures and districts had been set up in the south as the Ming gained firmer administrative control in that direction.[36] With peace restored, sweeping changes came, first in 1415, and again in late 1419. While some small prefectures were turned into independent subprefectures, the major changes took place at the district level. In this massive administrative rationalization, some districts were shifted to other prefectures (for the "convenience" of shorter distance), but the main change was the drastic reduction in the number of districts. In 1415, forty-one districts were abolished, twenty-one being merged with other districts and twenty becoming part of their respective subprefectures. From 1415 to 1419, then, the number of administrative offices was that which is generally given, seventeen prefectures, forty-seven subprefectures, and 157 districts.[37] The main reduction of districts had taken place in the old prefectures of the south and the north (almost half), while a large number (over a third) had disappeared from the Red River Delta. The newer prefectures in the south and the north, as well as the four autonomous subprefectures, had had none of their districts touched.

Thus, as the Chinese colonial effort reached its heyday, the Ming acted to bring their administrative structure more in line with the population spread of the Vietnamese. The Red River Delta prefectures retained proportionally more of their districts, and it is in this area that the main Chinese efforts of the years 1415 to 1419 would take place. The older prefectures in the outer areas tended to lose more, in all probability reflecting both the lower population in those areas and their lesser importance in the Chinese eyes. The newer border prefectures seemingly existed to Chinese satisfaction.

In the major reorganization of 1419, however, this ratio changed and the number of districts cut touched every prefecture except Thăng-hoa, no doubt reflecting the fiction of Chinese control in that border area. Eighty more districts and two subprefectures disappeared, forty-five of the districts going into subprefectures and thirty-five into other districts. The result was that, by 1420, the Red River Delta and the older outer prefectures had both lost about 75 percent of their original districts, with the other administrative units losing about half that. Consequently, the new Chinese administrative struc-

ture of fifteen prefectures, forty-six subprefectures, and
seventy-seven districts appears to represent a certain withdraw-
al of direct Chinese presence among the Vietnamese.[38] The heavy
majority of the subprefectures lost all, or all but one, of
their district offices, thus expanding their own direct jurisdictions, and the Chinese officials generally controlled their
territory from the somewhat more distant subprefectural level
rather than from the district seat in the crucial years of
the final revolt. Most particularly, the number of Chinese
administrative offices relative to the population dropped greatly in the lowland areas. After eleven years, the censor's advice
had been followed.

Yet, while the main administrative structure and its officials may have shrunk away from the level of the Vietnamese
populace, the lesser officers associated with the administrative
units fairly swarmed over the countryside and were the less
controlled as the district offices disappeared. By July 1408,
the Chinese had set up a salt distribution superintendency,
a maritime trade superintendency (at the old port of Vân-đồn),
seven mining offices in the mountains, 100 police stations,
ninety-two merchant tax offices, and a number of fishing tax
offices.[39] The most numerous of these, the police stations,
proceeded to double in number over the following decade and
were spread out at a variety of strategic points across Vietnam,
being located in every prefecture except the southernmost,
Thăng-hoa. They were meant to provide warning of any disturb-
ance and lay along the routes of communication. This meant
that they were mainly situated along, or at the mouths of,
the numerous watercourses and in the mountain passes, with
other stations scattered among the variety of highland and
lowland communities and outposts. For the central Delta, many
were at bridges. The original hundred probably lay in the Delta
and the northern mountains, while the following hundred were
concentrated to a certain degree in the strategic localities
of Thanh-hóa and its immediate southern neighbors (thirty-six)
or in the southern and eastern Delta (thirty-three). The pattern
of their establishment followed the fortunes and misfortunes
of the Trần resistance. Those in Thanh-hóa were set up in the
first two years of the conquest when the Trần were severely
pressing the Chinese, and the southern and eastern Delta sta-

tions arose in an attempt to control the Trần raids and their
local support over the following years.[40]

To further communications in the manner they thought necessary, the Chinese strove to overcome the great number of streams
by building or repairing bridges and to link the many offices
by establishing postal stations every ten li (approximately
three miles). Citing no less an authority than Mencius ("Build
bridges while you may, in the eleventh and twelfth months")
as well as the strategic need for bridges in Vietnam, the unknown Chinese author of the **An Nan Chih Yüan** tells how the
colonial regime put both men and women to work on them in the
dry season when they "had a high old time... without any great
hardship." The result was about three hundred bridges, with
their spread, as one might expect, depending on the hydrographic
nature of the terrain. The bulk of the bridges was in the central, eastern, and southern Delta, much smaller numbers existed
in the northern and western mountains and the southern prefectures. Anchoring the communications system were the major postal
offices (in over thirty localities) which connected the provincial capital with the outer areas, particularly it would seem
the eastern Delta prefecture of Tân-an and its port of Vân-
đồn, the Lạng-sơn link to China, the southern prefecture of
Thanh-hóa, and the western areas of Tam-giang and Quy-hóa,
the latter in the mountains. Linking these offices in constant
transmission were some three hundred eighty postal stations,
fifty-one in the central prefecture of Giao-châu, moderate
numbers elsewhere in the Red River Delta, and large numbers
in the northern and western mountains and the southern prefectures. There also existed transport offices which may have
provided links to ports on the coast and the maritime trade
offices there.[41]

In addition, the Ming set up other offices dealing with
economic matters. The main salt office had been established
in October 1407, though the **An Nan Chih Yüan** claims that it
was set up outside the Giao-châu citadel in May 1414. Branch
offices were scattered down the coast with several in Tân-an
and Nghệ-an. The main salt storage area lay west of the central
office with others in the producing areas. In 1418, eight tea
and salt control stations appeared in the east and southern
Delta and the southern prefectures as well.[42] About 100 merchant

tax offices were also set up, almost all before July 1408, apparently with one main office in each of the Red River Delta prefectures and local offices at the subprefectural, district, and local levels in various localities, mostly in the Red River Delta.[43] Another set of fiscal offices were the fishing tax offices, mainly it would seem in the central and eastern Delta.[44] With pacification and the administrative rationalization of 1415 and thereafter, a reduction occurred in tax offices as some thirty-three merchant tax offices, eighteen fishing tax offices, and three local salt stations were closed.[45] Finally, in September 1419, a pearl office appeared in Tân-an.[46]

With pacification also came the effort to control the cultural life of the province, as we shall examine below. There were the following numbers of schools: at least sixty-nine medical (i-hsüeh), fifty-four astrology (yin-yang-hsüeh), and 126 Confucian (ju-hsüeh). Buddhist religious registries existed in eleven, possibly twelve, prefectures, twenty-five subprefectures, and fifty-six districts and Taoist registries were located in twelve prefectures, but only in seventeen subprefectures and forty-one districts. Such institutions seem not to have been established south of Thanh-hóa.[47]

The range and depth of the Chinese administrative contact with the Vietnamese appears to have been great, if we judge by the details scattered throughout the Ming Shih Lu and the composite account in the An Nan Chih Yüan. Assuming that most or all of the bridges required local labor and that the postal and police stations, not to mention the variety of economic control offices, led to a potentially coercive and corrupt civilian Chinese presence beyond the district and subprefectural offices, we should have no doubt that the Vietnamese people had a greater contact with a governing force during this Chinese colonial period than at any prior time. Behind this local contact, of course, stood the occupying army, perhaps 87,000 strong after 1415. These troops were probably stationed in the thirty-nine solidly built citadels (ch'eng) and camps (pao) (twenty-seven more than in 1408) which were located either at the prefectural and wei offices or at particular strategic points. The troops were supposed to be, as the An Nan Chih Yüan claims, "always on the ready". Thirteen of these military bases were in the central Delta where the core of the Chinese military strength lay (five **wei**, one **so**). Here, west of the drum tower in the northern quarter of Tung-kuan, the military office was located, at least since December 1415, when Chang Fu had taken over the location of the administrative office. The parade ground and its twelve encampments lay southwest of the city. All in all, throughout the province there were eighteen **wei** and **so**, an increase of six over 1408. The only other major concentrations of military power existed in the distant southern prefectures.[48]

To fill these civil and military posts, a mixed variety of Chinese officials was sent south and a continued search was made for Vietnamese to be trained and used at the lower levels. The quality of the Chinese administrators in this "land of the fiery border" where, to quote the **An Nan Chih Yüan**, "there is no place farther than this", was uneven at best.[49] Many of them came to Vietnam under unfavorable circumstances (sometimes after having death sentences commuted), particularly before 1415. While some capable officials, like Huang Fu, were appointed from either the invading army or regular administrative positions in the early years, their number was soon to include many more who "were accused [and] banished to the frontier of Chiao-chih".[50] Indeed, through its first years as a colony, Chiao-chih seems not to have been a part of the regular promotion and transfer system of the Ming, though other southern provinces like Kuangsi and Yünnan were. While its officials did finally begin to come and go through regular administrative shifts, probably beginning with the nationwide evaluation of officials in 1411, there continued to be the threat from the capital that failure in the regular system, especially military, would lead to banishment in Chiao-chih.[51]

The conditions sustained by these officials are reflected in the plea of a Chinese prefectural officer in Thái-nguyên in 1412:

> Of the Chiao-chih officials and sub-officials, many have families which assist [them]. Of those who come, some die on the road and some die in office. [For] the wives and concubines left [here], the road is long [and they] are unable to return home. Badly lacking in food and clothing, they frequently yield [to male advances] and subsequently remarry, doing [great] damage to public

morals [specifically the requirements of chastity and the ban against remarriage for widows].[52]
Eventually, many of these undesirable posts were filled with unskilled and unsuccessful students from the southern regions of China (Kuangtung, Kuangsi, Yünnan) who wished to be closer to home than they otherwise would have been. By 1420, a regional inspector reported, such students held a good number of the prefectural and district offices and were, in Alexander B. Woodside's words, "not only inept and untrained, but neglected by those higher in authority".[53] Thus, in examining the Chinese administration, we must conclude with Wang Gungwu that "the shortage of good, trained staff remained a serious handicap to [Huang Fu's] provincial government throughout his stay".[54]

What balance existed between Vietnamese and Chinese administrators is impossible to say, but there can be no question that many of the middle-level positions were held by Vietnamese. At one time or another, indigenous figures seem to have occupied the major posts of prefect and vice-prefect in all the prefectures, not to mention the magistracies and clerical positions in the subprefectures and the scattered districts.[55] Most of the special offices and agencies, on the other hand, probably had the unsuccessful students, or even eunuchs, staffing them. In the military structure, Vietnamese seem to have filled secondary ranks in the guard units, being vice-commanders and assistant commanders, but generally not commanders, though there were two exceptions. Vietnamese also, of course, were used as officers in the battalions and companies.[56]

In finding such natives to aid the occupying forces, the Chinese drew heavily upon those who had rallied to their cause in the initial campaign and proceeded to reward the Vietnamese who helped in the continual suppression and pacification campaigns, as well as their kin. Besides such obvious recruitment, the Ming officials set out from the first months in a widespread search for "men of talent" who possessed any of a great variety of skills, hoping to bring them into the administration. In succeeding years, well over 9,000 Vietnamese were recommended for office and sent to Nanking to be confirmed.[57] Several Vietnamese even received promotions to posts within the regular Chinese system, both metropolitan and provincial; one of them was to serve as the chief engineer on the repair of the new

capital in Peking.[58] The Chinese also recruited among the continuing accumulation of the captured and surrendered from the
Trần campaign.[59] Once in the Chinese bureaucratic system, the
Vietnamese advanced in the standard ways, through the triennial
evaluations or through recognition of a memorial or some other
special achievement, and the Ming certainly strove to encourage
them via promotions and rewards.[60] Yet, in 1412, a major Chinese
official in Chiao-chih complained that the Vietnamese who had
taken official posts, "many of their own free will", were not
well versed in their tasks and had little influence with the
people.[61]

While preferring to stress those who refused to serve the
Chinese, the Vietnamese records grudgingly acknowledge that,
in fact, "a few with reputation accepted".[62] What the Ming sought
in their Vietnamese officials was the ability and the willing-
ness to rally the people, gather local troops, report what
they heard in their areas, round up or otherwise eliminate
opposition, and keep the local Chinese community in line as
well.[63] A certain group of Vietnamese fulfilled these aims and
came to occupy the top positions in the major prefectures.
Some even went beyond this level to serve in the three provincial offices: administrative, military, or surveillance. The
leading local family during the occupation was without doubt
the Mạc of Tân-an, descendants of a famous fourteenth-century
literati administrator, Mạc Đỉnh Chi. Mạc Thúy had been instrumental in the Ming success. He was celebrated at the Chinese
court and rapidly promoted from prefect of Lạng-giang to right
vice-commissioner of the administrative office before the end
of 1408. In 1411, he stood by himself at the top of the list
of rewards, and he died fighting a Lạng-sơn rebellion for the
Ming the following year.[64] Into his place stepped Nguyễn Huân,
a close associate of Thúy's who took the Mạc name. He too had
been promoted in 1408 (from subprefect in Lạng-sơn to right
assistant commissioner) and in 1411 had stood alone in the
second rank of those rewarded, behind only Thúy. In 1416, at
the great awards ceremony in Nanking following the pacification,
Huân reached the highest position held by a Vietnamese under
the Chinese, the rank 2b post of right administrative commissioner, theoretically second only to Huang Fu. He also received
an imperially inscribed poem.[65] Mạc Thúy's two brothers also

served the Chinese, Địch as a guard commander and Viễn as prefect of Tân-an and then as salt commissioner.[66]

A handful of others joined the Mạc as "very wealthy" officials in the colonial posts.[67] Immediately behind Huân in the
Ming estimation were Lương Như Hốt and Đỗ Duy Trung, prefects
of Thanh-hóa and Tam-giang respectively, who were promoted
in 1416 to assistant commissioners, with Như Hốt taking one
more step up to left vice-commissioner the following year.
The centrally located prefect of Giao-châu, Đỗ Hy Vọng, was
another in whom the Ming put great trust.[68] Several Vietnamese
appear to have held significant positions in the military office. In the first years men like Trần Phong and Trần Như Thạch
began to rise within the guard units. By 1415, following the
pacification, they had become assistant commissioners.[69] On
the other hand, only one Vietnamese is known to have been attached to the Censorate.[70]

In this period of Ming colonial security, many thousands
of Vietnamese journeyed to Nanking bearing gifts and thanks,
being rewarded and promoted, or serving the Chinese in some
capacity. The privileged returned with wealth and power to
become the central figures among their countrymen, yet they
were perpetually under the Chinese thumb. Without them, the
Ming would have had great difficulty in gaining or holding
the colony. The options of these collaborators would seem to
have been essentially two, either the cynical quest of this
relative wealth and power or a full commitment to the Chinese
pattern as provided by the Ming.

B. THE MING AIMS

In an ideological sense, the latter was the goal of the
Ming occupation—pushing the "egocentricity" of their cultural
position with little heed for the local patterns in order to
make Vietnam a part of the empire. Great effort was made, but,
as Woodside has noted, it was "vigor without perspective".[71]
What effect did this elaboration of the formidable administrative structure described above have on Vietnam and its people?
To what extent did it lead to changes in the Vietnamese world?

The Chinese were caught in a certain dilemma. Since Vietnam
had once been a part of their empire, indeed during the great
periods of the Han and the T'ang, it ought to have been civil-

ized. Yet, as any educated Chinese knew, Vietnam bordered on
the barbarian and was not a place esteemed for the level of
its civilization. Thus, while approaching the Vietnamese with
(in their terms) the highest possible motive, to establish
propriety among them, the Chinese all the while had doubts
that such people could ever learn the rudiments of true civilization.[72] This ambiguity is reflected in the contemporary **An
Nan Chih Yüan** when it discusses local customs. Borrowing from
such existing texts as the **Wen Hsien T'ung K'ao** and the **An
Nam Chi Lược** of the thirteenth and early fourteenth centuries,
the author gives a feeling of distance, cultural as well as
physical, of "worthless and cruel" people "who know neither
rites nor righteousness". Indeed, the Vietnamese were supposed
to have been lacking such a basic attribute as proper relations
between father and son with the result that "they cannot [even]
establish a system of laws by which to govern [themselves]".[73]

Then the author cites what may have been a contemporary
work, the **Chiao Chih T'ung Chih.** The passage starts in the
same vein: "[This] is a wild borderland where the common people
all go barefoot", and proceeds to describe the yearly cycle
of Vietnamese ceremony. The overall impression is one of a
mixture of beliefs, folk, Buddhist, Taoist, but not explicitly
Confucian, though ancestral ceremonies were noted. Our author
ends with a statement that, after the occupation, the Vietnamese
families of consequence, official and literary, lived close
to the towns where people congregated. "There are those," he
tells us, "who look [to us] with reverence, [and] may emulate
Chinese culture." On the other hand, the people of the villages
and the out-of-the-way places "still follow [their] old customs
[and we] have not been able to change [them] totally."[74]

Yet such was the Ming wish.[75] In a set of public proclamations
Huang Fu laid out the framework by which his officials, Vietnamese and Chinese, were to approach the problem. These "Notices
for the Clear Declaration of Our Civilizing Mission" began
with the statement: "The business of the administrative office
of Chiao-chih is to declare clearly our civilizing mission."[76]
Nevertheless, as he indicated time and time again, two aspects
of the situation stood in his way. First, Huang recognized
that the Chinese invasion had itself caused much disruption,
indeed had led to a "military transformation" within Vietnam,

a pattern that was then reinforced by the acts of corrupt officials.[77] The solution to this was merely to restore order once
again.   The second and more problematic of the two was the
fact that the Vietnamese had developed their own cultural patterns which did not mesh with the Chinese intentions. Huang
Fu saw his mission as overcoming these two obstacles by bringing
out the innate goodness of the Vietnamese and by leading them
into a state of peace and proper civilization. Liu Pen, Huang's
left administrative vice-commissioner, ably put the case for
a gradualist and tolerant approach before a receptive emperor
in 1411, an approach that Liu believed would avoid the "discon-
tented hearts" caused by the earlier "abrupt" Hồ reforms.[78]

The first step was the material one. The proper level of
civilization required both material comfort and stability for
the proper economic roles of the people. "Agriculture and seri-
culture are fundamental for food and clothing", went the standard Confucian formula, and each person had to maintain his
or her occupation (tilling or weaving) in order to achieve
sufficiency for all.[79] To maintain this situation, the Chinese
officials and their Vietnamese colleagues had to curb disruptions and banditry. Pacification had to be carried out with
good intentions, and the people cast adrift in the fighting
brought back to their proper places and occupations before
they turned into "bandits" and caused further chaos. All activities involving the people, such as corvée labor, had to be
performed in a manner that would not disturb them further.
Theoretically, any official guilty of disruptive activity would
be removed, and certainly any former rebel who went back into
resistance and was captured would be executed with his entire
clan.[80] The official activities were to include maintenance
of the commercial sector, both locally and beyond; establishment
of hospitals to care for the indigent; guidance for the populace
in times of flood, drought, and locusts; and control of bandits.
The police stations maintained control over movement; special
papers were needed to travel more than 100 li.[81]

"If the laws are clearly announced, then the protection
of the people will be systematic."[82] Basing himself on this
fundamental principle of bureaucratic administration, a clear
impartiality, Huang Fu set out to bring the Ming rule of law
into the new territory, "plagued by distance, wildness, and

evil customs". He promised that, if the Vietnamese would report
unjust matters to his office, even if they involved Chinese
officials, "[we] will bring out the entire truth".[83] By setting
a strict and just path, the rest would follow naturally, though
the reduction in administrative offices must have weakened
this effort considerably. Yet, in Huang's eyes, "in the relationship between customs and the way of ruling, [if] one loves
and esteems, seeing as superior, what is true, then the customs
will be pure".[84]

However, in this most imperfect of worlds, the evil customs
of the Vietnamese had to be actively countered: "... to care
for the people and to achieve order, [we must] first, with
caution, change the customs". "Until their social relationships
are put aside, the chaste and modest will not prosper."[85] By
evil customs the Chinese meant the whole pattern of tradition
in Vietnam. Huang Fu painted a picture of Vietnamese society
that, while undoubtedly overdone, had many elements of the
truth in it. Here we see a country dominated by the strong
and powerful with their followers and lands, while the poor
were obsequious and rendered service, suffering at the hands
of the great. Local chiefs and their people existed on the
one hand, and the great and their officials on the other. Such
indigenous strongmen had taken Vietnam away from the Chinese
sphere in the tenth century, had kept the Sinic influence out
in the following centuries, and were responsible for the spate
of rebellions that had been crushed since 1407. Every group
had its own military organizations and manufactured its own
warships and weapons. The local powers strove to build up their
personal followings and gain control over other local areas.
The Chinese warned the Vietnamese that there should be "no
handing over of your rights to the power of the chiefs" who
acted to bring as many such followers, not to mention lands
and ponds, under their control as possible.[86]

These aspects the Chinese could handle with police activity.
More difficult were the patterns of Vietnamese thought. Bare
feet, cut hair, and nakedness were signs of barbarity and de-
pravity; the sexes were not supposed to mix indiscriminately,
nor were father and son supposed to separate.[87] Vietnamese social
relationships did not match the Chinese ideal, and their religious beliefs were little better. In other parts of the An

Nan Chih Yüan, based to a certain degree on Vietnamese tradition, are descriptions of the local cults and beliefs, folk and Buddhist. The Vietnamese "believe strongly in ghosts and spirits, [with] a great number of licentious ceremonies". Shamanistic practices abounded, yet Huang Fu admitted "there is nothing completely weird [here]",[88] and he went on to state, at the end of his second proclamation, that the Chinese were to approach the local spirits and their cults with honesty and sincerity: "[We] ought to sacrifice to the spirits...; it is essential to do one's utmost in performing the ceremonies."[89] As for Buddhism, Vietnam was a land of many temples and famous monks, and its hold on the Vietnamese people seems to have been fairly strong. Taoism, on the other hand, was not nearly as entrenched, though a number of its temples did exist.[90]

The Chinese acted to control and transform these strange modes of behavior bureaucratically, legally, and academically. In Huang Fu's second cultural edict, he gave the Vietnamese in contact with the Chinese administration a month to change their clothing style to the "correct" (i.e. Chinese) style of dress. They could not cut their hair short, and the women had to wear a short jacket and a long skirt.[91] Acting "according to prefectural regulations", the Chinese moved to change local cult practices by setting up their own local altars, 444 of them, throughout the province and by performing spring and autumn sacrifices on them, as was done by the officials in their civil and military offices.[92] Buddhist and Taoist establishments were honored by the Ming authorities even as the same kinds of controls were extended to religious institutions as existed in China itself. While some of the Buddhist and Taoist prefectural and subprefectural offices appeared before the pacification ended, mainly in the Red River Delta, only in 1416 was the religious administrative pattern completed in the outlying areas. As noted above, the subprefectural and district levels had a greater preponderance of Buddhist than Taoist offices. The greatest concentration of offices lay in the upper Delta, though only slightly fewer existed in the southern and eastern Delta prefectures. Thanh-hóa, Thái-nguyên, and Tuyên-hóa had a few such offices, but the outer areas almost none at all. Later, in 1418, the Chinese Throne moved to control

Buddhist and Taoist monks throughout the empire. The restriction
of their numbers that took place presumably had an impact in
Vietnam as well, as no more than forty monks were allowed in
a prefecture, thirty in a subprefecture, and twenty in a district, and these were limited by age as well.[93]

In a parallel fashion, the sixty-nine schools of medicine
and fifty-four schools of astrology sprouted across Vietnam,
reaching down to the district level and undoubtedly bringing
some degree of control over local medical and magical practices
while imparting new information and techniques. Again the upper
Delta had the highest numbers, with the southern and eastern
Delta prefectures somewhat behind and a number spread out across
the northern and western mountains. Only one medical school
existed in Thanh-hóa, however, and nothing farther south. The
Ming sought Vietnamese to staff these religious and educational
positions.[94]

Yet the Chinese had to do more than control and suppress
the indigenous cultural patterns: they had to change them.
The Ming officials could rail against those who "dare to go
along with errors, do evil, cry rebellion, and hinder civilization"[95] and seek to punish them, but, as they themselves noted,
it was "essential" that the Neo-Confucian principles be implemented in Vietnam. Starting with the Mencian premise of the
inherent goodness and perfectibility of all men, Vietnamese
included, Huang Fu called in his edicts for the officials to
act as exemplars of proper behavior, for the local men of influence to propound the official doctrine, and especially for
schools to be set up. He ordered the officials to select "brilliant Neo-Confucians" to teach the "refined and elegant youth"
chosen from Vietnamese society. The Chinese officials were
not to approach this matter as they would an ordinary one,
but were to devote great effort to it.[96]

Upon their arrival in Vietnam, the Chinese had found what
in their jaundiced view were "mean and vulgar" schools of classical Chinese learning in which there was a "lack of reverence".
Yet the desire to learn was there, particularly in private
family sessions, and, as one high Chinese official admitted,
"the people of Chiao-chih know a bit about studying".[97] The
Ming administrators set out to permeate the land with their
schools, well over a hundred of them. They began their endeavors

in late 1410, though the schools themselves were not established until the pacification had been completed, in 1416. Again the largest number of schools (forty) lay in the upper Delta around the capital with twenty-nine in the rest of the delta. The twelve in Thanh-hóa, thirty-four in the northern mountains, and ten in the western mountains generally appeared somewhat later (1418-1419) as the Ming were undoubtedly striving to expand their influence. Only one school existed south of Thanh-hóa (in Thuận-hóa). A greater number of these schools (at least seventy-four) were at the district level than was the case with any of the other types. The teachers were probably a mixture of Chinese and Vietnamese as the Ming sought out learned local scholars. Accomplished students became assistant instructors.[98]

The time (ca. 1415) at which the Ming strove to bring their ideology into Vietnam was significant for two reasons, one institutional and the other philosophical. The Ming dynasty, from the day of its foundation, had been keenly interested in the spread of education. In 1369, the Hung-wu Emperor had ordered schools established throughout the empire at the district level in the belief that, to be governed, the people had to be reformed by means of education. As the Yung-lo Emperor was to state in 1415, "shaking up the customs of the gentry lies in promoting schools".[99] The state appointed and supported the instructors, gave stipends to chosen students, and set up detailed regulations for the schools which became part of the Hung-wu Emperor's final instructions in 1395 and which his son, the Yung-lo Emperor, continued. By the end of the former's reign, at least 1,200 schools had been set up.[100] Thus, at the time that the Ming had taken control of Vietnam, a major public school system existed in China and needed only to be implemented by the occupying officials for the Vietnamese to have a far greater access to Confucian education than had previously existed. Undoubtedly, the sons of the local officials and well-to-do Vietnamese took great advantage of this new system, especially since it gave exemptions from corvée service, though indeed any willing and intelligent young man would probably have found opportunity as well.

In the same years that the Ming completed the pacification of Vietnam and began to establish the school system there,

the Yung-lo Emperor was ordering the compilation of the defini-
tive edition of the Neo-Confucian canon: the Five Classics
and Four Books together with the commentaries of Chu Hsi and
the Ch'eng brothers. This was the culmination of a vigorous,
though selective, adoption of the Sung school as the standard
form of Confucianism by the first Ming rulers. In the Hung-
wu period, the emperor had actively taken up the debate over
the correctness of the variety of commentaries, Sung or otherwise, even arguing against Chu Hsi and criticizing 85 passages
of the **Mencius** for disrespectful tendencies. Yet he firmly
accepted the Neo-Confucian tradition and had the examinations
based upon it. The Yung-lo Emperor consequently moved to bring
out the official version of the Ch'eng-Chu school for use in
the educational system. His strong feelings on the matter may
be seen in the 1404 case where he severely castigated a scholar
who opposed the Sung views as "an enemy of scholars", not to
mention giving him one hundred strokes, having his writings
burned, and stripping him of his status as a teacher.[101] In
ordering the authoritative compilation in late 1414 the emperor
stated his belief: "The Five Classics and the Four Books are
all sacred and wise by nature and form the basis of morality
(**yi**). [In] the external commentaries (by Chou, Ch'eng, Chang,
and Chu), all the Neo-Confucian (**ju**) discussions are clearly
explained and all the details wrapped up." Working on it day
and night, the scholars finished the task in less than a year,
producing two outstanding volumes, **The Great Compilation of
the Five Classics** (113 chapters) and **The Great Compilation
of the Four Books** (36 chapters), for which they were richly
rewarded.[102] These two works, called collectively **The Great
Compilation of Neo-Confucianism**, became the standard text for
a well-defined state ideology. As Wing-tsit Chan has noted,
"it was designed not so much for the elucidation of the Neo-
Confucian doctrine as to put an official jacket on it."[103] In
April 1417, the books were sent out to the schools of the empire
with the Yung-lo Emperor's admonition that all teachers were
"to exhaust their hearts in propounding [the enclosed doctrine]
with clarity" and not to treat these volumes as they would
any other text.[104] The Vietnamese **History** states that the works
reached Vietnam in early 1419, carried by a National College
student.[105]

On the local scene, as Huang Fu and his compatriots saw it, "schools are the source of talent and the illumination of the [five] social relationships".[106] The latter, in the Chinese view, were exceedingly important, forming "the inherent principle (li) of man's moral nature and the way (tao) of his daily activity". If the Vietnamese were to be civilized, they had to accept these relationships so that father and son, older brother and younger brother, husband and wife, friend and friend would behave towards each other as they should. Severe punishment awaited violations of these principles.[107] Interestingly, the first of the five relationships, that between ruler and subject, was not mentioned, perhaps because the Chinese felt that leaving it implicit was the best approach to the recalcitrant Vietnamese. The official optimism of the Chinese was such that Huang Fu rhetorically declaimed, "How can [a society] be without filial sons, wise descendants, righteous men, virtuous wives, loyal ministers, illustrious gentlemen?", and concluded: "No generation is without men who possess the talent of the sage."[108] The schools with their rites and music were the "soil" out of which such people would spring as textual study and proper ceremony enlightened the innate goodness of the natives. The basis for this was to be the Hung-wu Emperor's Sacred Edict of 1385 and its expostulation of the social relationships.[109] In general, to quote Huang Fu further, "it is essential that [the Vietnamese] emulate China", and he felt the Ming administration to be close to achieving this goal.[110]

What was the educational situation in which the Vietnamese students (and some Chinese, as Huang Fu's son) found themselves? They wore a special form of dress which marked them higher than the local notables but below the officials.[111] In school, if we may consider the Vietnam situation as having been similar to that of China at the time, the students learned by rote as the teachers constantly went back and forth over the material. From this recitation, they were expected to gain a penetrating understanding of the texts. Writing style, too, was stressed in the proper approach to learning. Under the guidance of the teacher in the correct Confucian behavior, the whole person would be transformed, and the ritual of the Confucian cult set the form.[112] Equally if not more important for the Vietnamese were the libraries held by each of the schools.

Such collections as existed therein seem to have been the first major penetration of Confucian works into the rural areas across Vietnam.

The texts used were, first, the Hung-wu Emperor's proclamations, especially the Sacred Edict, and the Neo-Confucian works and commentaries, apparently in that order. Other works likely to have been found in the libraries were histories, statutes and laws, additional philosophical texts, and a mixture of Sung and Yüan textbooks for student use and other practical pursuits. Prominent among the writings for general consumption were the books of moral teachings, which were often illustrated. They included the Hung-wu Emperor's preaching, simple outlines of Neo-Confucian morality and studies, and lessons which were specifically directed as if written for children.[113] These were the lessons that Huang Fu and his officials wished to instill in the Vietnamese. In 1419 an imperial morality book with an introduction by the Yung-lo Emperor was distributed to all the schools of the empire.[114] Yet, for all the official Chinese input, the degree of local impact depended on the teachers, many of whom were probably Vietnamese, and the system left much room for their own approaches.[115]

In Ming times, the schools acted as much as a source of supply for the bureaucracy as they did in the moralizing mission of the new orthodoxy. For Vietnam, the two aspects served to reinforce each other. The tribute students (**kung-sheng**) drawn from the school system and sent to China not only would return to take up bureaucratic posts and aid the Chinese effort, but would also be more fully imbued with the ethics and ideology of the capital. With the school system established, the first Vietnamese students, thirty of them, traveled to Nanking in 1417 and entered the National College (**Kuo-tzu-chien**). They were governed by the same regulations as the Yünnan students and received summer and winter clothing. At first, each prefectural school was to supply two students per year, each subprefectural school three students every two years, and each district school one student per year, although these quotas were later cut in half. Overall, 161 such students are said to have gone to China, including Huang Fu's son.[116] Others went directly into the local administration. As Huang Fu stated in his first edict, "those with true talent and thorough scholarship are worthy of filling posts and being sent as tribute for [further] employment".[117] Another avenue to China was through the regular examination system, in which Vietnam had a quota of ten for the provincial examinations of 1425, the same number as Yünnan. The number of Vietnamese who actually served in the Chinese administration in China was, of course, very small.[118]

However the Chinese might have believed in their civilizing mission, the reality of their presence was the systematic economic exploitation of the new territory. According to Huang Fu's proclamations, the Ming economic stance was to maintain stability, ensure that all kept to their proper occupations, and develop the agricultural sphere as much as possible in the desired direction. But the other economic pursuits were to be strictly controlled.[119] As the Vietnamese described the situation, the Chinese sought to extend the farming acreage, at first requiring each household to open three **mou** of land for every one it held and then striving to get the family to open an equal amount every year. More seriously, the Chinese manipulated the existing acreage to gain what in effect was a much higher tax, particularly given the greater efficiency of the Ming administrative apparatus. Each **mou** became actually three **mou** and was thus taxed much more heavily than before.[120] Beyond this, the Chinese took steps to exploit the natural resources of the country, 79 different types ranging from gold, silver, and pearls to kingfisher feathers, peafowl, and parrots, ten kinds of fish and three kinds of rhinoceros.[121] Reinforced by the thick network of offices described above, the Ming, in the words of the Vietnamese **History,**

> got and assayed the gold and silver [as] [their] offices brought laborers [into the mountains] to pan and mine [the metals]. [They] also [had us] catch white elephants and dive for pearls. [They] laid such heavy taxes [on us] and plundered [us] so harshly [that our] people had nothing on which to live.[122]

In particular, the salt monopoly had a serious impact on the countryside and the mountains. As the salt offices imposed their quotas, the people were forced to buy at inflated prices. The Vietnamese were allowed to carry no more than three bowls of salt and one jar of fish sauce; anything more without the proper papers was considered a smuggling offense.[123]

The **An Nan Chih Yüan** provides a list of the annual revenues extracted by the Chinese, probably from the years 1416 to 1423 when they had their tightest control over Vietnam.[124] The gold and silver, about 500 and 1,100 taels worth respectively, came from the northern and southern mountains. The kingfishers, about 2,000, were caught all over the Red River Delta. Some 1,200 catties of silk were produced mainly in the central Delta with a bit coming from Thanh-hóa, while 10,000 paper fans were made in the eastern and central Delta regions. Commercial taxes worth about 34,000 strings of cash, made up of 3,800 in copper cash and over 30,000 in paper money, came mostly from the same area. The salt production, on the order of 41,000 catties, was concentrated along the coast, particularly in Tân-an and as far south as Nghệ-an. The mainstay of the regime was the rice production from both the public lands and the private farms. The registered land, both public and private, totaled approximately 1.7 million **mou** and was fairly evenly spread across the Red River Delta with lesser amounts to the north, west, and south. Of the 70,000 piculs of rice produced by the private lands, proportionately more came from the immediate capital area than from the eastern and western Delta. Fishing taxes from the central and southern Delta and from Thanh-hóa brought in an amount worth 12,000 strings of cash (about 3,900 in cash, 8,300 in paper). The rice, metals, and cash were generally used within the province. From 1416 to 1423, the locally produced silk and fans, together with the kingfisher feathers, lacquer, and sapanwood, went yearly to China.[125]

This income was, of course, merely the official revenue and gives no hint of the private peculation thriving in the same period. Given the generally low caliber of the Chinese officials and the use of eunuchs in the salt and tax offices, there was much opportunity for corruption, particularly as the reduction of district offices weakened direct supervision.[126] The most notorious case was that of the eunuch Ma Ch'i. His greed in obtaining the exotic goods of the area and lining his sleeves in the process epitomized the evil of the occupation. The arrangement of which Ma took advantage was the **shang-kung** or contribution of local goods to the imperial household. The Vietnamese saw it as nothing more than outright exploitation.[127]

Idealistic, yet greedy and shortsighted, the Ming administration failed to implement its program to the degree desired.[128]
One may note the cautionary statement made by Huang Fu in
his first proclamation: "Remember that these are newly dependent
people who are still infected with [their] old customs and
are not going to change [their] hearts entirely."[129] Even in
1419 Vietnamese officials and students were quite lax in their
observance of mourning for their parents. According to a com-
plaint by the assistant in the supervisorate of judicial proceedings:

> The men of Chiao-chih [still] practice [their] barbarian
> customs. When [their] father or mother dies, they only
> wear black clothing [as opposed to the Sinic white for
> mourning]. The local officials, students, and clerks...
> do not go into [proper] mourning, [going on with their
> duties].[130]

That even this cardinal principle of Confucian belief had not
taken root shocked the emperor who responded, "How can there
be men who [in effect] have no father or mother?" Yet the official clung to what was perhaps the optimistic official dogma:
"[We] are almost on the point of transforming, [however] slowly,
the barbarian practices."

Yet such philosophical principles would not be installed
in Vietnam for another half century and, following the Ming
occupation, the Vietnamese pattern of the fourteenth century
was reasserted. The Vietnamese victory statement of 1427, the
Bình Ngô Đại Cáo, began with a reference to the classic Chinese
principles of **jen** (humanity) and **yi** (righteousness), but it
also made the point that fundamental differences existed between
China and Vietnam:

> Our state of Đại Việt is truly a cultured land. Our moun-
> tains and rivers have long been different, as likewise
> have the customs of South [Vietnam] and North [China].
> The Triệu, Đinh, Lý, and Trần established our state,
> co-existing with the Han, T'ang, Sung, and Yüan [of Chi-
> na], the ruler of each having his own territory.[131]

For the Vietnamese of the time, the immediate impact of the
close contact with the Chinese was highly negative. They felt
strongly the pressures of the heavy administrative structure
resting on them and, particularly, the exploitative acts which

arose from that structure. The sufferings of the local populace were great, whether from the bloody retributions of Chang Fu or the relatively efficient labor services and tax collections organized by Huang Fu. Turning Vietnamese against Vietnamese, the Chinese encouraged local participation in office and in the army. Everywhere, the "poison" of the "mad Ming" seeped through the land. So the Vietnamese saw it and so they remembered it.

Taken together, the Hồ effort at reform and the Ming attempt to transform Vietnam cover only thirty years, and neither may be said to have achieved any clearly and identifiably lasting results. Yet both formed part of a longer and major transformation in the history of Vietnam. The court at Thăng-long which suffered the Cham blows in the 1370s and 1380s and crumbled before them was a decidedly different entity from the court which, one hundred years later (1471), would crush the Cham threat once and for all. In this coming century, the king Lê Thánh-tông would change the philosophy of government decisively and with it the philosophy of interstate relations. Matching these changes would be far-reaching and equally decisive innovations in the government structure and in the relationship between the capital and the provinces.[132]

Despite the negative epitaphs of the fifteenth century historians,[133] Hồ Quý Ly's role in this transformation was significant. Both his successes and his failures helped pave the way for the establishment of Lê Thánh-tông's bureaucratic, Neo-Confucian state which would generally follow the contemporary Ming model. Quý Ly's regime overcame the critical dangers of decentralization and foreign invasion and acted against the growing local autonomy. Furthermore, Quý Ly's moves to limit local control of land and manpower and to bring this control into the capital meant that Vietnam would not be following the pattern of disintegration to be seen in fourteenth-century Angkor, Pagan, and Majapahit.[134] Indeed, these moves were the beginning of the decades-long reform aimed at centralizing control. Yet this period of initial centralization saw little change in the structure of central power from previous centuries and little resolution concerning the question of a new state ideology. Quý Ly formed his regime around people personally and directly loyal to him. Nevertheless, he abolished the blood oath and sought legitimacy not via traditional indigenous patterns, but in terms of a peculiar interpretation of the Chinese classics. While encouraging such classical learning, he allowed the scholars to play only ornamental roles in his state.

In this way, Hồ Quý Ly disrupted the old pattern of the Trần aristocrats, their landed estates, and their numerous followers. This in turn led members of the old aristocracy either to be co-opted by the Ming colonial forces or to resist and be crushed by the Ming army. The consequences of the Hồ failure to deal with the Ming were, first, that much more Chinese learning (and a more orthodox Confucian kind at that) entered Vietnam during the occupation and, second, the successful resistance to the Ming, when it did arise, came from the fringe of Vietnamese society. Quý Ly's seizure and development of central power consequently led in an indirect manner to the formation of a group of Vietnamese literati much more attuned to the contemporary beliefs of China and equally prepared to carry on the concentration of power at the center. Quý Ly's coeval success and failure also meant that the group which succeeded the Ming would be peripheral to the old ideological pattern of central power and would be very likely open to the blandishments of the group of Neo-Confucian ideologues.[135]

The Ming occupation itself had a major effect on Vietnam, in essence marking a watershed in the style of government employed by the Vietnamese. It opened Vietnamese society in a greater degree than before to the contemporary East Asian philosophy of Chu Hsi's Neo-Confucianism and to the bureaucratic pattern of government. While Vietnamese adoption of Chinese precedents might have occurred in any event, it would appear that the brief but intensive exposure to Ming government hastened the process considerably.

Thus, the fifty years examined here, from the Cham conquest of Thăng-long in 1371 to the heyday of the Ming colonial period in 1421, mark the first half of this major transformation. The great crisis of the last third of the fourteenth century brought Hồ Quý Ly's efforts at reform, centralized control of resources, and shoring up the weakening central ideology. These efforts undercut the power of the Trần aristocracy and in turn brought about the confrontation with Ming China, the defeat of the Vietnamese state, and the shattering of the Trần attempts at restoration. The resulting colonial rule would come to a violent end before Lê Lợi's maneuvers from the hinterlands. In the following half century, the Lê dynasty would fulfill the aims of both the Hồ and the Ming, concentrating power at the center and adopting Neo-Confucianism as the orthodoxy of the land. The Lê rulers thus would eventually forestall the threat from the crisis of the fourteenth century on the foundation laid by both the Hồ and the Ming.

N O T E S

Abbreviations

ANCY	An Nan Chih Yüan (see following entry)
Aurousseau	L. Aurousseau, Ngan Nan Tche Yuan
BEFEO	Bulletin de l'École Française d'Extrême-Orient
BK	Thiên Nam Lịch Triều Liệt Huyện Đăng Khoa Bị Khảo
Chú	Phan Huy Chú, Lịch Triều Hiến Chương Loại Chí
CM	Khâm Định Việt Sử Thông Giám Cương Mục
DMB	L. G. Goodrich and Fang Chao-ying, eds., Dictionary of Ming Biography
ĐKL	Đại Việt Lịch Triều Đăng Khoa Lục
HĐBĐ	Hồng Đức Bản Đồ
KNLS	Phan Huy Lê and Phan Đại Doan, Khởi Nghĩa Lam Sơn
MHY	Lung Wen-pin, Ming Hui Yao
MS	Chang T'ing-yu, comp., Ming Shih
MSL/YL	Ming Shih Lu (Yung Lo)
NÔML	Lê Trừng, Nam Ông Mộng Lục
NTTT	Nguyễn Trãi Toàn Tập
TKML	Nguyễn Dữ, Truyền Kỳ Mạn Lục
TS	Lê Quý Đôn, Đại Việt Thông Sử
TT	Phan Phu Tiên and Ngô Sĩ Liên, Đại Việt Sử Ký Toàn Thư
YCS	Li Wen-feng, Yüeh Ch'iao Shu

INTRODUCTION

1. The **Toàn Thư** (**TT**) used here is a microfilm copy from the Toyo
   Bunko in Tokyo (X-85), together with the first edition of
   the Hanoi translation, 1967-1968. For comments by Phan Phu
   Tiến and Ngô Sĩ Liên, see below, especially chap. 2, n. 50,
   as well as chap. 2, nn. 2, 39, 42, 44, 48, 51; chap. 3, nn.
   9, 14, 20, 27, 30; chap. 4, n. 1; chap. 5, n. 20; and chap.
   6, n. 133. On these two historians, see John K. Whitmore,
   **Transforming Đại-Việt: Politics and Confucianism in the Fif-
   teenth Century** (forthcoming), chaps. 3, 5.

      A good example of the results of this general pattern of
   thought may be seen in Nguyễn Dữ's early sixteenth century
   work, **Truyền Kỳ Mạn Lục** (**TKML**), Vietnamese trans. (Saigon,
   1963), II, 54-58; French trans. by Nguyễn Trần Huân, **Le vaste
   recueil de légendes merveilleuses** (Paris, 1962), 170-171. For
   a subtler example, see **TKML** (Saigon), II, 107-122; (Paris),
   199-204, where Quý Ly is outfoxed by two forest spirits.

2. See below, chap. 4, nn. 5 and 25, and Ngô Thì Sĩ, **Việt Sử Tiểu
   Án,** Vietnamese trans. (Saigon, 1960), 254-286.

3. See the imperial comments in the **Cường Mục (CM)**, Vietnamese
   trans. (Hanoi 1958?), VII, 10, 21, 23, 99, 104, 106 (see n.
   10 below). The anonymous **Hoàng Việt Xuân Thu** [Royal Vietnamese spring and autumn annals], most likely from some time in
   the nineteenth century, gives a poor but typically Confucian
   rendering of the Hồ; Vietnamese trans. (Saigon, 1971), 11-49;
   Chinese 1-36; on this work, see L. Cadière and P. Pelliot,
   Bulletin de l'École Française d'Extrême-Orient (BEFEO), 4
   (1904), 660, no. 118.

4. Trần Trọng Kim, **Việt Nam Sử Lược**, 7th printing (Saigon, 1964),
   170-190. For a rather inadequate English adaptation of this
   text, see Nguyễn Văn Thái and Nguyễn Văn Mừng, **A Short History of Vietnam** (Saigon, 1958), 129-141.

     Two other interesting Vietnamese histories, both from 1914
   and perhaps the last written in Chinese characters, are Hoàng
   Cao Khải, **Việt Sử Yếu**, Vietnamese trans. (Saigon, 1971), 299-
   304, Chinese 47a-50a, and Nguyễn Văn Mại, **Việt Nam Phong Sử**,
   Vietnamese trans. (Saigon, 1972), 163-164, 290, Chinese 74a-
   b, 132a, which deal with the Hồ in standard fashion. Short
   texts written in French by Vietnamese maintain this version
   in brief; see, for example, Dương Quảng Hàm, **Leçons d'histoire
   d'Annam** (Hanoi, 1936), 56-58. A recent publication is Quốc Ấn,
   Hồ Quý Ly, nhân-vật lỗi-lạc nhất thời-đại từ Đông sang Tây
   (Saigon, 1974).

5. See, for example, G. Maspero, "Histoire générale", in G. Maspero, ed., **L'Indochine** (Paris, 1929), I, 111-112; A. Masson,
   Histoire du Vietnam (Paris, 1960), 21; and J. Chesneaux, **Contribution à l'histoire de la nation vietnamienne** (Paris,
   1955), 37, among the French works, and C. A. Bain, **Vietnam:
   The Roots of Conflict** (Englewood Cliffs, N.J., 1967), 57; P.
   J. Honey, **Genesis of a Tragedy** (London, 1968), 16; and D. J.
   Duncanson, **Government and Revolution in Vietnam** (New York,
   1968), 41.

6. Lê Thành Khôi, **Le Việt Nam: Histoire et Civilisation** (Paris,
   1955), 195-206 (quotation, p. 197); Joseph Buttinger, **The
   Smaller Dragon** (New York, 1958), 153-156, 188-189; **A Dragon
   Defiant** (New York, 1972), 44-45.

7. M. Durand, review of **Văn Sử Địa** [Literature, history, geogra-
   phy], nos. 10-20 (Sept.-Oct. 1955 to Aug. 1956), **BEFEO**, 50,
   2 (1962), 547. The article was Minh Tranh's "The development

of our country's feudal system and the role of Hồ Quý Ly at
the end of the 14th and the beginning of the 15th century" (in
Vietnamese), **VSĐ**, 11 (1955), 5-19.

8. See, for example, Trường Hữu Quỳnh, "A re-evaluation of the reforms of Hồ Quý Ly" (in Vietnamese) in the journal **Nghiên Cứu
Lịch Sử** [Historical Research] (issue no. 20 in 1960), and
various other articles in the same journal in 1961 (nos. 22-
33), dealing with the question, "How do we appraise the role
of Hồ Quý Ly in Vietnamese history?" Other references on this
matter are "Ten years of historical research in the Democratic Republic of Vietnam", **Vietnamese Studies** 4 (1965), 138, and
Phan Gia Bền, **La recherche historique en République Démocratique Vietnamienne** (Hanoi, 1965).

9. Ủy Ban Khoa Học Xã Hội Việt Nam, **Lịch Sử Việt Nam** (Hanoi, 1971),
I, 229-235. The most recent article was unavailable to me;
this was Tống Trung Tín, "Recently discovered materials on Hồ
Quý Ly" (in Vietnamese), **NCLS**, 195 (1980), 77-82.

10. Émile Gaspardone, "Bibliographie annamite", **BEFEO,** 34 (1934),
51-58. The **Khâm Định Việt Sử Thông Giám Cương Mục (CM)** is
the nineteenth-century historical chronicle, rather poorly
derived from the **TT** for this period.

11. **Sinologica**, 11, 3-4 (1970), 113; **Annuaire du Collège de France,**
56 (1956), 292-294; 57 (1957), 358-360.

12. Viện Sử Học, **Nguyễn Trãi Toàn Tập (NTTT)** (Hanoi, 1969).
The edition of the **Ming Shih Lu** used here is the Hung-ke
text of the National Library of Peking, edited by the In-
stitute of History and Philology, Academia Sinica, Taipei,
1962, and has **ch'uan** (chapter) numbers at variance with the
standard edition. Volume 9 ("Mu-lu"), pp. 1-23, gives both
the standard **ch'uan** numbers and the new numbers.
The major modern work on the late fourteenth and early fifteenth century in Vietnam is Phan Huy Lê and Phan Đại Doan,
Khởi Nghĩa Lam Sơn... [The Lam-sơn uprising]; used here is
the second edition (Hanoi, 1969); the third edition (1977)
was available too late for me, but has some interesting
changes and additions.

13. John K. Whitmore, "Vietnamese Historical Sources for the Reign
of Lê Thánh-tông (1460-1497)", **The Journal of Asian Studies,**
29, 2 (1970), 387. Used here is the four-volume translation
in modern Vietnamese (Hanoi, 1961), referred to hereafter as

Chú (Hanoi).

14. Whitmore (1970), 381. The works used are the Đại Việt Lịch Triều Đăng Khoa Lục (ĐKL) (Saigon, 1962), and the Thiên Nam Lịch Triều Liệt Huyện Đăng Khoa Bị Khảo (BK), Document A.485, EFEO microfilm #253.

15. O. W. Wolters, "Assertions of cultural well-being in fourteenth-century Vietnam: Part I", Journal of Southeast Asian Studies (JSEAS), 10, 2 (1979), pp. 435-450; "Part II", JSEAS, 11, 1 (1980), pp. 74-90; History, Culture, and Region in Southeast Asian Perspectives (Singapore, 1982A), pp. 73-82, 105-107; "Phạm Sư Mạnh's poems written while patrolling the Vietnamese northern border in the middle of the fourteenth century", JSEAS, 13, 1 (1982B), pp. 107-119, published again in a revised version in The Vietnam Forum (TVF), 4 (1984), pp. 45-69; "Celebrating the educated official: A reading of some of Nguyễn Phi Khanh's poems", TVF, 2 (1983), pp. 79-101; and his essay to appear in D. G. Marr & A. Milner, eds., Southeast Asia, Ninth to Fourteenth Centuries (Singapore, forthcoming).

I. ĐẠI VIỆT IN THE FOURTEENTH CENTURY

1. Kenneth R. Hall, "An Introductory Essay on Southeast Asian Statecraft in the Classical Period", in Kenneth R. Hall and John K. Whitmore, eds., Explorations in Early Southeast Asian History (Ann Arbor, Mich., 1976), 1-24.

2. See the descriptions in John K. Whitmore's manuscript, Transforming Đại Việt, chap. 1, and in his article, "'Elephants can actually swim!'—Contemporary Chinese accounts of late Lý Đại Việt", in Marr & Milner, eds. (forthcoming). On the blood oath, see Chú (Hanoi), II, 206, and Raymond Deloustal, BEFEO, 10 (1910), 21-22.

3. TT, 5:44b-45a; (Hanoi), II, 51, 263, n. 87; Chú (Hanoi), IV, 5-6. In 1284 the king stated in poetic form, "Everyone should remember the old feats of Cối Kê;/ the South [Nghệ-an and Diễn-châu] maintain 100,000 men." Cối Kê was K'uai-chi, a classical Chinese reference to The Spring and Autumn Annals where Yüeh was defeated by Wu.

4. TT, 5:46bff; (Hanoi), 54-56. See Yamamoto Tatsuro, Annanshi Kenkyu [Research on the history of Vietnam] (Tokyo, 1950), 45-261, and Hà Văn Tấn and Phạm Thị Tâm, Cuộc Kháng Chiến

Chống Xâm Lược Nguyên Mông Thế Kỷ XIII [The resistance against
the Yüan/Mongol invasions of the thirteenth century] (Hanoi,
1968) for authoritative examinations of the Mongol invasions.
On Trần Quang Khải, the Chiêu Minh Prince, see Gaspardone (1934),
87-88, no. 46, and Chú (Hanoi), I, 184-185; for Trần Quốc
Tuấn, the Hưng Đạo Prince, see Gaspardone (1934), 144-145,
nos. 147-148, and Chú (Hanoi), I, 249-251.

5. **TT**, 5:27a; (Hanoi), II, 32. It is curious to note the positive
   value placed by Ngô Sĩ Liên on the princely position in the
   state, considering that he wrote in the 1470s, a time when
   bureaucratic participation was at a very high level.

6. Gaspardone (1934), 49, 144. The princes apparently helped their
   favorites among the literati to gain success and administrative position, marking the development of a patron-client
   relationship between the two groups.

7. **TT**, 6:11b-14a; (Hanoi), II, 82-85. For an introduction to and
   translation of this proclamation, see Trường Bửu Lâm, **Patterns of Vietnamese Response to Foreign Intervention** (New
   Haven, Conn., 1967), 49-54, or **Vietnamese Studies** (Hanoi),
   21 (1969), 59-60.

8. **TT**, 6:1b-2a, 17b, 44a; (Hanoi), II, 72-73, 88, 116. Quang Khải
   (1241-1294) took the administrative reins away from the civilian Counsellors (**Hành-khiển**) and applied the term "inside"
   (**nhập-nội**) strictly to aristocrats. Quang Khải's descendants,
   Trần Văn Bích and especially Trần Nguyên Đán, wielded great
   influence in later reigns.

9. **TT**, 5:60a-b; 6:8a-b; 7:4a-b; (Hanoi), II, 68, 79, 126.

10. Chú (Hanoi), II, 69; **TT**, 6:11a, 37b-38a, 41b; (Hanoi), II, 82,
    110, 113. In the first quarter of the fourteenth century,
    veterans who had served the Hưng Đạo Prince such as Trần Thì
    Kiến and Phạm Ngũ Lão, top winners in the classical examina-
    tions such as Mạc Đĩnh Chi and Nguyễn Trung Ngạn, students
    such as Trường Hán Siêu and Phạm Sư Mạnh, and Thanh-hóa na-
    tives like Lê Quát and Lê Duy were major figures in the court.

11. Paul Demiéville, "Les versions chinoises du Milindapanha",
    BEFEO, 24 (1924), 217; Gaspardone (1934), 88-91, nos. 47, 50,
    51; Louis Bezacier, **L'art vietnamien** (Paris, 1954), 122-123.
    See also Keith W. Taylor's essay in Marr & Milner, eds.
    (forthcoming).

12. **TT**, 6:19a-b; (Hanoi), II, 90; Chú (Hanoi), II, 7-8; III, 8, 37;

Gaspardone (1934), 49, 144.

13. **TT**, 5:15b; (Hanoi), II, 20; Gaspardone (1934), 49-50, no. 27;
John K. Whitmore, "Note: The Vietnamese Confucian Scholar's
View of His Country's Early History", in Hall and Whitmore
(1976), 193-199; O. W. Wolters, "Lê Văn Hưu's Treatment of
Lý Thần-tông's Reign (1127-1137)", in C. D. Cowan and O. W.
Wolters, eds., **Southeast Asian History and Historiography**
(Ithaca, N.Y., 1976), pp. 203-226, and "Historians and em-
perors in Vietnam and China: Comments arising out of Lê Văn
Hưu's history presented to the Trần court in 1272", in A.
Reid & D. G. Marr, eds., **Perceptions of the Past in South-
east Asia** (Singapore, 1979), pp. 69-89.

14. A correlation exists between the development of **nôm** literature
and the rise of the classical literati in terms of the area
from which they came—Hải-dưởng to the east. The first records
of this indigenous literature appear in the last decades of
the thirteenth century and in the beginning of the fourteenth
century. The three persons mentioned (excepting the King)—
Miss Điểm Bích, Nguyễn (or Hàn) Thuyên, and Nguyễn Sĩ Cố—
all appear to have come from Hải-dưởng. [Nguyễn Sĩ Cố, who
may have been Trần Cố of Hải-dưởng, first in the examinations
of 1266, is known to have been the teacher of the Phạm
brothers of Hải-dưởng. See **TT**, 5, 30a, 41b; 6, 41b; (Hanoi),
vol. 2, pp. 35, 48, 114; **ĐKL** (Saigon), p. 16; Gaspardone,
"Bibliographie annamite", pp. 88-89, no. 49.] See Phạm Thế
Ngũ, **Việt Nam Văn Học Sử...**, vol. 2, pp. 51-54.

   In addition, as Woodside (1971), 52-53, points out (from
Bửu Cầm, "Nguồn gốc chữ nôm" [The origins of the **nôm** script],
Văn Hóa Nguyệt San, 50, 1960, pp. 347-355), "... **nôm** characters [are] known to have existed in a list of the names of
twenty villages on a stone monument in Ninh Bình province,
erected in the fourteenth century". Ninh-bình was, at the
time, the northern part of Thanh-hóa province and also a
locality from which came some of the earliest scholars (like
Trưởng Hán Siêu). Since that article appeared, earlier finds
have come from the same area. I tend to agree with Woodside
that **"nôm** was surely a consequence of Vietnam's Sinicization
...",** and, I might add, its localization of classical Chinese
scholarship.

15. Keith W. Taylor, **The Birth of Vietnam** (Berkeley, Cal., 1983).

Chapters 1 and 4 in particular describe the pattern of myth
passed down through the centuries by the Vietnamese; see also
his appendices.

6. In general, a most suggestive pattern seems to appear. Lê Tắc
in his early fourteenth-century work, the **An Nam Chí Lược**
(new edition, Hue, 1961), Chinese, p. 30, has given us the
following formula: "Men of Giao [the central Delta] and Ái
[Thanh-hóa] are full of energy and love to plot; men of Hoan
[Nghệ-an] and Diễn are genuine and accomplished and love to
study" (as corrected from the **Ta Ming I T'ung Chih** [1461],
90:3a). Rather than accepting the geographical lines drawn
by Tắc, we might see the division lying between the old Buddhist area of Kinh-bắc and Sơn-tây, north and west of the
capital respectively, and the newer developing areas east
(Hải-dương) and south (Sơn-nam and the southern provinces) of
the capital. The results of the classical examinations that
are known show a heavy predominance of successful candidates
from the southern and eastern provinces until the final quarter of the fourteenth century. In the examination of 1304,
for example, Mạc Đỉnh Chi of Hải-dương placed first, a Sơn-
nam scholar second (Nguyễn Trung Ngạn), and a Thanh-hóa scholar fourth (**ĐKL**, Saigon, 17; Chú, Hanoi, III, 8-9).

7. **TT**, 6:41b; (Hanoi), II, 113-114; Chú (Hanoi), I, 185-190, 289-
290; II, 69; Gaspardone (1934), 44, 93, nos. 17, 57. As Ngô
Sĩ Liên described the Vietnamese post of **Hành-khiển** (**TT**, 7:
32b-33a; Hanoi, II, 158), its function was "to give aid on
the major matters in the land". At first, in Lý times, an office held by eunuchs, it was given to literati in the thirteenth and fourteenth centuries and became "an important
road for the classical scholars" (Chú, Hanoi, II, 21). See
also Wolters (1979), p. 436.

The prominence of Thanh-hóa scholars (Lê Văn Hưu, Trương
Hán Siêu, Lê Quát) and their anti-Buddhist stance may not be
mere coincidence. The literati administrative road to power
opened the door to the capital that had apparently been blocked
for men of the south under the Lý. At the same time, the southern view of life in the capital might easily have predisposed
it to an anti-Buddhist sentiment. One gets a strong feeling
from these scholars of being isolated in a thorough Buddhist
land; see Chú (Hanoi), I, 188; **TT**, 7:17a-18a, 36a-b; (Hanoi),

II, 160-161; **Vietnamese Studies**, 21 (1969), 56-57. Wolters (1979), 446-447, offers another perspective.

18. **TT**, 7:21a-b; (Hanoi), II, 145. The incident was not recorded in the text of the **Toàn Thư**, but in a comment by the Vietnamese historian of the 1450s, Phan Phu Tiên, following the entry on Minh-tông's death in 1357. Presumably the event took place before Minh-tông's abdication in 1329 (the official involved died in 1330). See also Wolters (1979), 444, 447, and his essay in Marr and Milner, eds. (forthcoming).

19. Gaspardone (1934), 126-128, 130, no. 127; Demiéville, "Versions chinoises", 216; Taylor (1983), 352-354. This work was written in Chinese as the Buddhist/indigenous patterns of thought located in the old aristocratic areas north and west of the capital appear to have continued to use this medium as opposed to the development of **nôm** in the literati area of the east (see note 14 above).

20. From the 1120s to the 1210s, episodic warfare had occurred among Khmers, Chams, and Vietnamese for political (and perhaps economic) dominance of the eastern mainland; see **TT**, chapters 3 and 4, **passim.**, and G. Maspero, **Le Royaume de Champa** (Paris, 1928).

21. **TT**, 6:16b, 18a, 21a-23b; (Hanoi), II, 87, 89, 92-94; G. Maspero (1928), 189-191.

22. **TT**, 6:28a-30a, 35a, 40a; (Hanoi), II, 99-102, 107, 117; G. Maspero (1928), 194-195, 197-199.

23. The Vietnamese records state that the major rival crushed by the surging Ming forces of Chu Yüan-chang was Trần Hữu Lượng (Ch'en Yü-liang), who claimed to be the son of the traitor Vietnamese prince Chiêu, Trần Ích Tắc, an émigré to China during the Mongol wars. Hữu Lượng, according to the records, sought aid from his supposed kin on the Vietnamese throne and was rejected (**TT**, 7:17a, 22b-23a, 24a, 26b-27a, 27b; Hanoi, II, 140, 146, 147, 159, 162). For a discussion of the revolts against the Mongols and Ch'en Yu-liang's part in them, see John W. Dardess, "The Transformations of Messianic Revolt and the Founding of the Ming Dynasty", **The Journal of Asian Studies**, 29, 3 (1970), 539-558, especially 551-552. The Chinese records show Ch'en as having been the son of a (presumably Chinese) fisherman (**ibid.**, 544). See also the Editor's Note to R. Taylor, "Ch'en Yu-liang", **Dictionary of Ming Bio-**

graphy (**DMB**) (New York, 1976), I, 185-188.

24. Though the Cham raids began in 1361, there is no evidence of
    the year in which Chế Bồng Nga ascended the throne of Champa.
    The first mention of him comes in 1369 when the new Ming rul-
    er conferred the title upon him. His name does not appear in
    Vietnamese records until 1376 (Jean Boisselier, **La statuaire
    du Champa**, 1963, 352; G. Maspero, 1928, p. 204).

25. **TT**, 7:24b, 25a, 26b, 27b, 28a, 37a-b; (Hanoi), II, 148, 150,
    151, 152, 162.

26. Lê Trừng, **Nam Ông Mộng Lục** (**NÔML**) (in the Chinese collection
    Chi Lu Hui Pien, 50), 2a, translated with help from Charles
    O. Hucker. We will meet the author, eldest son of Lê Quý Ly,
    later. He wrote the piece while in China (the preface was
    signed in 1438). For more on the Trần pattern of succession,
    see Wolters (1976), 223-226, and (1979), 79-80.

27. **Ibid.**, 2a-b. The death of Minh-tông brought a full-fledged Sin-
    ic mourning period of three years during which "tears were
    unceasing, food could not be heavy or tasty, and such south-
    ern delicacies the fruit of the mango and the sea slug were
    absolutely not to reach the mouth from this time".

28. **TT**, 7:16b, 23a-b, 36b-37a; (Hanoi), II, 139, 147, 161; R. De-
    loustal, **BEFEO**, 8 (1908), 192.

29. **TT**, 7:24a-b, 25b-26b, 27b; (Hanoi), II, 148, 150, 152; Chú (Ha-
    noi), I, 163; **NÔML**, 7a, 15b. See E. Gaspardone, "Le théâtre
    des Yuan en Annam", **Sinologica**, 6, 1 (1959), 1-15, for a
    translation of this passage and an account of the introduction
    of this style of drama into Vietnam a century earlier. Liu
    Wu-chi, **An Introduction to Chinese Literature** (Bloomington,
    Ind., 1966), 169-184, has a chapter on Yüan drama and de-
    scribes a number of plays.

    E. Gaspardone, **Annuaire**, 58 (1958), 393-395, provides a
    good description of the life of these times. An early six-
    teenth-century view of the behavior of court officials in
    this period may be seen in **TKML** (Saigon), II, 73-104; (Paris),
    187-196. See also the story of Ô-lồi (below, n. 41).

30. **TT**, 7:37a; (Hanoi), II, 161-162. The poem is quoted in part
    from Huỳnh Sanh Thống, ed., **The Heritage of Vietnamese Poetry**
    (New Haven, Conn., 1979), 41. For more on Chu Văn An, see
    Wolters (1979), pp. 448-449; (1980), 78, 85, 88.

31. **TT**, 7:16b, 17a, 23a, 27b, 30a; (Hanoi), II, 140, 147, 152, 155;

NÔML, 2b, 18b; Chú (Hanoi), II, 8, 19-20, 63.

32. **TT**, 7:15b, 18b, 22b, 23am 25a-b, 27a-b; (Hanoi), II, 139, 142,
146, 149, 151, 152; Chú (Hanoi), II, 8, 21-22; H. Maspero,
"La géographie politique de l'empire d'Annam sous les Lì, les
Trần, et les Hồ", **BEFEO**, 16 (1916), p. 46. In 1366, two counsellors (**tả** and **hữu bộc xạ**) were sent to check the census in
Thanh-hóa province. The following year, a **hành-khiển** led the
Vietnamese army against the Chams, only to be badly beaten.
Unfortunately, little is known of the **Khu-mật-viện** (the
translation comes from the name rather than its activities),
only that the most important counsellors seem to have been
involved with it. Chú (Hanoi), vol. 1, p. 191, comments on
the quality of ministers during the middle of the fourteenth
century, and Wolters' discussion of his "witnesses" (1979;
1980; 1982A, pp. 73-82, 105-107; 1982B; 1983, pp. 85-87) is
a good introduction to the literati who filled these positions.

33. **TT**, 7:23a, 25b, 28a, 34a; (Hanoi), II, 146, 149, 152, 159;
NÔML, 15b, 16b; Chú (Hanoi), II, 8, 21ff, 87.

34. **TT**, 7:22b, 27b; (Hanoi), II, 146, 151; Chú (Hanoi), II, 8.

35. The following description is drawn from the later (ca. 1419)
Chinese work, the **An Nan Chih Yüan [ANCY]** (as edited by L.
Aurousseau, **Ngan Nan Tche Yuan**, Hanoi, 1932). For an analy-
sis of this text and its information, see chapter 6, note 37.

36. Aurousseau (1932), 132-133; see also 208-212, on the major
Vietnamese monks, and **NÔML**, 12b-13a, which provides the story
of a major Buddhist nun, contemporary of Nguyễn Trừng. For
an early sixteenth-century impression of the Buddhist practices, see **TKML** (Saigon), II, 63; (Paris), 177.

37. **TT**, 7:16b, 23b; (Hanoi), II, 139, 149; **TT**, 8:2a-b; (Hanoi), II,
174, is a most interesting passage for its description
of local obligations. Evidently, there was an hereditary
class of soldiers who could not enter official ranks.

38. **TT**, 7:22b, 25a; (Hanoi), II, 146, 149. A poem on the calamities, dating to 1362, may be found translated in Nguyễn Khắc
Viện et al., **Anthologie de la littérature vietnamienne** (Hanoi, 1972), I, 123.

39. **TT**, 7:28b. The Hanoi translation (II, 153) has omitted this
eclipse which, according to Ho Peng Yoke, in "Natural Phenomena Recorded in the Đại Việt Sử Ký Toàn Thư", **Journal of**

the American Oriental Society, 84, 2 (1964), 140, was real
and occurred in the region south of the Yangtze River.

40. **NÔML**, 2a-b. This text ignores Nhật Lễ's name, using instead
the phrase "forgotten name" (**vong danh**), though in another
location it uses his posthumous title, Hôn Đức Vương (15b).

The pattern of succession to the throne in Vietnam had,
since Lý Công Uẩn's oldest son took the throne on his death
in 1028, generally been that the eldest son succeeded his
father (Chú, Hanoi, II, 160-163). Only when Anh-tông abdicated in 1314 did there begin a series of younger sons of a
young age (Minh-tông, fourteen years old; Hiến-tông, ten
years old; and Dụ-tông, five years old) being placed on the
throne by their abdicated fathers. This meant that elder
brothers were shunted aside and a tradition established of
making them ineligible for the throne.

41. **TT**, 7:11a, 28b-30a; (Hanoi), II, 133, 153-155; **NÔML**, 2a-b
(quotation), 3a; Gaspardone (1959), 11-12. A story, said to
relate to Nhật Lễ and his rise to power, is that of Ô-lôi in
the late fourteenth century collection of Trần Thế Pháp, **Lĩnh
Nam Trích Quái** (Saigon, 1960), 14-15, 93-97, Chinese 37-40;
see also Taylor (1983), p. 356. On the literati in the early
1370s, see Wolters (1979), pp. 448-449; (1980), pp. 78-79.

42. As Gaspardone (1959), 12, suggests, this would appear to be a
formula for a bad king.

43. **TT**, 7:30a-32a, 39b; (Hanoi), II, 155-157, 164; **NÔML**, 2b-3a;
R. B. Smith, "Thailand and Vietnam: Some Thoughts toward a
Comparative Historical Analysis", **Journal of the Siam Society**, 60, 2 (1972), 17. As Smith notes, this move to Thanh-hóa
had, for the first time, "the effect of giving Việt-Nam two
political centers of gravity instead of one". The informer
at the court was Nguyễn Nhiên of Kinh-bắc, to whom Phủ remained grateful for at least a decade after (**TT**, 8:5a; Hanoi,
II, 177).

For a nearly contemporary biography of Trần Phủ (Trần Nghệ-
tông) by the son of his client Lê Quý Ly, see **NÔML**, 2a-4b.

44. **TT**, 7:32a-33b; (Hanoi), II, 157-159; **NÔML**, 3a-4a. The latter
work records a very emotional meeting between Phủ and Nhật
Lễ on Phủ's return. Embracing his enemy, Phủ said, "What have
you, the ruler, done to come to this? I, your servant, am
most distressed. How would I have even thought that there

would be a day (like this)?" Kinh promptly broke it up and
had Nhật Lễ dragged away. It would appear from this account
that Kính was the prime mover in Phủ's actions, given the
degree of distress over the day's events felt by Phủ. Indeed,
Kính may well have placed his older brother on the throne and
then forced him to step aside for himself.

A rather flowery **phú** poem from the Lê period may be found
on this whole episode in Bùi Huy Bích, **Hoàng Việt Văn Tuyển**
(Saigon, 1971), I, 37-43, Chinese xv-xviii.

45. **TT**, 7:33a-b; (Hanoi), II, 158-159; also see **NÔML**, 4a, and O.
W. Wolters (1979), 444, 447-448. Ironically, as the Vietnamese court was making this statement of purpose, the Chinese
court, under the recently enthroned Ming Hung-wu Emperor, was
binding "An-nan" more tightly into its theoretical world
order. As in Korea, Vietnam had its topography (mountains and
rivers) placed on China's maps and received word that higher
standards of tributary behavior were expected of it. Moreover, the Vietnamese and the Chams received "copies of all the
major edicts concerning the Ming empire" for several years
(Wang, 1968, 51, 55). That this latter act had some effect
in the Vietnamese court may be seen in the use of Ming phrase-
ology by a Vietnamese official when presenting a memorial to
the Throne concerning the Chams **(TT**, 7:44b-45a; Hanoi, II,
169-170; Wolters, 1970, 51). At the same time, Korea, Vietnam, and Champa were informed "that they could send their
most promising scholars—the cream of their examination
systems--to Nanking as 'tribute' to compete in the Chinese
metropolitan examinations" (Alexander B. Woodside, "Early
Ming expansionism, 1406-1427: China's abortive conquest of
Vietnam", **Papers on China**, Harvard University, Cambridge,
Mass., 1963, p. 6). The Hung-wu Emperor also took it upon
himself to prescribe the proper Confucian mourning customs
for the Vietnamese court.

46. **TT**, 7:34b-36b; (Hanoi), II, 160-161; **NÔML**, 6b-7b; Chú (Hanoi),
I, 289; Vũ Tuấn Sán, "Chu Văn An, thầy dạy học và nhà trí-
thức nổi tiếng cuối đời Trần [Chu Văn An, noted teacher and
intellectual of the late Trần period]", **Nghiên Cứu Lịch Sử**
[Historical research], Hanoi, 137 (1971), 43-53; Phạm Đình
Hổ and Nguyễn Án, **Tang Thương Ngẫu Lục**, Vietnamese trans.
(Hanoi, 1972), 79-80. Trần Nguyên Đán, in the opening lines

of a poem to An, declared, "...the current has changed; (our)
customs return to their purity of earlier times"; **Anthologie**,
I, 125. See also Huỳnh (1979), 31, and Wolters (1979), 448-449.

47. **TT**, 7:32b, 36b-37a; (Hanoi), II, 158, 161-162. For Trần Nguyễn
 Đán, see **NÔML**, 15b; Chú (Hanoi), I, 191; and **NTTT**, 77-79.

48. Vietnamese joined the Cham forces twice in the late tenth century and once in the early twelfth century (**TT**, 1:8a-b, 19a-
b; 3:15a; Hanoi, I, 160, 173, 244).

49. **TT**, 7:37a-b; (Hanoi), II, 162; **NÔML**, 4a; Gaspardone (1959),
12; G. Maspero (1928), 206. As a result of the destruction,
all articles and books within the palace were lost.

Ngô Sĩ Liên, from his vantage point of success a century
later, took the opportunity to chide the Trần court for having been so unobservant of such a powerful enemy and so un-
prepared both at the border and around the capital. Basically, it seemed to him that too much attention had been paid
to literary affairs and not enough to military strategy.

II. THE SUCCESS OF LÊ QUÝ LY

1. **TT**, 7:37b-38a; (Hanoi), II, 162; **NÔML**, 4a, 6a.

2. **II**, 7:31a, 36b, 37b-38b; 8:13a, 38b; (Hanoi), II, 156, 161-163,
185, 209-210; **NÔML**, 18a; E. Gaspardone, "Deux essais de biographie annamite: Hồ Quý Ly", **Sinologica**, 11, 3-4 (1970),
101, and **DMB**, I, 797-800. The marriage between Quý Ly and the
princess was most disgustedly received by the fifteenth century Ngô Sĩ Liên as un-Confucian and a violation of human
principles. Sĩ Liên foresaw the incident as leading to rebellion since it broke the bonds between a husband who had died
only six months defending the state and his mourning wife.

That Quý Ly was already married at this time is apparent
in that his eldest son, Nguyễn Trừng, is never said to have
been born of this princess and, indeed, is passed over for
the throne on that account.

3. Gaspardone (1970), 101. The **NÔML**, 7b-8a, and **TT**, 8:38a; (Hanoi), II, 209, indicate that Quý Ly's father married a woman
of the Phạm family, probably court doctors; the latter source
also shows that his mother's father married a woman of the
Chu family; and the **NÔML**, 18a, and **TT**, 5:34a; 7:31a; (Hanoi),
II, 40, 156, provide evidence that his paternal grandfather
took a wife from the family of Nguyễn Thánh Huấn, a palace

scholar.

4. **TT**, 7:38b-39a; (Hanoi), II, 163.

5. **TT**, 7:14a, 23a, 24a, 25a-b, 27b, 38b-39a; (Hanoi), II, 137, 146, 148, 149, 151-152, 163. For Nguyễn Nhiên, see chap. 1, n. 43 above.

6. **TT**, 7:39a; 8:9a-b; (Hanoi), II, 163, 181. For Hồ Tông Thốc, see below, p. 25.

7. **TT**, 7:39a-b, 40b-41a; (Hanoi), II, 164-166; **NÔML**, 3a-4a. A century later, the Confucian historian Ngô Sĩ Liên could see Hán Siêu merely as a boastful man who pushed devious doctrines, despising and falsely accusing his own kind. Immediately thereafter, Sĩ Liên (**TT**, 7:40a; Hanoi, II, 165) also took the Trần rulers to task for using the same honorific name for two queens in their line, and condemned the act as a violation of ritual.

   Phan Huy Chú (Hanoi, II, 9, 37) states that the abdicated ruler Nghệ-tông sponsored the 1374 examination and held it at his palace in Sơn-nam province, though the **TT** gives no evidence to support this.

8. **TT**, 7:44b-45b; (Hanoi), II, 169-170. See chap. 1, n. 45 above for the first Ming initiatives towards its immediate eastern and southern neighbors. The official, Trưởng Đỗ (or Xã), came from Hải-dương and successfully passed the classical examinations though it is not known when (probably 1363). He served only in the capital. Ngô Sĩ Liên naturally spoke quite favorably of Đỗ's act, praising it as a good example. See also Wolters (1980), 79, 85; (1983), 86.

9. **TT**, 7:40b-42a; (Hanoi), 165-167, 277. The southern provinces supplying armies were: Thanh-hóa, Nghệ-an, Hóa-châu, Thuận-châu, and Tân-bình. Most of the units appear to have been from the capital and to have worn three characters (as in the tenth century, **Thiên Tử Quân**, "Army of the Son of Heaven") tattooed on their foreheads. The supporting units apparently did not have the tattoo.

   There is a problem as to just which southern households had to provide soldiers. The **CM**, 10:36a; (Hanoi) VI, 68, has a note stating that only the households using hired labor were required to send men.

10. **TT**, 7:40b-42a; (Hanoi), II, 165-167; Wolters (1980), 81.

11. O. W. Wolters, "The Khmer King at Basan (1371-1373)", **Asia**

Major, n. s., 12, 1 (1966), 48.

Excellent descriptions of early Ming diplomacy and its historical antecedents are provided by Wang Gungwu, "Early Ming Relations with Southeast Asia, A Background Essay", in John K. Fairbank, ed., **The Chinese World Order** (Cambridge, Mass., 1968), 34-62, and O. W. Wolters, "The Founder of the Ming Dynasty and the Malays", chap. 5 in his work, **The Fall of Srivijaya in Malay History** (Ithaca, N.Y., 1970), 49-76.

For a statement of this principle in the first year of Ming rule, see Li Wen-feng, **Yüeh Ch'iao Shu (YCS)**, 2:9b, as quoted in Lo Jung-p'ang, "Intervention in Vietnam: A Case Study of the Foreign Policy of the Early Ming Government", **Tsing Hua Journal of Chinese Studies**, n. s., 8, 1-2 (1970), 156.

12. Lo (1970), 157, 163 (as taken from **YCS**, 2:11a-b).

13. G. Maspero (1928), 205, 207-208; Wolters (1970), 54; Lo (1970), 155, 158, 160, 163-164. For a general description of early Ming China's strategic and diplomatic concerns, see Charles O. Hucker, **The Ming Dynasty: Its Origins and Evolving Institutions** (Ann Arbor, Mich., 1978), 62-66.

In the Chinese edict of 1373, the Chinese reflected the ambiguity of their feelings towards the Vietnamese whom they saw as "barbarian" but not "wholly barbarian, for in the end it is a country of culture and letters and can be guided by polite usage" (from Chang Ching-hsin, **Yu Chiao Chi**, 3:35).

14. **TT**, 7:42b-43a; (Hanoi), II, 168; G. Maspero (1928), 208-209. See also Wolters' discussion (1980), 79, 85.

15. **TT**, 7:43b-44b; (Hanoi), II, 168-169; **NÔML**, 4a; G. Maspero (1928), 209-210.

16. **TT**, 8:1b, 2b; (Hanoi), II, 174, 175. The aristocratic title was **Tiểu Tử-không**, a Vietnamese use of an old T'ang title.

17. **TT**, 7:45b; 8:1a, 13a; (Hanoi), II, 170, 173, 185; **NÔML**, 4a, 6a-b. The Lê queen, Quý Ly's cousin, took the robes, shaved her head, and became a Buddhist nun, predicting in tears that her child, and the country, would suffer only misfortune as a result.

Again we have the non-Confucian pattern of treating the same year as the last of the old ruler and the first of the new, instead of waiting until the following year to proclaim the new reign period. As Ngô Sĩ Liên stated, "one year cannot have two rulers" (**TT**, 2:14a; Hanoi, II, 202). To do so was a violation both of propriety and of filial piety.

Following the mission to China proclaiming the change of rulers, a cautionary statement from a member of the aristocracy has been inserted in the record (**TT**, 7:46a; Hanoi, II, 171): "Your younger brother (Duệ-tông) has died, the country is in a state of misfortune, and you have placed your son on the throne. The affairs of men are like this. The will of Heaven can be known and matters will gradually comply therewith." Given its context in the **TT**, this comment appears to say that the Vietnamese were not dependent on the Throne of China for the designation of the will of Heaven (that is, who shall sit on the throne of Vietnam); rather they can see for themselves and can handle their own affairs.

18. **TT**, 7:45b-46a; (Hanoi), II, 170; G. Maspero (1928), 210.

19. **TT**, 8:1a-2a; (Hanoi), II, 173-174; Chú (Hanoi), I, 317; G. Maspero (1928), 211; Wolters (1980), 88. In the transliteration of names, the usage of the Hanoi translation has been followed as opposed to that in Maspero's text.

20. Wolters (1966), 85-86. Burma too would fit this scenario; see G. E. Harvey, **A History of Burma** (London, 1925), 79-87.

21. **TT**, 8:2b-3b, 5a; (Hanoi), II, 174-177; G. Maspero (1928), 211.

22. **TT**, 8:2a-3a; (Hanoi), II, 174-175. Strictly speaking, the phrase means, the clash of two different types (the square and the round). See n. 4 in the Hanoi translation, II, 278.

23. **TT**, 8:3a-b, 4b-5a; (Hanoi), II, 175-177; **CM**, 10:23a, 47a, 48a-b; G. Maspero (1928), 211-213. At least three of the Trần royal tombs, those of Anh-tông, Minh-tông, and Dụ-tông (grandfather, father, and brother respectively of Nghệ-tông and Duệ-tông) were on Mount Yên-sinh (**TT**, 6:38b; Hanoi, II, 111). This mountain is located on the northern edge of Hải-dương province (**CM**, Hanoi, VI, 59) and would have been well out of the path of the invading Cham armies (see **HĐBĐ**, Saigon, 33, 6B).

The Vietnamese fear in the latter case might well reflect one aim of the Cham raids. Besides gaining loot and manpower while destroying that of the Vietnamese, the Chams may also have aimed to destroy the sacred centers of the ruling dynasty and hence moved on the royal tombs.

Ngô Sĩ Liên's comment on the transfer of the treasury was

that this was not the way to accomplish the goal. Instead,
he urged, the Son of Heaven should preside over a well-ruled
state so that men of later generations would not ridicule
such actions.

There is no evidence as to the result of the command to
the Buddhists. Note that the "Master of the Realm" was located in the vicinity of the major Buddhist temples of earlier
centuries.

24. Huỳnh (1979), 154. Yen refers to the area of present-day Peking and Pan to K'ai-feng, capital of the Northern Sung dynasty in China. Both fell in 1126 when north China was lost.

Another indication of the impact made by the Cham wars on
the Vietnamese mind may be seen in Trần Thế Pháp's **Lĩnh Nam
Trích Quái** (see above p. 26). Originally, the second tale,
behind that about the original Vietnamese dynasty, was "King
of the Demons" (Dạ-xoa-vương), derived from the **Ramayana** of
India. This tale "explained" the nature of the Chams as
"simian". A century later, following the Vietnamese victory
over the Chams in 1471, the tale apparently lost its significance and was relegated to the twenty-first position; (Saigon), 10, 98, Chinese 40; see also Taylor (1983), 356-357.

25. **Anthologie**, I, 124.

26. **TT**, 8:3b-7a; (Hanoi), II, 176-179; G. Maspero (1928), 211-214.
Some of Maspero's description does not seem to match the
Vietnamese text.

The horse in question saved the life of an officer on patrol who was being chased by the Chams by leaping a canyon.
As a consequence, the horse was named "Better than Bất-tề",
one of Confucius' best students (**TT**, Hanoi, II, 279, n. 13).

Ngô Sĩ Liên's comment on the ex-king's behavior (**TT**, 8:6b;
Hanoi, II, 178) was a simple "Nghệ-tông had no courage...
How can he be compared with his countrymen?"

The **TT**, 8:6a-b; (Hanoi), II, 178, describes the Vietnamese
view of the Cham resurgence as follows: "Champa, ever since
the tenth century (Lê and Lý times), has had weak and timor-
ous soldiers. Whenever our army approached, the people either
fled or surrendered. But when Chế Bồng Nga and La Ngai (the
chief general) appeared, they brought the people together
and taught them gradually changing their old customs. Brave,
ruthless, and tough, they have frequently raided us and made

our country grieve." Perhaps the historians of the fifteenth
century saw a lesson therein. The final word of the quotation
(hoạn) is the same used by the Ming dynasty in application
to the "misfortunes" caused by the Central Asian peoples
(Wolters, 1970, 53).

27. **TT,** 7:46a; (Hanoi), II, 171; G. Maspero (1928), 210-214;
Wolters (1970), 52, 66, 69; Woodside (1963), 9. According to
the Vietnamese **History,** the Chinese could not have cared less
about Duệ-tông's death, although they did finally send a mission of condolence. This may have been due to the Hung-wu Emperor's strong desire to preserve borders (Wolters, 1970,
66). In any case, Vietnamese historians have looked back to
this episode as marking the Ming designs on Vietnam and that
dynasty's wish to make a "blood sacrifice" of the Vietnamese
state. The Chinese view, on the other hand, was that "An-
nan" was a recalcitrant vassal which had paid no heed to its
warnings about attacking Champa and even refused to negotiate
on border territory claimed by China (Lo, 1970, 158, 178, n.
16).

No mention is made of the 1382 Vietnamese mission in the
TT. The Vietnamese had occupied land during the collapse of
the Yüan dynasty which the Ming claimed to be in Kuangsi
province and continued to argue that it was their territory.
The Ming emperor gave orders in 1381 to reject the Vietnamese tribute.

28. **TT,** 8:7a, 9b; (Hanoi), II, 179, 182; Gaspardone (1934), 93-94,
no. 59. The officials involved in Nghệ-tông's project were
Nguyễn Mậu Tiến of the Secret Council, Phan Nghĩa of the
Ministry of Rites, and an unidentified official from the
staff of a local lord.

Phan Nghĩa served as First Secretary of the Ministry of
Rites from 1371 to at least 1384 (**TT,** 7:38b; 8:7a; Hanoi,
II, 163, 179), while Trần Đình Thâm, third in the examination
of 1374, had been the chief envoy in the mission to China on
Duệ-tông's death in 1377 and was promoted on his return (**TT,**
7:40b, 46a; Hanoi, II, 165, 171).

29. **TT,** 8:4a-b, 7a-b; (Hanoi), II, 176, 179; **ĐKL** (Saigon), 19; Gaspardone (1934), 94. Tử Bình originally was a palace scholar
in the 1340s (**TT,** 7:14a; Hanoi, II, 137). Both Phan Phu Tiến
and Ngô Sĩ Liên expressed their strong displeasure at the

move; instead, as the latter intimated, Tử Bình should have
been executed.

The Vạn-Phúc Temple was built by Lý Thánh-tông in 1057;
see L. Bezacier, **L'art vietnamien** (Paris, 1954), chap. 6.

30. **TT**, 8:7b-8a; (Hanoi), II, 179-180; Chú (Hanoi), I, 164, 191;
CM, 11:2b. For more on Trần Nguyên Đán, see Wolters (1979),
448-449; (1980), 78-79, 88-89; (1982A), 77; (1983), 79ff.

An early nineteenth-century collection of tales, the **Vũ
Trung Tùy Bút** by Phạm Đình Hồ, Vietnamese trans. (Hanoi,
1972), 125, contains a discussion of an inscription set up
by Nguyên Đán in Hải-dương, which tells how his mother's
younger brother, Châu Tung Trinh, commander of the Tam-sưởng
Imperial Guard (**Cấm-binh**), turned Nguyên Đán's poems over to
Quý Ly and presumably smoothed the way for a rapprochement
between the two.

Mộng Dư's wife was the daughter of Nhẫn Vinh, killed by
Nhật Lễ, with his widow married to Quý Ly thereafter (**TT**,
7:38a; Hanoi, II, 162); see p. 12 above.

Ngạc's reference to "past years" is most likely to the
aristocratic coup of 1370.

Note that the Vietnamese style of writing (**nôm**) was now
being used by the aristocracy as well as by the literati.

31. **TT**, 8:8b; (Hanoi), II, 181, 279; Chú (Hanoi), I, 191; **CM**,
11:41a-b. Nguyên Ứng Long later changed his name to Phi
Khanh; his son was the famous minister and scholar Nguyên
Trãi. Gaspardone (1934), 94, saw Phi Khanh as a graduate of
1374. See also Wolters (1982A), 75, 76, 79-82, 106-107, and
(1983), 79-101, for more on Phi Khanh.

A tale in the early sixteenth-century **TKML** (Saigon), I,
189-211; (Paris), 131-142, which is linked to the 1390s, tells
the story of a mortal married to a spirit. It reflects the
same sort of misgivings as seen here for intermarriages between scholars and aristocrats.

32. **TT**, 8:9a-b; (Hanoi), II, 181; **NÔML**, 17b-18a; **ĐKL** (Saigon), 25;
BK, "Nghệ-an", 31b-32a; Chú (Hanoi), IV, 72-73; see above.
Some write his personal name as Xác. **Đại Nam Nhất Thống Chí**,
15:16b-17a, even goes as far as to give Tống Thốc the same
tenth-century ancestry as Quý Ly.

The fact that the texts of both the **TT** and the **NÔML** are
almost identical here raises interesting questions: did the

fifteenth-century authors of the **TT** have access to the **NÔML**, or did the authors of both works use an identical source?

For a tale of a century or so later concerning Tống Thốc, see **TKML**, (Saigon, I, 15-30; Paris, 35-42). Here Tống Thốc talks with the spirit of a defeated Chinese claimant for the throne, perhaps meant to be Quý Ly himself. The story was probably a comment on Quý Ly, placed in the famous Tống Thốc's mouth.

33. **TT**, 7:40b-41a, 46a-b; 8:5a, 7a, 21a, 22b; (Hanoi), II, 165, 171, 177, 179, 192-193, 194; **ĐKL** (Saigon), 18-19. Note that during the last two decades of the fourteenth century. in the examinations of 1384, 1393, and 1400, a greater geographical spread took place among the known successful candidates. For the first time, these scholars began to come from the north and west, from varied districts in Kinh-bắc and Sơn-tây, as well as from Hải-dương, Sơn-nam, Thanh-hóa, and Nghệ-an. See above, chap. 1, n. 16.

34. **TT**, 8:9b; (Hanoi), II, 181; Chú (Hanoi), IV, 63, 73; Gaspar-done (1934), 94-95, nos. 61, 62; Wolters (1980), 88; (1983), 83.

35. Chú (Hanoi), IV, 61. Wolters (1983), 84, notes how sounds were used to indicate general discontent and confusion in the 1380s.

36. Chú (Hanoi), IV, 74; Gaspardone (1934), 95-96, no. 63; quoted from Huỳnh (1979), 70. This poem came from 1385, since it refers to a six-year-old boy (Chinese style) which might have been Nguyễn Trãi (born in 1380); see Wolters (1983), 97, n. 11. An-jen was a Chinese of the Chin dynasty (A.D. third-fifth centuries) who wrote a poem entitled "At Rest". Wolters (1983), 79-85, describes Phi Khanh's "embittered poetry" of these years.

37. Chú (Hanoi), IV, 46, 118; Gaspardone (1934), 50, no. 28, 128-130, no. 127; H. Maspero, "Le royaume de Văn-lang", **BEFEO**, 18, 3 (1918), 1-8; Taylor (1983), 306-311, 351-357. See also Wolters (1980), 75-77, 80-81, 86. Neither of Tống Thốc's works is extant.

According to Maspero, 4, 6, n. 1, 8, n. 1, and Taylor (1983), 357-359, the fifteenth-century author of the **TT** drew its chapter on Văn-lang and the Hùng kings from these works; see **TT**, 1:3a; (Hanoi), I, 59-63.

38. **TT**, 8:7a-b, 9a; (Hanoi), II, 179, 181; G. Maspero (1928), 214;

DMB, I, 781. According to the Vietnamese, they attempted to comply with the Chinese request for rice in 1384, only to have many of their escort fall ill in the mountain miasmas and die. How real this attempt was we do not know.

The two eunuchs, Tổng Đạo and Toán, both stayed in China and later served as agents for the Ming attack (**TT,** 8:45a; Hanoi, II, 216).

39. **TT,** 8:9a-10a; (Hanoi), II, 182. The bestowal of a sword and declaration of military ability for Quý Ly is ironic concerning his apparent lack thereof. Ngô Sĩ Liên, in his comment, demonstrates a much lower regard for the future usurper and his invidious subversion.

The eunuch (**nội-nhân**), Nguyễn Vị, apparently became chief of the palace staff, Trần Ninh took a position on the Secret Council, and Lê Dử Nghi took Vương Như Chu's place as Counsellor. Vị and Ninh would serve the new Hồ dynasty, while Đỗ eventually took his stepfather's name.

Ho (1964), 132, n. 36, states that no comet is known for this time, though one had appeared in March. Thus, the comet, with its western direction, is probably a symbolic historiographic device to indicate the beginning of Quý Ly's rise to power, the west (or southwest) becoming a representation of Quý Ly's strength and future capital in western Thanh-hóa (see Ho, 129).

40. **TT,** 8:9b, 10b-11a, 12a; (Hanoi), II, 182-183, 184.

41. **TT,** 7:42a; 8:5a; (Hanoi), II, 167, 177. Apparently the then nineteen-year-old king had taken it upon himself to plot Húc's execution in 1381. The **CM,** 10:49a-b, however, did not believe that this could possibly have been the case.

42. **TT,** 8:11a-12b, 13b, 20a; (Hanoi), II, 183-184, 185, 192. The three generals apparently shared the same nursemaid with the future king (see above p. 20; **TT,** 8:2b; Hanoi, II, 174). The coup took place in the twelfth month and may well have been symbolically foreshadowed by a total eclipse of the moon two months earlier; Ho (1964), 143, notes that the eclipse did occur.

Quý Ly's son, Lê Nguyên Trừng, author of the **NÔML,** refused to give Ngung a royal title à la Nhật Lễ and recorded the event this way (4a): "After a while, Nghiễn (began) to listen to perverse ministers (whose) actions did not follow the Way

(Đạo). The ruler (Nghệ-tông) feared for the safety of the national altars (i.e., the state), wept, and dismissed him."
   Ngô Sĩ Liên, in his comment on the matter, scolded the plotters for their failure.

43. **TT**, 7:2b; 8:13b-14b, 38b; (Hanoi), II, 174, 185-186, 210; G. Maspero (1928), 215.

44. **TT**, 8:14b-16b; (Hanoi), II, 186-188; G. Maspero (1928), 215-217. Ngô Sĩ Liên roundly condemned the military disasters and political machinations of Quý Ly and Đa Phương as well as Nghệ-tông's weakness, making his usual classical references.

45. **TT**, 8:16b-18a; (Hanoi), II, 188-190; **CM**, 11:11a-b; G. Maspero (1928), 217-219.

46. **TT**, 8:18a-b, 20a, 21a; (Hanoi), II, 190, 192, 193; **BK**, "Thanh-hóa", 36b-37a. La Tu is mentioned in the **NÔML**, 10b, as a descendant of an eleventh-century Vietnamese Taoist. This act put aside the special commissioners (**kinh-lược-sứ**) who had served in the provincial areas.

47. **TT**, 8:18b-19a; (Hanoi), II, 190-191; **CM**, 11:10a. See pp. 20-21 above for the burying of the treasure. Trần Khất Chân, a Thanh-hóa man, was a descendant of the prince Trần Bình Trọng. He came from the same district that Quý Ly had been prepared to flee to earlier.
   Khất Chân's ancestor, Bình Trọng, was a descendant of the tenth-century king Lê Hoàn. He received the royal name from his father who had served as an official under Trần Thái-tông, married a princess, and gained eternal fame in Vietnam for his answer to the Mongols when they captured him and offered him the title of prince (**vương**) in China: "I would rather be a ghost in the South than a prince of the North." (**TT**, 5:47a; Hanoi, II, 53)

48. **TT**, 8:19a-20b; (Hanoi), II, 191-192; G. Maspero (1928), 219; Boisselier (1963), 355; Wolters (1970), 66-68. The weariness of the elderly Nguyễn Đán may be seen in his poem, "Sleepless Night": "Before my eyes, nothing but affliction! The illness gone, life is yet worse than during the illness!"; **Anthologie**, I, 124.
   The difference between the praise of Trần Nguyễn Đán in the text and Ngô Sĩ Liên's extensive criticism of him in the comment may be laid to Nguyễn Đán's grandson, Nguyễn Trãi.

Trãi wrote a handsome eulogy of his grandfather in the 1420s
(**NTTT**, 77-79), and this probably influenced Phan Phu Tiên in
writing the text, while the later Sĩ Liên castigated anyone
who tolerated the evil Quý Ly.

49. **TT**, 8:18a, 20b-22a; (Hanoi), II, 190, 192-193; **CM**, 11:16a-b.
Ngô Sĩ Liên's comment on Nghệ-tông in these actions was that
he must have been extremely senile to have done them. On
Trần Thiên Bình, see chap. 5 below.

50. **TT**, 8:22a; (Hanoi), II, 193-194. Phan Phu Tiên's comment,
rather more objective on Quý Ly than the later Ngô Sĩ Liên,
noted: "The Trần dynasty, ever since Dụ-tông's wildness, had
also been invaded by Champa and assaulted by increasing numbers of bandits. In broad daylight, (they) plundered (our)
people (and) the law was unable to prevent it. (When) Quý Ly
took control of the government, he began by establishing
stations to uphold the law and was able to curb (the abuses)
somewhat."

    For the classical references, see **The Analects,** Book 6,
Chapter 26; Book 15, Chapter 1; Book 17, Chapters 5, 7 (James
Legge, **The Chinese Classics,** Hongkong, 1960 reprint, I, 193,
294, 319-320, 321). The seven philosophers listed after Han
Yü were Chou Tun-i, Ch'eng Hao, Ch'eng I, Yang Shih, Lo
Ts'ung-yen, Li T'ung, and Chu Hsi in that order.

51. **TT**, 8:22a-23a; (Hanoi), II, 194. Wolters (1983), 88, also discusses the displacing of Confucius with the Duke of Chou.
Ngô Sĩ Liên predictably denied Quý Ly's formulations.

52. The pairs of ministers and monarchs were as follows: the Duke
of Chou and King Wen (Chou), Huo Kuang and Chao-ti (Han),
Chu-ko Liang and Hou-chu of Shu (Three Kingdoms) of Chinese
history; Tô Hiến Thành and Lý Cao-tông of Vietnamese history
(the late twelfth century).

53. Actually, the term **Ch'ih-tsui** means the Fire-red Constellation,
no. 20 among the Twenty-Eight Constellations, which has as
its element fire and as its animal the monkey. See also **TKML**
(Saigon), II, 190, 192, 194, n. 3. The "White Cock Tower"
apparently meant the old man born in the year of the cock;
CM, 11:21a.

54. **TT**, 8:23b-24b; (Hanoi), II, 195-196; **NÔML**, 4a. See also Wolters
(1980), 79. As noted above, Yên-sinh was located in northern Hải-dương. For the oath ceremony, see chap. 1, n. 2 above.

In Ngô Sĩ Liên's terms, the old ruler had failed: "Nghệ-
tông was by nature vacillating and affable. He maintained a
respectful and timid manner. Thus, [his] authority and military [ability] were not enough to repulse foreign enemies,
(and his) firmness and intelligence were not sufficient to
discern slander. There was one man (capable of this), (Trần)
Nguyên Đán, and (Nghệ-tông) was unable to use him. Thus, (he)
entrusted the government to his maternal relatives (and)
caused the royal altars of the Trần family to fall into a
gradual decline and danger. It has been said that earlier
there had been slander, yet he had not seen it, (while) later there was rebellion, yet he did not know it." One should
consult the NÔML, with its pro-Hồ bias, as a counter to this
interpretation of Nghệ-tông; yet a certain consensus appears
which indicates a lack of forcefulness and a susceptibility
to persuasion in this figure who may have reached the throne
only to facilitate his younger brother's ascension.

III. QUÝ LY IN POWER

1. **TT**, 8:23a; (Hanoi), II, 194-195.

2. **TT**, 8:24b,, 25b-26a; (Hanoi), II, 196, 197; Chú (Hanoi), II,
   24-25. For Nguyên Bửu's background, see **TT**, 8:34b, 46b; (Hanoi), II, 206, 218.

3. The quotations are from Legge, I, II, 427, 442 (**Shu Ching**, Part
   V, Book 12, 12, Book 13, 13) respectively. On the career of
   the Duke of Chou, see the **Shu Ching**, Preface, 39-40, 42-43,
   46-49, 52, 54, 57, 58; Part V, Books 6, 9 (1), 12-19; Legge,
   III, 9-12, 351-361, 381, 423-522. A brief sketch of the image
   of the Duke of Chou in official Chinese historiography may
   be found in Chan Hok-lam, **Liu Chi (1311-1375): The Dual Image
   of a Chinese Imperial Advisor**, Ph.D. thesis (Princeton University, 1967), 14.

4. **TT**, 8:25a; (Hanoi), II, 196-197. For the Nhật Chưởng affair,
   see above chap. 2, p. 33.

5. **TT**, 8:25a; (Hanoi), II, 197. His full title was **Nhập-nội Phụ-
   chính Thái-sư Bình-chương-quân-quốc-trọng-sự, Tuyên-trung-vệ-
   quốc Đại-vương** (Grand Preceptor, Prime Minister, and Prince),
   and he was granted permission to wear a golden unicorn tab-
   let.

6. **TT**, 8:25a-b; (Hanoi), II, 197. The Vietnamese work was entitled

For the Support of the State and the Instruction of the Emperor (Phụ-chính Cai-giáo Hoàng-đế).

For the text and translation of this chapter, see Legge, III, 464-473. What this section argued against was, to quote Legge, III, 464, an idleness "in which, while the proper duties are neglected, improper lusts and gratifications may be eagerly sought..."

7. The quotations are from Legge, III, 471-472, 465-466, 473, respectively.

8. **TT,** 8:25b; (Hanoi), II, 197; Gaspardone (1970), 105; Woodside (1963), 9; Lo (1970), 162-164. For the Hung-wu Emperor's feelings in this direction, as stated in 1375, see above chap. 2, n. 13.

9. **TT,** 8:27b-28a; (Hanoi), II, 199. Ngô Sĩ Liên's comment of less than a century later was lengthy and in sharp disagreement with Quý Ly's philosophical position. For Sĩ Liên, Chinese thought had fragmented and become hair-splitting, if not positively wrong, following the death of Mencius; only when Chu Hsi came on the scene was Chinese thought reintegrated in its original simplicity. "[Chu Hsi's] words probe deeply [and] his teachings are broad. [We] may say that [his] works are the great accomplishment (đại-thành) of all Confucianism." And Sĩ Liên ended by stating: "After him, the works [of some] were vast and they were capable of being greater than he [while others] were fruitful and brilliantly propagated his [thought], [but] this was all. Having achieved it, how could they criticize and examine it [without accepting it]?"

Also contrast Quý Ly's anti-Neo-Confucian stance with the fervent (if censored) Neo-Confucianism of the Hung-wu Emperor in China at the same time as well as that of his son, the Yung-lo Emperor. Anyone who "made light of the canon" or "defamed the sages" was punished (Ku Chieh-kang, "A Study of Literary Persecution during the Ming", translated by L. C. Goodrich, **Harvard Journal of Asiatic Studies,** 3, 1938, 279, 293).

10. **TT,** 8:25b-27a; (Hanoi), II, 197-199. See also Wolters (1979), 444-445. Hucker (1978), 56-57, shows that the Hung-wu Emperor in China forbade all religious orders to recruit monks younger than forty or nuns under the age of fifty.

11. **TT,** 8:26b; (Hanoi), II, 198; Chú (Hanoi), III, 9; **CM,** 12:5a;

(Hanoi), VII, 92; **Ming Hui Yao** (Peking, 1956), 869. Yet, according to Chú, the Vietnamese pattern of the examinations
"followed the examination rules of the Yüan dynasty". Previously, from the early Trần on, "the literary pattern (of
the examinations) had not been established." In the first
field, the Vietnamese scholars were to explicate the theme,
link the words, examine the text in detail, find the origin
of the theme, give an overall rendering of the passage whence
it came, and show its relevance to themselves.

The length of the various sections was: five hundred characters and over for both the first and second fields, and one
thousand characters and over for the fourth field.

12. **TT**, 8:27a-b, 31b; (Hanoi), II, 199, 202; G. Maspero (1928),
220-221.

13. **TT**, 8:26a-b; (Hanoi), II, 198; Chú (Hanoi), III, 61-62. Chú's
comment reflects a strong mistrust of such currency, seeing
it as disturbing the social situation. A recent article is
Đỗ Văn Ninh, "Tiền cổ thời Hồ" [Money in the Hồ period],
NCLS, 191 (1980), 50-54.

For a description of the paper currency in China under the
Yüan dynasty (into the second half of the fourteenth century),
see H. F. Schurmann, **Economic Structure of the Yüan Dynasty**
(Cambridge, Mass., 1956), 131-145. Hucker (1978), 60, briefly
describes how the Hung-wu Emperor first used copper cash, but
soon (1375) began to use a new paper money to relieve the demand on the coins. To quote him, "Private ownership of gold
and silver was forbidden; all supplies were ordered turned in
to the government." Ultimately, the Chinese (as later the
Vietnamese) designated that the paper money was to be used
in paying some taxes and in making some government payments,
though, as Hucker notes, "by the end of his reign [1398] it
was apparent that paper money was doomed." Quý Ly, as we shall
see, apparently viewed it as an aid to his own goals.

The seven denominations were ten **văn** (aquatic plants drawn
on cloth), thirty **văn** (waves), one **mạch** (clouds), two **mạch**
(a turtle), three **mạch** (a unicorn), five **mạch** (a phoenix), and
one **mân** (a dragon).

14. **TT**, 8:28a-29b; (Hanoi), II, 200, 281, n. 53. The old saying
was that of Wu Ch'i's in conversation with the Marquis Wu of
Wei, fourth century B.C.

Phan Phu Tiên's mid-fifteenth-century comment also made
use of a Chinese historical allusion, this time from the Han
where he saw the fall of the Han (and the Trần) as having
been based in such a movement of the ruler by a powerful
minister (equating Quý Ly with the legendary Ts'ao Ts'ao?)
"in order to command all the nobility". "But," in Phu Tiên's
words, "what generation does not have a rebellious minister
causing grave trouble for the Emperor? The ruler of men (must
be) decisive in order to stop him and clear in thought in
order to know him, then there will be no later worries."

The memory of this attempt to move the capital out of the
Red River Delta remained negative; the early sixteenth-century **TKML** (Saigon), II, 56; (Paris), 171, contains such a
reference.

15. **TT,** 8:27b, 28b; (Hanoi), II, 199, 200; Charles Robequain, **Le
Thanh Hóa** (Paris, 1929), II, 284-285; Bezacier (1954), 83-84,
96 (quotation). The latter's description of the physical site
of the citadel is invaluable. Also, see L. Bezacier, "Conception du plan des anciennes citadelles-capitales du Nord Viet-
Nam", **Journal Asiatique,** 240, 2 (1952), 185-195.

For the general location of the citadel, see **HĐBĐ** (Saigon),
10 (10C-D); according to H. Le Breton, **Revue Indochinoise,**
35, 3-4 (1921), 169, it sat three kilometers northwest of
the seat of Quảng-hóa prefecture and one kilometer from the
left bank of the Mã River, or as Chú (Hanoi), I, 40, stated,
"to the left and the right of the citadel, close to the mountains, flowed the Mã and Lương Rivers, coming together in
front of it".

16. Legge, III, 431.

17. Bezacier (1954), 84-86; (1952), 191; Gaspardone (1970), 103;
TT, 8:31a-b, 40a; (Hanoi), II, 202, 211. In the repair, brick
was used for some of the rock in the walls which had crumbled.
All the bricklayers of the country were called together for
the work. Bezacier (1954), Pl. VII, 8, is a photograph of
the main gate.

18. Bezacier (1954), 84, 85-86, 190, 200; Chú (Hanoi), I, 40. Bezacier (1954), Pl. VII, 9, is an aerial photograph of the
citadel.

19. **TT,** 8:29a-30a; (Hanoi), II, 200-201; Chú (Hanoi), I, 35, 257.
H. Maspero (1916), 46-47, has been most helpful in straight-

ening out Quý Ly's administrative approach.

20. **TT**, 8:30a-b; (Hanoi), II, 201. The reference in the quotation
    to the different types of schools would seem to come from
    Mencius (see S. Couvreur, **Dictionnaire classique de la langue
    chinoise**, 1963, 277, under **siang**). See also Wolters (1979),
    447-448.

    The amounts of public land given were fifteen **mẫu** in a
    large prefecture, eleven in a medium one, and ten in a small
    one.

    Ngô Sĩ Liên, in the next century, asked what good all this
    was; while admitting that he could not really grasp what was
    going on, he did not think that it could have been the young
    king's doing, rather that it was merely Quý Ly's idea "in
    order to gain the hearts of the people".

    An odd aspect here is that the three provinces where the
    educational officials were to be appointed are all given late
    fifteenth-century, rather than late fourteenth-century, names:
    Sơn-nam, Kinh-bắc, and Hải-đồng (Hải-dương?).

21. **TT**, 8:30b, 32b-33a; (Hanoi), II, 202, 204; Chú (Hanoi), III,
    66. Chú remarked that the system of the Lý and the Trần dy-
    nasties was merely to tax the peasants on the amount of land
    they claimed to have rather than to try to control the hold-
    ings. In his eyes, Quý Ly acted in accord with activities of
    earlier periods, such as those of Wang Mang (usurper of the
    Han dynasty, A.D. 9-25). In sum, Chú thought these measures
    "vainglorious", there being no reimbursement for lost land
    and the "poor" thus having to suffer. However, as he so right-
    ly concluded, "...in what way would [the restrictions on land-
    holding] block the methods for annexing [land] and equalize
    the gain for the people?!"

    In contrast with Vietnam, early Ming China redistributed
    the land confiscated from the government-owned lands of the
    Yüan dynasty and the estates of the large landholders who
    had supported the Mongols (Hucker, 1978), 58, as Lê Lợi would do
    in the late 1420s.

22. Lo (1970), 159, 165, 178-179, n. 20; Gaspardone (1970), 105.
    The Hung-wu Emperor merely stated: "At all times barbarians
    have quarreled with each other, [but] this defies destiny.
    Let us wait." (Quoted in Gaspardone, 1970, 105, n. 46, and
    Lo, 1970, 159.)

The Vietnamese **History** (**TT**, 8:31b; Hanoi, II, 202) only
mentions the Ming sending two Mongols who had served the old
Yüan dynasty "to pacify and put in order" the Vietnamese
situation. As Wang (1968), 52, indicates, the Hung-wu Emper-
or had begun to revive activities involving all of his rest-
less border states, but never to the point of physical intervention; thus, the border states proceeded their own ways.

23. **TT**, 8:31a-32b; (Hanoi), II, 203-204.

24. **TT**, 8:32b, 33a-b; (Hanoi), II, 203, 205; Gaspardone (1970),
112, n. 94. As Gaspardone notes and as Vietnamese literati
indicated in the **Toàn Việt Thi Lục** [Complete record of Vietnamese poetry], Quý Ly's poetry was of a rather dull and
tedious style better suited for prose.

25. **TT**, 8:33b-34a; (Hanoi), II, 205-206. A tale about this event
may be found in the **TKML** (Saigon), II, 163-199; (Paris),
227-235.

26. **TT**, 8: 30b-31a; (Hanoi), II, 202. The text gives the name Đỗ
Thế Mẫn, but it would appear that this man, together with Đỗ
Tử Mẫn, a favored choice for Quý Ly's faction (see **TT**, 8:14b;
Hanoi,   II, 186), was the Đỗ Mẫn who becomes more signifi-
cant from this time.

27. **TT**, 8:34a; (Hanoi), II, 205. As examples of the backgrounds of
these men, Trần Khát Chân was a third-generation high general (see chap. 2, n. 47 above) and Lương Nguyên Bưu was the
sixth generation of an aristocratic family that went back to
the late Lý dynasty (including another hero in the wars against
the Mongols).

    Ngô Sĩ Liên (**TT**, 8:35a; Hanoi, II, 206) complained that
the group should have learned of the plot, disrupted it by
stopping Phạm Khả Vĩnh, and exposed Quý Ly's machinations,
"then the names would have been rectified, words would have
conformed [to propriety], and the [entire] matter would have
ended well [with Quý Ly in his place]. It is regrettable that
their hesitancy and timidity resulted in this defeat."

28. **TT**, 8:25a, 39b; 9, 1b; (Hanoi), II, 197, 211, 227-228. For more
on this group of officials, see chap. 4 below.

29. **TT**, 8:34a; (Hanoi), II, 206.

30. **TT**, 8:35a; (Hanoi), II, 206. Ngô Sĩ Liên (**TT**, 8:35a-b; Hanoi,
II, 206) referred to a case of the same sort (a powerful
minister wearing royal garb and having guards before seizing

the throne) in the **Tso-ch'uan,** first year of Duke Chiao
(Legge, V, 576, 581) where the opposition vanished, giving
tyranny its chance: "This matter of the Hồ family went the
same way!"

31. **TT,** 8:35b, 36a; (Hanoi), II, 206, 207.

32. **TT,** 8:35b-36a; (Hanoi), II, 207, 277, n. 60. The various loca-
    tions mentioned are difficult to place.

33. **TT,** 8:36b, 37b, 38b, 47a; (Hanoi), II, 207-208, 209, 219. There
    is no explicit indication why Quý Ly chose his second son
    over his eldest, except that the former was the son of the
    Trần princess while the latter was not (Gaspardone, 1970,
    111).

IV. THE HỒ REGIME

1. **TT,** 8:36b-37a; (Hanoi), II, 208; Gaspardone (1970), 101, 103.
   For a mention of Yao and Shun by Trần Nguyên Đán, see chap.
   2, p. 21, above. Wolters (1980), 79-80, places Hồ Quý Ly in
   relation to the Vietnamese literati of the fourteenth century,
   and (1983), 88, also notes the role of Shun and Ta Yü in
   Vietnam.

   The reasoning behind the adoption of Đại Ngu follows Phan
   Phu Tiên's comment of some fifty years later. Phu Tiên did
   not, however, agree and quoted Confucius (**The Analects,** II,
   xxiv; Legge, I, 154), "To take a man's spirit not [in one's
   line of descent] and worship it, [that] is flattery!" and
   listed a number of Chinese examples of men who had refused
   to go along with such attempts. Ngô Sĩ Liên merely quibbled
   with one of Phu Tiên's examples while noting that even the
   great Chu Hsi had made the same mistake.

   On the career of Shun, see the **Shu Ching,** Preface, 2; Part
   I, Chapter III, 12; and especially Part II, Book I, "The
   Canon of Shun" (Legge, III, 2, 26-27, 29-51). The Preface, in
   summary, stated: "Shun of Yu was in a low and undistinguished
   position, when Yao heard of his comprehensive intelligence,
   and wishing to make him successor to the throne, made proof
   of him in many situations of difficulty" (Legge, III, 2).
   What Quý Ly appears to have been doing was using the myth of
   Shun to place his mentor, Nghệ-tông, in the position of Yao
   and himself in the role of Shun. Like Shun, Quý Ly was raised
   by the ruler, married to a princess, tested "reluctantly",

inherited the throne, put the state in order, controlled the local powers, revamped provincial administration, deepened waterways, properly instructed the people, and held examinations. This image allowed Quý Ly to rule, whereas that of the Duke of Chou would have forced him to step aside eventually for the young king.

2. **TT,** 8:37b, 38a, 38b, 39a; (Hanoi), II, 208, 209-210.

3. Legge, I, 295, 398-400, respectively.

4. **Shu Ching,** Part II, Book I, Chapter 1; Legge, III, 29.

5. **TT,** 8:41b-42a; (Hanoi), II, 212-213; Chú (Hanoi), II, 121-122; Gaspardone (1970), 112, n. 94. Later commentators (Ngô Thì Sĩ of the eighteenth century and Phan Huy Chú of the early nineteenth) remarked on the poor and confused way in which the ceremony was held (as, for example, including women) as well as on the impropriety of a usurper attempting to hold such a ceremony. As Thì Sĩ exclaimed, "Civilized ceremonies were greatly lacking!" all the way up to the late fourteenth century.

6. **TT,** 8:42b, 43b; (Hanoi), 214-215.

7. **TT,** 8:39a, 40b-41a, 42a-b, 44b, 46a-b, 47a-48b; (Hanoi), II, 210, 212, 213, 216, 218-220. For the poem, see chap. 3, above, p. 56.

8. **TT,** 8:49a; 9:1a-2a; (Hanoi), II, 221, 227-229. In the Sinic style of counting years, Quý Ly's seventieth year was celebrated in 1405. He granted all males seventy and over one additional rank, awarded their wives with the paper money, and held a great celebration in the Western Capital to bestow the ranks.

   Gaspardone (1970), 113, n. 96, gives all Nguyễn Trừng's titles.

9. **TT,** 8:38a, 43a, 44b, 46a; 9:1a-2a, 5b, 7a; (Hanoi), II, 209, 214, 216, 217, 227-229, 231, 233. The case of Phạm Xạ, who received the royal name, is curious since his elder brother, Phạm Ông Thiện, was executed for plotting against Quý Ly in 1399; see chap. 3, above pp. 53-54.

10. **TT,** 8:39a, 42b-43a, 50a; (Hanoi), II, 210, 214, 222; Chú (Hanoi), I, 35; III, 49. In the re-organization, Quý Ly seems to have split Thanh-hóa (then Thanh-đô) province into three smaller units (the **Tam-phụ** for which the separate army was created): Thiên-xương, presumably in the western part of the

province around Tây-đô, and the old Chinese administrative
territories of Cửu-chân and Ái-châu, in all likelihood along
the coast; Diễn-châu was made the fourth unit under the name
Linh-nguyên (all four units being referred to as the **Tứ-phụ**).
This pattern of the capital and the four supporting units,
west, north, east and south, matches the Southeast Asian use
of the number five. At the same time as the organization occurred, the name of Đại-lại Mountain in the vicinity of the
Western Capital was changed to that of Kim-âu (Golden Bowl),
perhaps an allusion to the golden bowl plowed up by Lê Hoàn,
400 years earlier in the ceremony on the mountain (see **TT**,
1:18a; Hanoi, I, 171).

11. **TT**, 8:21b-22a, 38a, 39a, 40a, 44a, 47a-b, 49a-b; 9:5b; (Hanoi), II,
     193, 209, 210, 212, 215, 218, 219, 221, 231. According to
     the **TKML** of a century later (Saigon, II, 57; Paris, 172), Lê
     Cảnh Kỳ "was a good strategist, but lacked decision-making
     ability".

12. **TT**, 7:46b; 8:39b, 40b; (Hanoi), II, 171, 211, 212. Hoàng Hối
     Khanh was a graduate of 1384, Đồng Thức in 1393, and Nguyễn
     Hy Chu probably also in 1393 (**ĐKL**, Saigon, 19-20, 25). Hối
     Khanh, in the negative words of the **TKML** (Saigon, II, 57;
     Paris, 172), "was learned but abstruse (in his thought)".
        Đồng Thức was being likened to Wei Cheng (Ngụy Trung),
     trusted counsellor of the founder of the T'ang dynasty and
     especially of his son, T'ang T'ai-tsung (cf. H. A. Giles,
     A Chinese Biographical Dictionary, London, 1898, 856-857, no.
     2264, and H. J. Wechsler, **Mirror to the Son of Heaven** (New
     Haven, Conn., 1974). Such a comparison was flattering to the
     Hồ, father and son, as well, since it set them beside the
     first two rulers of the great T'ang dynasty.

13. **TT**, 8:28b, 29b, 32b, 40a, 45b-46a, 48b-49a, 51b-52a; 9:1b; (Ha-
     noi), II, 200, 201, 203, 211, 217, 220, 224, 228.

14. **TT**, 7:46b; 8:38a; (Hanoi), II, 171, 209. Yet many of the older
     officials like Nguyễn Phi Khanh would have relished finally
     serving under a dynamic king; on Phi Khanh in the years 1401-
     1407, see Wolters (1983), 79, 83-85.

15. A good example is the case of Nguyễn Đại Năng, a sorcerer
     (**phương-sĩ**) who used a "fire-needle" to heal the ill and was
     appointed by Hán Thương to a position as a special aide with
     his own bureau and clerks; despite his "false" credentials,

as the **TT** states, he moved up eventually to command an army
(**TT**, 8:44b; Hanoi, II, 216).

Of the men who served the Hồ regime, very little is known
of their backgrounds and how they came to serve it. A few,
like Hoàng Hối Khanh, can be followed from having passed an
examination under the Trần or from their service; most, however, simply appear in the positions they had already received.

16. **TT**, 8:37b-38a, 45b-46a, 48b; (Hanoi), II, 209, 217, 220, 282,
    nn. 74-75; Chú (Hanoi), III, 9.

17. **TT**, 8:45b; (Hanoi), II, 217.

18. **TT**, 8:37b, 38a, 40a, 47b; (Hanoi), II, 209, 211, 219; **ĐKL**
    (Saigon), 17, 20-21, 24-25; Chú (Hanoi), I, 192, 290, 293;
    Gaspardone (1934), 96-97.

19. Chú (Hanoi), IV, 81-82, for the first reference, and I, 290-
    292, for the quotations. Both Chou Tun-i and Chu Hsi lived
    in Sung China. The "stone drums" refer to texts carved on
    them in the Temple of Confucius, the "clear thinking" to the
    story of Ch'eng T'ang of the Shang dynasty. Han Yü lived dur-
    ing the T'ang dynasty, and Mr. Li was the son of Confucius
    who always told him to study the **Shih** Ching and the **Li Chi**.

20. Phạm Thế Ngũ, **Việt Nam Văn Học Sử** (Saigon, 1961), II, 82.

21. Lê Quý Đôn quoted in Gaspardone (1934), 8; specifically listed
    were Nguyễn Trãi, Lý Tử Tấn, and the later Phan Phu Tiến;
    Ngô Thì Sĩ, quoted in Chú (Hanoi), III, 9.

    Maurice Durand and Nguyễn Trần Huân, **Introduction à la lit-
    térature vietnamienne** (Paris, 1969), 63, make the following
    statement concerning Nguyễn Trãi's **Quốc Âm Thi Tập** [Collec-
    tion of poetry in the national language], including poems of
    the late Trần, Hồ, and early Lê periods: "The language is
    still under the hold of Chinese: the literary allusions (per-
    sonages from the Confucian classics or from Chinese history)
    abound; one often senses that the Vietnamese expressions
    closely follow Chinese expressions; the syntax in numerous
    cases is Chinese."

22. Chú (Hanoi), II, 9.

23. **TT**, 8:14b, 23a, 37b, 41a-b, 46b-47a; (Hanoi), II, 186, 194,
    209, 212, 218; **ĐKL** (Saigon), 19, 25; Gaspardone (1970), 104.
    Hucker (1978), 47, notes how the Hung-wu Emperor in China
    liked to use National College students for investigation in

the empire.

24. **TT**, 8:39a-b; (Hanoi), II, 210-211; Chú (Hanoi), III, 49. The term **kinh-nhân,** literally "men of the capital", meant the lowland Vietnamese as opposed to their upland neighnors.

About the officials who urged Quý Ly to this action, see pp. 63-64 above.

Both these acts (the census and the limitation on controlled manpower) are similar to acts of the Ming, though the Hung-wu Emperor abolished all forms of slavery. He held a huge cadastral survey in 1387. See Hucker (1978), 47, 55, 58.

25. **TT**, 8:42a; (Hanoi), II, 213; Chú (Hanoi), III, 54. To quote Ngô Thì Sĩ's eighteenth-century comment, "Exempting the landless, orphans, and widows from taxes was certainly a compassionate policy towards the people, but [the fact that] those with land had to pay taxes, [that] those with bodies had to endure, was certainly a law no one could change. As to the land taxes which reached one mạch per sào, in some places that was excessively heavy, in others far too light; none of it was correct."

The head tax schedule was as follows:

.1 - .5	mẫu of land	...	.5 **quan** (strings of cash)
	(= 5 **sào**)		(= 5 **mạch**)
.6 - 1.0	mẫu	...	1.0 **quan**
1.1 - 1.5	mẫu	...	1.5 quan
1.6 - 2.0	mẫu	...	2.0 quan
2.1 - 2.5	mẫu	...	2.6 quan
2.6 and up	mẫu	...	3.0 **quan**

The Hung-wu Emperor, too, had sought an equalization of land tax burdens (Hucker, 1978, 58).

26. **TT**, 8:42b, 46a, 47a; (Hanoi), II, 213-214, 217, 218. The idea of transfering landless peasants to border territory most likely came from the numerous moves ordered by the Hung-wu Emperor in China (1370, 1371, 1382, 1388, 1390); Hucker (1978), 57.

27. **TT**, 8:40a, 41a, 42b, 48a; (Hanoi), II, 211, 212, 214, 220.

28. **TT**, 8:38b, 43a; (Hanoi), II, 210, 214.

29. **TT**, 8:38a-b, 39b-40a, 40b-41a, 44a-b, 46a; (Hanoi), II, 209-212, 215-217; G. Maspero (1928), 221-223; Boisselier (1963), 356; Wolters (1966), 51. Two campaigns seem to have been sent out in 1400-1401, though, as Maspero indicates, a case

may be made for only one.

For Tân-bình and Thuận-hóa, see **HĐBĐ** (Saigon), 48 (6B, 7C) (where the maps of Thuận-hóa and Quảng-nam should be reversed, pp. 47-48).

30. **TT**, 8:40b-41a, 42b, 44a, 47a; (Hanoi), II, 212, 214, 215, 218; G. Maspero (1928), 222-223. For the area colonized, now in southern Quảng-nam and northern Quảng-ngãi (**TT**, Hanoi, II, 282), see **HĐBĐ** (Saigon), 47 (3C, 4B); see previous note as well.

The **Ming Shih Lu**, Yung-lo period (**MSL/YL**), 149:4b-5a, notes that men who were important in the Trần revolts against the Chinese occupation (Nguyễn Súy, Hồ Bối, Nguyễn Cảnh Dị, son of Cảnh Chân, and Đặng Dung, Tất's son) were established in Thăng-hoa from this time.

Exactly what the term **Xiêm-la** (Ch. **Hsien-lo**, Siam) refers to is difficult to say, though it may mean an extension of Thai power into what is now southern Laos.

31. **TT**, 8:49a; (Hanoi), II, 221.

32. **TT**, 8:19a, 31b, 39b, 40b, 46a; (Hanoi), II, 191, 202, 211, 212, 218; G. Maspero (1928), 221-222.

7. DESTRUCTION OF THE VIETNAMESE STATE

1. D. B. Chan, "The Problem of the Princes as Faced by the Ming Emperor Hui (1399-1402)", **Oriens**, 11 (1958), 183-193; and "The Role of the Monk Tao-yen in the Usurpation of the Prince of Yen", **Sinologica**, 6 (1959), 83-100; Ed. L. Farmer, **Early Ming Government** (Cambridge, Mass., 1976); H. L. Kahn, **Monarchy in the Emperor's eyes** (Cambridge, Mass., 1971), 17-21; Wang Gungwu, "China and Southeast Asia, 1402-1424", in J. Ch'en and N. Tarling, eds., **Studies in the Social History of China and Southeast Asia** (Cambridge, 1970), 378; Lo (1970), 159; **DMB**, I, 355-360.

2. Charles O. Hucker, **Traditional China in Ming Times** (Tucson, Ariz., 1961), 78.

3. Lo Jung-p'ang, "Policy Formulation and Decision-Making on Issues Respecting Peace and War", in Charles O. Hucker, ed., **Chinese Government in Ming Times** (New York, 1969), 51-55; Wolters (1970), 155; Wolters (1966), 50; Wang Gungwu, "The Opening of Relations between China and Malacca, 1403-1405", in J. Bastin and R. Roolvink, eds., **Malayan and Indonesian**

Studies (Oxford, 1964), 89-91, 99.

4. Farmer (1976), 88-96, 101; Wang (1970), 378-380, 400; Wang (1964), 89, 91-93, 99-100; Wang (1968), 53. The quotation is translated in Wang (1970), 379.

5. Lo (1970), 156, 165, 166. The quotation is translated in Lo, 166.

6. Wang (1970), 399. See also below, chap. 6, p. 97.

7. Gaspardone (1970), 106, 111; Wang (1970), 379, 381; Lo (1970), 166; **TT**, 8:43b-44a; (Hanoi), II, 215. The Vietnamese embassy sent in 1400 may well have been received by the young Chinese emperor but no record survives (cf. Wang, 1964, 91).

   The Vietnamese text, written presumably in the 1470s, gives an interesting account of the rise of Chu Ti: "At that time, the Ming emperor had established the capital in Ch'in-ling [when] Ti, Prince of Yen, revolted, killed the officials of the Three Offices (**San-ssu**), and brought [his] troops toward the capital. Upon reaching it, he vanquished the loyalists and entered the city, indiscriminately killing [his opponents]. Ch'ien-wen killed himself in the fire." Chu Ti is here referred to by his original posthumous title of T'ai-tsung, while a few pages later (**TT**, 8:45a; Hanoi, II, 216) he is given the later (sixteenth-century) posthumous title of Ch'eng-tsu, thus posing an intriguing historiographical problem.

8. Lo (1970), 166, 168; Gaspardone (1970), 106; Woodside (1963), 10; Wang (1970), 381, 399; **TT**, 8:45a-b; (Hanoi), II, 216, 217. The Vietnamese stated that the Chams had presented the elephants, together with the territory, as tribute to the Vietnamese ruler "seeking to put off our armies" and had then "falsely" reported to China that the Hồ had seized the land and intercepted the tribute meant for China. Yet the passage ends, "therefore [we] returned them". See above chap. 4, pp. 73-74.

   The Chinese records profess that the court had no knowledge at that time of the Hồ seizure of power and change of name for the state.

9. **TT**, 8:39a, 44b-45a; (Hanoi), II, 210, 216-217; Wang (1964), 92; G. Maspero (1928), 223; Woodside (1963), 10; Lo (1970), 167. The requests for monks et al. came in the 1380s and in 1395. According to the Vietnamese records (**TT**, 8:7b, 9a; Ha-

noi, II, 179, 181), Nguyễn Tống Đạo and Nguyễn Toán had perhaps gone to Nanking in 1381 (at least prior to 1385) to
serve as personal attendants to the emperor, and Tống Đạo
had eagerly bragged about the quality of Vietnamese Buddhism
and fruit.

The question about the Vietnamese version is that there
seems to be no substantiation of it in Chinese records. Also,
as noted above, the fact that the posthumous title Ch'eng-
tsu (from the sixteenth century) is used instead of T'ai-
tsung to refer to the Yung-lo Emperor arouses the suspicion
that this passage may have been added later.

10. **TT**, 8:46a-b; (Hanoi), II, 217-218; Gaspardone (1970), 105; Lo
    (1970), 171.

11. Lo (1970), 168-169; G. Maspero (1928), 223. The quotation is
    Lo's translation.

12. Translated from the **MSL/YL**, 33:5b-6a, by Lo (1970), 169. For
    the Vietnamese view of Bá Kỳ, see **TT**, 9:8b; (Hanoi), II,
    234, which claims that he did not know Trần Thiên Bình when
    the latter arrived at the Ming court, and Chú (Hanoi), I,
    317, who states that Bá Kỳ and Cảnh Xuân were in the plot
    together.

13. Lo (1970), 169, 180, n. 50; Woodside (1963), 10; Gaspardone
    (1970), 106; **TT**, 8:16a, 18b, 51a; 9:8b; (Hanoi), II, 188,
    190, 223, 234. For Yamamoto's arguments, see his work **Annan-
    shi Kenkyu** (Tokyo, 1950), 281-286. The Vietnamese records re-
    fer to the pretender as Trần Thiêm Bình.

14. Wang (1970), 393; W. Franke, "The Veritable Records of the Ming
    Dynasty". in W. G. Beasley and E. G. Pulleyblank, eds., **His-
    torians of China and Japan** (London, 1961), 68-71; Kahn (1971),
    22-29.

    About the **MSL/YL**, note that the Chinese commander, Chang Fu,
    "was one of the directors of the commission which compiled the
    shih-lu of Chu Ti's reign" and that a controversial execution
    of one of the Chinese generals by Chang is conspicuously
    missing from the account (Wang Gungwu, "Chang Fu", **DMB**, I,
    67, and below chap. 6, n. 21).

15. Lo (1970), 165, 169-170; Woodside (1963), 10; Gaspardone (1970),
    106; Wang (1964), 102-103; **TT**, 8:48b-49a, 51a; (Hanoi), II,
    220, 223. While the Vietnamese mission of Phạm Canh and Lưu
    Quang Đình is recorded for later 1405, it would seem to ac-

cord better with the New Year mission of late 1404 as recorded by the Chinese. We will see another case of transposition
(that of Li I) below.

16. Lo (1970), 170, 171; **TT**, 8:46b; (Hanoi), II, 218; Woodside
    (1963), 10. The quotation is translated by Lo, 170. The Viet-
    namese annals place the mission of Li I in the second half
    of 1404, though the Chinese records (**Shih-lu** and **Ming Shih**)
    indicate quite clearly that it left Nanking in the first
    lunar month of 1405.

    Another curious point about the Vietnamese text is that it
    states that Li I went "from Đông-đô to Tây-kinh", thus using
    the term later applied by the Lê dynasty to its own Western
    Capital.

    Curiously, neither of Nguyễn Cảnh Chân's missions to Nan-
    king is mentioned in the Vietnamese annals which make him
    appear to have remained at his southern post in Thăng-hoa.

17. **TT**, 8:47b-48a; (Hanoi), II, 219; Lo (1970), 170-172; Woodside
    (1963), 10-11. Interestingly, the only matter brought up by
    the Chinese mission was that of Kuangsi; the Yünnan issue was
    not mentioned and may have been merely another self-justifi-
    cation for the Chinese case, though the Vietnamese reply held
    in the Chinese records does mention it. On the other hand,
    crime number thirteen of the "twenty crimes" listed by the
    Ming does seem to be a confirmation of this act (**MSL/YL**,
    60:3a).

18. Lo (1970), 172; Gaspardone (1970), 106; **TT**, 8:48b; (Hanoi),
    II, 220. The quotation is translated by Lo.

19. **TT**, 8:48a-b; (Hanoi), 219-220; Chú (Hanoi), IV, 7; Lo (1970),
    171. According to the **TT**, each **vệ** had eighteen **đội** (squads),
    and each **đội** had eighteen men, thus each **vệ** had 324 men and
    the armies had 6,480 men. For the rest, the large armies had
    thirty **đội** (540 men), the medium-sized ones twenty **đội** (360
    men), the **dinh** or camps fifteen **đội** (270 men), and the **đoàn**
    or troops ten **đội** (180). The Palace Guard (**Cấm-vệ-đô**) had
    five **đội** (90 men). One wonders if each **đội** should have had
    80 men, thus making the army count larger.

20. **TT**, 8:49b-50a, 51a-b; (Hanoi), II, 221-223; Gaspardone (1970),
    105-106; Lo (1970), 171. For the location of Đa-bang, see
    HĐBĐ (Saigon), 25 (6D), and for Bạch-hạc (7D).

    Ngô Sĩ Liên, in a comment, could not bring himself to

praise Nguyễn Trừng, though he liked the statement.

21. Lo (1970), 172-173; Woodside (1963), 11, n. 28; Gaspardone
    (1970), 106-107; **TT**, 8:50a; (Hanoi), II, 222. The quotation
    is from the New Year's message delivered by Nguyễn Cảnh Chân
    and is translated by Lo, 172.

    The Chinese records speak in terms of the third lunar month
    with the attack on the sixteenth day (April 4), while the
    Vietnamese records refer to the fourth lunar month with the
    attack on the eighth day (April 26).

    The Vietnamese records (**TT**, 9:8b; Hanoi, II, 234) claim
    that the Chinese asked Thiên Bình how many troops would be
    needed and he replied only a few thousand because the people
    would willingly take him back. Bùi Bá Kỳ is said to have
    disputed this and to have gone into disfavor until the am-
    bush.

22. Lo (1970), 173; **TT**, 8:50a-51a; (Hanoi), I, 332, n. 27; II, 222-
    223; **HĐBĐ** (Saigon), 128. Following the titles of the Vietnam-
    ese generals mentioned, at least some of the units involved
    were the **Nhị-vệ** (Second Royal Guard Unit), the **Chấn-cường
    Quân** (Terror-Striking Iron Army), the **Tam-phụ Quân** (Three
    Pillars Army—of Thanh-hóa—which protected the territory
    around the Western Capital), the **Tả Thần-dực Quân** (Left Spirit
    Wing Army), the **Tả** and **Hữu Thánh-dực Quân** (the Left and Right
    Sacred Wing Armies), and the **Bắc-giang Thánh-dực Quân** (Sacred
    Wing Army of Bắc-giang [Kinh-bắc] province, north of Thăng-
    long).

23. **TT**, 8:51a, 51b-52a; 9:4a, 6b-7a; (Hanoi), II, 223-224, 230,
    232-233. It was Cẩn who had been ordered to kill the young
    king in 1399; see above, chap. 3, p. 51.

24. **TT**, 8:27b, 52a-b; (Hanoi), II, 199, 224-225, 283 (which quotes
    a section from the **MSL** describing the results of these act-
    ivities); Gaspardone (1970), 106; Phan Huy Lê and Phan Đại Doan,
    Khởi Nghĩa Lam Sơn (Hanoi, 1969), 16, 18, where the Hanoi
    historians take the Hồ to task for their static defense and
    lack of guerrilla tactics.

    Two curious incidents are recorded at this point in the
    TT: the tip of the Báo-thiên (Buddhist) Tower, built in the
    mid-eleventh century (**TT**, 3:1a; Hanoi, i, 229) fell off, and
    Quý Ly dreamt of a spirit. Regarding the tower, the same
    thing had occurred in 1258 before the Mongol invasions when

a strong wind blew it off (**TT**, 5:24b; Hanoi, II, 29), while
in 1322 lightning struck it, knocking off a corner (**TT**, 6:40b;
Hanoi, II, 113).

In Quý Ly's dream, which took place in the sixth month
(June/July), the spirit recited a poem to him, as follows:
"In the second month, [you] were among your family./ In the
fourth month, there were troubles and glory./ In the fifth
month, wind and floods./ In the eighth month, mountains and
rivers./ In the tenth month, the Dragon Vehicle." As the Hanoi translation of the **TT** notes, "[this] is translated [lit-
erally] with [its] obscure meaning. It is not clear what the
entire verse means".

25. **MSL/YL** 52:2a, as translated by Lo (1970), 173.

26. Wang (1970), 381-382; **MSL/YL**, 60:2b-3b (the quotation is taken
    from 3a); Gaspardone (1970), 108.

27. Wang (1970), 390-392; Lo (1970), 174; **TT**, 9:8b, 18b; (Hanoi),
    II, 234, 243; Chú (Hanoi), I, 317. The quotation is translat-
    ed by Wang, 390. The Vietnamese information appears trust-
    worthy (at least in terms of the Vietnamese view) since it
    most likely comes from Lê Cảnh Tuấn's contemporary document.

28. Woodside (1963), 11 (from Yamamoto, 1950, 307-309); Lo (1970),
    173; Wang (1970), 395; Gaspardone (1970), 107; **DMB**, I, 146.
    The propagandistic number of 800,000 soldiers was used in
    official Chinese records, while the Vietnamese match that
    figure with 400,000 men in each of the eastern and western
    armies (**TT**, 8:52b; Hanoi, II, 225).

    The Yung-lo Emperor later made a general reference to the
    Cham participation in responding to a tribute mission from
    Champa; see **MSL/YL**, 84:1a. The Cham aid was, to all appear-
    ances, of little consequence.

29. Woodside (1963), 11-12; Wang, **DMB**, I, 65; **TT**, 8:53a; (Hanoi),
    II, 225; **ANCY**, 117.

    An apparent further indication of the importance for this
    enterprise of those men who had stood by the Prince of Yen
    in his conquest of the throne is that seven of the nine mil-
    itary figures whose biographies are included in the **ANCY**,
    came from Chih-li province around Peking in the north, the
    other two being from the same prefecture in Anhwei.

30. Gaspardone (1970), 107, 123; Lo (1970), 173-174; **TT**, 8:52b;
    (Hanoi), II, 225, 283-284 (translation of a section from the

sixteenth-century **YCS**); Wang, **DMB**, I, 65; Wang (1970), 399. As the latter source indicates, the Ming asked the Javanese for 60,000 ounces of gold "to compensate for [our envoys'] lives and to redeem your crime", though they ultimately were satisfied with less.

Woodside (1963), 6-7, notes a source which says that the Chinese ruler "demanded, but did not receive" a golden effigy of the Hồ ruler.

31. Gaspardone (1970), 107-108; **TT**, 8:53a-b; (Hanoi), II, 225, 284 (translation from the **YCS**). The Vietnamese troops were said to have hated "the strange government of the Hồ family".

32. **TT**, 8:53a-b; (Hanoi), II, 225; Lê Quý Đôn, **Đại Việt Thông Sử** (A.1389), 31 ("Rebels"), 22a; **DMB**, I, 689; **ANCY**, 205-207, gives brief biographies of six Vietnamese including Mạc Thúy, who joined the Ming at the time of this attack and who continued to serve them afterwards.

33. Gaspardone (1970), 107-108; Lo (1970), 174; **TT**, 8:53b-54a; (Hanoi), II, 226, 284-285 (translation of sections of the **YCS**); Wang, **DMB**, I, 65; Woodside (1963), 12, 24; Ed. L. Farmer, "Juan An", **DMB**, I, 687-688, on Nguyễn An who was later to be the chief engineer during the re-construction of the Ming capital at Peking in the 1430s and 1440s, and **ibid.**, I, 691-692; II, 1363-1364, on three other Vietnamese who became eunuchs at this time and went on to become imperial favorites in China.

34. Gaspardone (1970), 108-109, n. 75 (quotation translated from the **MSL/YL**, 68); **TT**, 9:1a-b; (Hanoi), II, 227-228. The latter instance of rebellion seems to have occurred in eastern Sonnam. While no Kiến-hưng can be located, in the one region existed Kiến-xương and Tiên-hưng (see **HĐBĐ**, Saigon, 18, 7G), and the former name is perhaps a combination of the latter two.

35. Gaspardone (1970), 109, 111; **TT**, 9:1a-3a; (Hanoi), II, 227-229, 285 (translation of **YCS**); Wang, **DMB**, I, 65. A few years later, the poet Vũ Mộng Nguyên would write, "A mouse's courage moved Minister Hồ" (Huỳnh, 1979, 12), in reference to Hồ Đỗ's role in the battle. On Đồng Thức, see above, chap. 4, n. 12.

36. **TT**, 9:4a-5a; (Hanoi), II, 230-231, 286 (translation from **YCS**); G. Maspero (1928), 224. Later this refugee, Nguyễn Rỗ, would

be brought to Nanking, so the Vietnamese record tells us, serve as an official (Hu-Kuang guard commander), and be executed. In retaliation for Rỗ's defection to Champa, Hoàng Hối Khanh executed his mother and father.

37. **TT**, 9:3b; (Hanoi), II, 230; **NÔML**, 9a-b; Gaspardone, **Annuaire**, 57 (1957), 358. The **TT** appears to have taken its section of the text dealing with Ngô Miễn from the **NÔML**; see chap. 2, n. 32, above.

38. Gaspardone (1970), 109-110; **TT**, 9:3a-4a, 5a-b, 6b; (Hanoi), II, 229-230, 231-232, 286-287 (translations from **YCS** and **MS**); Wang, **DMB**, I, 65. The quotation is from **TT**, 9:3b; (Hanoi), II, 230.

The Vietnamese listed as taken to Nanking were: Quý Ly, his four sons (Nguyên Trừng, Hán Thương, Triệt, and Uông), his stepson Đỗ, four grandsons (including Nhuế), his younger brother Quý Tỳ, the latter's six sons, the Counsellors Nguyễn Ngạn Quang and Lê Cảnh Kỳ, and three other officials. The exact fate of Quý Ly, Hán Thương, and the others is unknown, though they were probably executed. It is known, however, that Lê Cảnh Kỳ refused food and starved to death.

Nguyên Trừng is believed by Gaspardone (1970), 113, to have been the author of the **NÔML**, finished in 1438. Also see Gaspardone, **Annuaire**, 56 (1956), 292-294; 57 (1957), 358-360.

39. **MSL/YL**, 72:5a. The seven honored in November 1407 were Thúc Ngạc, Hẵng, Uyên, Tế, Nhật Chương, Cáng, Dận, and Quốc Thôi. Prince Ngạc lost to Quý Ly in 1391 and died (see above, chap. 2, p. 33). Nhật Chương was executed by Quý Ly in 1393 for plotting (see above, chap. 2, p. 33), Nguyên Uyên and Nguyên Dận died following Nghệ-tông's death in 1395 because they alluded to Nhật Chương's death (see above, chap. 3, pp. 39-40), and Hẵng fell in the purge of 1399 (see above, chap. 3, pp. 53-54). Tế and Quốc Thôi undoubtedly died in one or another of these executions.

The positions bestowed posthumously upon each of the Trần were a prestige title ("Great Officer", **Ta-fu**) and a position in the provincial administrative office (either vice-commissioner or assistant commissioner). See Hucker (1958), 17, 43.

Indeed, the Trần Thúc Bừng who led an unofficial delegation of ninety men and women to China in June 1408 may well have been a member of the old royal clan; **MSL/YL**, 79:2b.

40. Wang, **DMB**, I, 65-66; Gaspardone (1970), 110-111; **TT**, 9:2b, 8a-
    b, 9a, 18b; (Hanoi), II, 229, 233, 234, 243; **MSL/YL**, 68:1a;
    Chú (Hanoi), I, 317; Woodside (1963), 13. It is curious that
    the **TT** accepts the story of the Vietnamese élite requesting
    the colonial status with no question at all.

    In 1413, a Vietnamese envoy from the Trần pretender, angered
    by Chang Fu's keeping of the tribute goods, scolded him: "In-
    ternally, [you] have a scheme to seize [our country]; extern-
    ally, [you] carry on as a righteous (**jen-i**) teacher. [You]
    promised to establish the Trần line [on the throne]; [you]
    also set up your own prefectural (**chun-hsien**) system. Not
    only do [you] seize [our] wealth, [you] also injure [our]
    people. [You] are truly a tyrannous bandit." He was executed.
    TT, 9:22a; (Hanoi), II, 246; Chú (Hanoi), I, 318; **KNLS**, 73-
    74. The **TKML** (Saigon), I, 181-188; (Paris), 121-127, con-
    tains a hint of such a usurpation of authority by a Chinese
    officer on the local level, deceiving the emperor in the
    process.

41. Translated from **NÔML**, 1b, by Gaspardone, **Annuaire**, 56 (1956),
    293.

42. **TT**, 9:2b, 3a, 3b, 5a, 6b-7b; (Hanoi), II, 229-232, 286-287
    (translation of **YCS**); Gaspardone (1934), 96-97; Chú (Hanoi),
    I, 192, 290-293; **NTTT**, 11.

VI. CHIAO-CHIH AND MING COLONIALISM

1. Wang (1970). 386-387.
2. Wang (1964), 96-98; Chang Kuei-sheng, "Cheng Ho", **DMB**, I, 194-
   200.
3. **TT**, 9:2b; (Hanoi), II, 229; Wang Gungwu, "Chang Fu", **DMB**, I,
   66; "Huang Fu", **DMB**, I, 653; Aurousseau, 166-167; **MSL/YL**,
   69:7a-b; 80:3b; Yamamoto, 495-499; Woodside (1963), 13-15.
   According to Woodside, at least four prefectures, seven subprefectures, and twenty-seven districts had their names
   changed by the Chinese. He observed by way of example that
   the characters meaning "peace" (**p'ing**) or "harmony" (**ho**) were
   commonly substituted for "prosperity" (**hsing**). The Ming essentially took over the Hồ administrative structure and elab-
   orated on it. The provinces of Giao-châu (Đông-đô), Bắc-giang,
   Tam-giang, Tân-an, Lạng-sơn, Thanh-hóa, Diễn-châu, Nghệ-an,
   Tân-bình, and Thuận-hóa appear as prefectures in the Ming

system. Lạng-giang was probably taken out of Bắc-giang, and
the Hồ southern Delta province of Thiên-trường seems to have
been split into the four Ming prefectures of Kiến-bình, Kiến-
xương, Phụng-hóa, and Trấn-man. For the Hồ system, see H.
Maspero, 16, 1 (1916), 47. Yamamoto, 500-570, gives the locations of each district, subprefecture, and prefecture in the
Ming structure.

4. Woodside (1963), 14 (cf. Yamamoto, 594-595), 18-21 (describing
the t'un-t'ien system and its application in Vietnam), 24,
27; Wang, DMB, I, 66, 653-654; TT, 9:2b; (Hanoi), II, 229;
MSL/YL, 87:4a.

5. See Mu Sheng's brief description in MSL/YL, 86:1a (January
1409) where he stated: "After a short time in office, [these]
officials brought the proper order to [local] affairs (li-
shih)."

6. Wang, DMB, I, 654; TT, 9:1b, 6b, 15b; (Hanoi), II, 228, 232,
240. For the general pattern of the "native officials" (t'u-
kuan), see Hucker (1958), 78.

7. TT, 9:6a-b; (Hanoi), II, 232. The use of the term Ngô (Ch. Wu)
for the Ming is a derogatory one referring to the Ming founder's original position as Duke of Wu under another claimant
to the Chinese throne, thus implicitly bringing out his lack
of loyalty and faithfulness.

8. KNLS, 35-39.

9. TT, 9:1a, 8a-b; (Hanoi), II, 227, 233-234, 287 (translation of
MS); Chú (Hanoi), I, 165; KNLS, 38-39. There seems to be a
mistake in the text of the TT (9:8a; Hanoi, II, 233) where
it states that "in the fourth month" the Ming attacked.
"Fourth month" makes no sense here, and it might be a mistake
for "fourth day [of the tenth month]; KNLS, 39, n. 1.

10. TT, 9:5b-10b, 19a; (Hanoi), II, 232-236, 243; Chú (Hanoi), I,
318; KNLS, 32-33, 37, 39-41. Ngô Sĩ Liên felt that the two
assassinations were justified, considering the times, when
no one knew who was the proper ruler. Yet, he felt, the
slaughter of the others showed that the Trần forces were not
the Humaneness-Righteousness Army (Nhân Nghĩa Quân).

11. TT, 9:10a-12a; (Hanoi), II, 235-237, 287, 288 (translations of
MS); Wang, DMB, I, 66; KNLS, 41-44; MSL/YL, 82:5a-b, 6b, 86:
6b-7a. Phan Phu Tiên and Ngô Sĩ Liên both saw Tất's failure
to advance as unfortunate. Phu Tiên noted: "The situation of

the Eastern Capital is such that if [you] seize it, the provinces will not be able to withhold support and the local notables will flock to you." Sĩ Liên, however, excused Tất
since his troops had come a long way and might have run out
of supplies. The Hanoi historians (**KNLS**, 44) agree with Phu
Tiên, seeing it as a major tactical error.

12. **MSL/YL**, 79:2a.

13. **TT**, 9:9b, 12a-13b; (Hanoi), II, 235, 237-238; Chú (Hanoi), I,
    165-166, 318-319; **MSL/YL**, 92:13b; **KNLS**, 45-47.

14. **TT**, 9:13a-15b; (Hanoi), II, 237-240, 288-289 (translations of
    MS, YCS, MSL/YL); Wang, **DMB**, I, 66, 146; **KNLS**, 47-53, 55-57,
    60. **KNLS**, 54-55, 58-60, describes the variety of local re-
    volts throughout Vietnam in the period 1409-1411. The horror
    of these years was remembered and expressed a hundred years
    later by the Vietnamese scholar Nguyễn Dữ in two tales of his
    TKML (Saigon), II, 174-177, 233-245; (Paris), 230, 251-259.

15. On this matter of presenting gold and silver human images, see
    Woodside (1963), 6, and Trường Bửu Lâm's discussion of the
    Tây-sơn episode, "Intervention vs. Tribute in Sino-Vietnam-
    ese Relations, 1788-1790", in John K. Fairbank, ed., **The
    Chinese World Order** (Cambridge, Mass., 1968), 175, 324, n.
    53, where he states, "The gold statue may have been intended
    to replace the Vietnamese king who did not want to come to
    the Capital, or it may have represented the Chinese general
    or generals who had been killed by the Vietnamese." Our pas-
    sage, together with the Chinese statement quoted by Lâm in
    his note, would indicate that the former postulation was the
    case.

16. **TT**, 9:17a-b; (Hanoi), II, 242, 289, n. 39 (translation of **MS**);
    Gaspardone (1970), 113, n. 96; **KNLS**, 60-61, 73. The Ming ver-
    sion has Quý Khoáng offering to surrender, and the Chinese
    emperor, "knowing it to be false", trying to lure the Viet-
    namese leader into the open with the positions in the colo-
    nial administration. Other posts offered were regional mil-
    itary commissioner for the major leaders, and administrative
    vice-commissioner or assistant surveillance commissioner for
    others. The **MSL/YL**, 111:6a, has Hồ Ngạn Thân's mission and
    the offer of the positions to Quý Khoáng in early 1411. The
    Hanoi authors of **KNLS**, 61, n. 1, accept this date, as opposed
    to that of the **TT** later in 1411, in correlation with other

evidence.

17. **MSL/YL,** 113:4a; Woodside (1963), 27.

18. **TT,** 9:16a; (Hanoi), II, 241; **KNLS,** 62-63; see also Aurousseau, 245. By 1417, this reference had become much more specific: "Chiao-chih was originally [part of] China's territory [and] its people are all the children of [this] Court." (**MSL/YL,** 185:2a).

19. **TT,** 9:16a; (Hanoi), II, 241. The three edicts may be pieced together from **TT,** 9:16a-17a, and **MSL/YL,** 113:4a-b, 114:6b-7a. The interrelationship of these documents provides solid evidence of the general reliability of the **TT** for these years. The first edict is complete in **MSL/YL,** 113:4a-b, with a direct quote appearing in **TT,** 9:16a. The second edict, quoted above, exists only in the **TT,** 9:16a-b, while the third document is found mainly in **TT,** 9:16b-17a, with an excerpted version of it in **MSL/YL,** 114:6b. Where the same lines appear in both texts, there is no variation, and the two together appear to provide us with a complete set of the edicts. Thus, particularly in the case of the third edict, the Vietnamese text for these years may be seen as having been derived from original materials.

20. **TT,** 9:15b, 17a, 19b-21b; (Hanoi), II, 240, 241, 244-245; **KNLS,** 62-66, 69-72.

21. **TT,** 9:25a; (Hanoi), II, 249, 290 (translation of **MS**); Chú (Hanoi), I, 318-319; Wang, **DMB,** I, 66, 146; **KNLS,** 66-76. Chang Fu is portrayed by the Vietnamese as fearless and bloodthirsty: he ate the liver of one Vietnamese rebel leader after executing him. Chang also executed Huang Chung, one of the top military men in the colony, and apparently suppressed this fact at a later date when he was involved in the compilation of the **MSL/YL;** see Wang, **DMB,** I, 66-67. In the Vietnamese version (**TT,** 9:23a-b; Hanoi, II, 247), Huang commanded one of the forward positions through which the Vietnamese sent assassins to kill Chang. The next day, at a staff meeting, Huang disagreed with Chang on a point and Chang exploded, accusing him of negligence at his post, and had him executed. "All the [other] officers turned pale." **KNLS,** 78-85, analyzes the failure of the resistance movements before 1418, the major reasons being that they were locally based and lacked organization and decisive, prestigious leadership (due

to social contradictions).

22. **TT**, 9:23b, 24b-25b; (Hanoi), II, 247, 249-250; **MSL/YL**, 149:4b-5a, 152:2b, 155:1a; **DMB**, I, 146-147; G. Maspero (1928), 225; Woodside (1963), 30-31; **KNLS**, 84, 87. For the lack of Ming control, see E. Gaspardone, "Le **Ngan Nan Tche Yuan** et son auteur", in Aurousseau, 36-37.

23. **TT**, 9:25a; (Hanoi), II, 249; **MSL/YL**, 151:2a, 154:1a; Chú (Hanoi), I, 318-319; **KNLS**, 76. The Ming text makes two references to Chang Fu sending Quý Khoáng and his lieutenant to Nanking, neither of which makes any mention of suicide. The first, May 30, 1414, states that they were taken to the capital in a cage, together with the nine Trần royal seals. The second mention, presumably of their arrival, comes on August 16, seventy-eight days later, and simply notes that they were then executed.

24. Wang, **DMB**, I, 66-67. **KNLS**, 77-78, notes the occasional troubles following the fall of Trần Quý Khoáng. A younger brother of Quý Khoáng was captured in the far south in 1414, and three other revolts were dispersed in 1415 (Tân-an, Giao-châu, and Thanh-hóa, the last being that of Trần Nguyệt Hồ). On Trần Nguyệt Hồ, see **MSL/YL**, 169:1a. According to the **TT**, 9:28a; (Hanoi), II, 252, 291, n. 51, the eunuch Ma Ch'i got Chang out of Vietnam by sowing doubt about the latter in the emperor's mind. Chang was alleged to have used Vietnamese for his own purposes. The emperor, while questioning the charge, recalled Chang and replaced him with Li Pin.

25. **MSL/YL**, 80:3b; chüan 71-216, **passim**; Woodside (1963), 13-14; Aurousseau, 39-40, 108-109, 128-129. For the basic outline Of Ming administration, see Hucker (1958).

26. The **ANCY** (Aurousseau, 212-216) notes the strange differences of the mountain peoples and the various myths surrounding them. To quote the unknown author (212), "The mountainous landscape of Chiao-chih is strange, indeed, and the types of people [there] also differ [from one another]. [Their] customs are not the same [as those of the lowland]."

27. **MSL/YL**, 80:3b; **TT**, 9:4a; (Hanoi), II, 232; H. Maspero, **BEFEO**, 10 (1910), 681; Aurousseau, 104-106. The precise Ming figures given are: pacified population, 3,120,000+; captive barbarians, 2,087,150+; grain, 13,600,000 catties; elephants, horses, and cattle, 235,900+; boats, 8,677; weapons, 2,539, 852.

The **TT** has: population, 3,129,000; elephants, 112; horses,
420; cattle, 35,750; boats, 8,865. The **ANCY** has a set of population figures, said to be from 1415, that are of interest,
though apparently corrupted at certain points (Aurousseau,
104-106); the overall figure given is 450,288 in 162,558
households (only 2.77 persons per household), whereas the
somewhat shaky prefectural figures add up to about 500,000
in 120,000 households (about 4.2 persons per household). These
figures were probably for tax purposes rather than any attempt at total population. For a general discussion of "The
Nature of Ming Population Data", see Ho Ping-ti, **Studies on
the Population of China, 1368-1953** (Cambridge, Mass., 1959),
3-23.

28. Aurousseau, 60-63, 104-106, 246-254. E. Gaspardone discusses
the relevance of the **ANCY** in Aurousseau, 7-43, as well as in
a later article, **"Ngan Nan Tche et Ngan Nan Ki Yao", Journal
Asiatique,** 233 (1941-42) , 167-180. His conclusion is that
the main body of the work, apart from the two introductions
(both late seventeenth century), comes from the heyday of the
brief Chinese colonial period—the years 1415 to mid-1419—
the rest having been borrowed from earlier texts such as Lê
Tắc's **An Nam Chí Lược.** My own investigation strongly agrees
with Gaspardone's conclusions and suggests that the text
may have been compiled in 1418 to cover the years 1414-1417.
A note in **MSL/YL,** 196:1a, refers to information gathered in
1417 for those years. The total number of **xã** in the **ANCY** is
2,533 out of a total of 3,359 communities, though the total
proclaimed by the text is 3,385. These figures include all
the prefectures but the southernmost, Thăng-hoa, which the
Ming only nominally controlled. See Gaspardone, in Aurousseau, 36, and Aurousseau, 82. The tax figures, Aurousseau,
82-100, confirm this pattern.

29. Aurousseau, 125. The **ANCY,** 125-126, goes on to list the different buildings of the administrative office and how many rooms
each had. These buildings included a registry, a record office, a supervisorate of judicial proceedings, and a prison
office, as was standard in Ming provinces. See Hucker (1958),
43. There were also two storehouses and a legal record office.

30. Hucker (1958), 54-55.

31. Aurousseau, 129-130; **MSL/YL,** 76:2b; Hucker (1958), 49-52, 53-
    55; Charles O. Hucker, **The Censorial System of Ming China**
    (Stanford, 1966), 47-54. According to Hucker, each provincial
    surveillance office had one surveillance commissioner (Huang
    Fu), several surveillance vice-commissioners (here four),
    several assistant surveillance commissioners (perhaps eleven),
    a registry, a record office, and a prison office. The **ANCY**
    states that the Chiao-chih provincial surveillance office had
    fourteen buildings, including the above registry, record of-
    fice, and prison office, and that the regional inspector's of-
    fice had four buildings. The **MSL/YL,** 163:3a, states that four
    investigating censors from different circuits in the capital
    had been sent for punishment in 1406 to Chiao-chih, whence
    they returned in 1415 to their old jobs once peace had been
    established. Would they have staffed the Chiao-chih office?
    Thereafter censorial transfers in and out of Chiao-chih seem
    to have been normal.

32. **MSL/YL,** 76:1b; Yamamoto, 501-502. The author wishes to thank
    Yu In-sun for help on the Japanese portions of the Yamamoto
    work.

33. **MSL/YL,** 80:3b; Yamamoto, 495-499. While the **MSL** states that
    there were 208 districts, Yamamoto has compiled a list of
    210. For a discussion of the administrative divisions in the
    Ming period, see Gaspardone, in Aurousseau, 35-37. **KNLS,** 20,
    n. 1, gives the general location of each prefecture.

34. **MSL/YL,** 84:1b-2b. At the same time, the northern mountain sub-
    prefectures of Thái-nguyên and Tuyên-hóa became prefectures.

35. **MSL/YL,** 87:3b, 106:3a, 118:4a. February 1409 saw five districts
    in the northern mountain prefecture of Lạng-sơn merged into
    either other districts or into the particular subprefectural
    office. In the following year (August 1410), as the Chinese
    hold on Thanh-hóa was being tightened, one district in each
    of its three subprefectures was merged with the higher office
    and, a year after that, one district became part of a neigh-
    boring district in the eastern Delta prefecture of Tân-an.

36. **MSL/YL,** 121:3b, 149:4b-5a, 163:1a-b; Yamamoto, 570. By this
    time, Thăng-hoa prefecture had ostensibly been organized in
    the far south with four subprefectures and eleven districts,
    while elsewhere in the south two subprefectures in Nghệ-an and
    one in Diễn-châu and a fourth autonomous subprefecture (Ninh-

hóa) with three districts had been set up.

37. **MSL/YL,** 167:2a-b; Woodside (1963), 14; **YCS,** 1:7b-10a; Aurous-
    seau, 34-36. The administrative lists given in the latter two
    sources are essentially the same, though five major prefec-
    tures have been lost from the **ANCY,** and reflect the adminis-
    trative structure following the major changes of 1415, but
    not those of 1419, thus reinforcing Gaspardone's conclusions
    on the dating of the **ANCY.** See n. 28, above. As Huang Fu pro-
    claimed, "we have restored the frontiers of old and set up
    a reformed administration"; Aurousseau, 245. Diễn-châu, Phụng-
    hóa, and Trấn-man were the three small prefectures which be-
    came independent subprefectures. While the Red River Delta
    prefectures lost another nineteen districts, making a total
    of thirty-eight out of 107, the old prefectures in the south
    (Thanh-hóa, Nghệ-an, Tân-bình, and Diễn-châu) and Lạng-sơn
    in the north lost twenty-two districts or thirty out of sixty-
    four. The newer prefectures in the south (Thuận-hóa, Thăng-
    hoa) and the north (Thái-nguyên and Tuyên-hóa), as well as
    the four autonomous subprefectures, had none of their fifty-
    four districts touched.

38. **MSL/YL,** 216:1b-3a; Yamamoto, 274-278. Yamamoto missed two dis-
    tricts which had been abolished in Tuyên-hóa prefecture, thus
    having a total of seventy-nine surviving districts. The Red
    River Delta prefectures lost forty-one districts, the older
    outer areas nineteen, and the other, previously untouched ad-
    ministrative units twenty. Thus the Red River Delta and the
    older peripheral prefectures lost seventy-nine of 107 and
    forty-nine of sixty-four districts respectively, and the other
    units twenty of fifty-four. Of the 148 districts abolished,
    ninety-four eventually became part of a subprefecture and
    only fifty-four remained in other districts. According to
    Yamamoto, 580, the Ming appear not to have attempted any
    changes at the sub-district level, leaving the village or-
    ganizational patterns essentially intact.

39. **MSL/YL,** 71:1b, 75:2b, 80:3b; Hucker (1958), 46-47.

40. **MSL/YL,** 84:2a-b, 4b-5a; 87:3a-b; 96:4b; 106:3a; 111:1b-2a;
    115:2b, 4b; 129:4b; 130:1b; 132:1a; 140:6b; 159:2b; 164:1a;
    167:3a; 173:1a; 189:1a-b; 203:1a-b; Woodside (1963), 28-29;
    MHY, 738. Aurousseau, 128, gives a total of 187 stations.
    The southern stations and five of the eastern and southern

Delta stations appeared in 1408-1409; eleven stations were
set up in Kiến-bình and Tân-an in late 1410, and in 1417
eleven more appeared in Tân-an.

41. Aurousseau, 128, 131-132, 133-134 (quotation); **MSL/YL**, 87:3b;
106:3a; 132:1a; 176:3a; 181:1b; 203:1a-b; 211:1a; Woodside
(1963), 19; **TT**, 9:26b; (Hanoi), II, 251; **KNLS**, 87. In the
ANCY, the proclaimed totals differ from the added sums of
the prefectures (bridges—335 as opposed to 296; post stations—374 as opposed to 384). The higher ground to the northwest of the Red River Delta (Bắc-giang) had only fourteen
bridges, the riverine prefectures of Tam-giang, Giao-châu, and
Lạng-giang thirty-three, thirty-one, and twenty-nine respectively, and the lower Delta forty-four in Tân-an to the east
and seventy in the four prefectures to the south. On the
other hand, only twenty-three existed in the northern mountains and twenty-six in the southern prefectures though the
strategic subprefecture of Quy-hóa in the western mountains
had sixteen. Aurousseau, 134, actually has twenty-nine bridges for Lạng-sơn and only five for Lạng-giang, but lists them
in reverse of the usual order. Given the nature of the terrain in each area, I take this to be a mistake and have reversed them. Regarding the post stations, Tam-giang, Bắc-
giang, Lạng-giang, and Tân-an averaged twenty apiece. Kiến-
bình, Kiến-xương, Trấn-man, and Phụng-hóa eight apiece; Lạng-
sơn, Thái-nguyên, and Tuyên-hóa, Thanh-hóa and Nghệ-an twenty-
eight apiece, and Tân-bình and Thuận-hóa nineteen apiece;
there were none in Thăng-hoa, with seventeen in Quy-hóa and
ten in Gia-hưng in the western mountains. The **ANCY** gives totals of thirty-seven post offices and eight transport offices,
while the numbers found in the **MSL/YL** are twenty-nine post
offices (nineteen land and ten water) and four transport offices. Thanh-hóa and Lạng-sơn each had at least four land
post offices, Tam-giang three water stations, Quy-hóa eight
land stations, and Tân-an six water stations and three transport offices. There were maritime trade superintendencies at
Vân-đồn in Tân-an and in Tân-bình and Thuận-hóa in the south;
they were accompanied by produce levy offices. See Hucker
(1958), 36; Aurousseau, 128; **MSL/YL**, 80:3b, 84:5a; Woodside
(1963), 25.

42. Aurousseau, 127-128; **MSL/YL**, 71:1b; 87:5b; 96:4a-b; 115:4b;

167:3a; 192:4b; 196:4a-b; 205:1b. The **ANCY** states that there
were six tea and salt control stations. There were several
branch offices in Tân-an and in Nghệ-an with one each in
Kiến-xương, Kiến-bình, Thanh-hóa, and Diễn-châu. Nghệ-an also
had two storage areas and Tân-an, Kiến-bình, and Thanh-hóa
one each.

43. **MSL/YL,** 80:3b; 84:2a-b; 87:3b; 96:4b; 106:2b-3a; 164:1a; 167:
2b-3a; 193:1b; 216:3a; Aurousseau, 128. The **ANCY** gives figures
of ten major offices, but only nine local offices.

44. **MSL/YL,** 84:2a; 167:3a; Aurousseau, 128. The **ANCY** gives a total
of only three fishing tax offices, which may have been the
number left after the reduction in 1415.

45. **MSL/YL,** 167:2b-3a.

46. **MSL/YL,** 215:1a.

47. **MSL/YL,** 96:4a; 131:3b; 132:1b; 176:1b-3a; 193:1b; 198:2b; 210:
3a; Aurousseau, 107, 129; Woodside (1963), 22-23. The **ANCY**
gives totals of seventy-eight medical, sixty-eight astrology,
and 161 Confucian schools; fourteen prefectural, thirty-four
subprefectural, and 113 district Confucian schools; eleven,
twenty-four and sixty-five Buddhist registries, and twelve,
twenty-four and fifty Taoist registries. We will examine the
geographic distribution of these schools and registries below.

48. Aurousseau, 38-40, 107-109; **MSL/YL,** 68:8b; 71:6b; 73:4a; 74:1a;
76:2a; 80:3b, 6a; 84:5a; 106:2b; 107:6a; 152:2b; 155:1a;
176:3a; 204:1b; **KNLS,** 87. In the south, Thanh-hóa, Diễn-châu,
and Nghệ-an had two **wei,** one **so,** and eight bases and the border areas of Tân-bình and Thuận-hóa two **wei,** one **so,** and five
bases. The **MSL/YL** notes two **wei** in Lạng-sơn and Tân-bình,
which the **ANCY** does not record. There was also a **so** established in Quy-hóa in 1417 which was attached to the Yünnan
military office. The military office had fifteen buildings,
including a registry, a court-martial hall, and a prison office. The number of soldiers is guessed at from **MSL/YL,** 178:
5b, which states that the government gave 37,065 uniforms to
the Chiao-chih army and ordered Kuangtung, Kuangsi, Hukuang,
and Kiangsi to provide 50,000 more.

49. Aurousseau, 125; **DMB,** I, 146, 654.

50. For example, see **MSL/YL,** 87:5a; 97:1b; 99:1b; 101:2b-4b; 102:
2a-b, 5a; 109:2a; Woodside (1963), 15-16. Hucker, **Censorial**

System, 267, states that during the period of the 1420s "both investigating censors and surveillance commissioners were most commonly demoted to county magistrates, often in Annam". A good example of the circumstances leading to a Chinese official being sent south was Hsieh Chin, a top **chin-shih** from Kiangsi in the Hanlin Academy, posted to Chiao-chih as an assistant administrative commissioner for speech displeasing to the emperor. Hsieh is said to have written a poem challenging Chu Ti's succession to the throne and his cruelty, although such a poem, if known, would surely have led to the author' immediate execution. Once in office in Vietnam, Hsieh sent a memorial to the Throne which, according to the Vietnamese **History,** stated: "Chiao-chih is divided into administrative units differently from the way it was before. [We should] enfief the local notables so that [they can] control themselves for us. Let [them] have what they have achieved; do not make [them] pay for what they have lost. [Otherwise] that which is beneficial will not remedy that which is harmful." The Yung-lo Emperor is said to have been furious at Hsieh for "being partial towards the Trần family and not working for the benefit of the state". Hsieh was arrested, returned to Nanking, and thrown in jail where he died. **TT,** 8: 43b-44a, 9:17b; (Hanoi), II, 215, 242. We might ask whether the Chinese emperor was rather sensitive about having been turned aside from the initial path which he had proclaimed. For more on Hsieh Chin, see **MSL/YL,** 116:5a-b; **DMB,** I, 556-557; Woodside (1963), 16; and Gaspardone, **"Ngan Nan Tche",** 169-171.

51. **MSL/YL,** 114:4a; 129:4b; 134:2b; 176:1a; 208:1b; 223:2b-3a; Woodside (1963), 16. The **ANCY,** Aurousseau, 166-170, has brief biographies of fourteen Chinese administrators which provide a good sample of the best officials in the new province. Unlike the Chinese military figures, see 118-125, most of whom came from Chih-li province in north China and were close to the emperor, the civil officials came from across China.

52. **MSL/YL,** 126:4b. The request was then made that these women be given more food and helped to return to China. The emperor accepted it.

53. Woodside (1963), 17; **MSL/YL,** 219:6a. See also Wang, **DMB,** I, 654-655; Gaspardone (1970), 115, n. 10. Hucker (1958), 50-51,

provides a vivid discussion of the powers of a regional inspector. He was sent out from the Censorate to a province
for a full year, during which time he was on his own, checked
all records and every locality, inspected the local government offices, observed what was going on around him, and reported directly to the emperor.

54. Wang, **DMB**, I, 654. See Woodside (1963), 17-18.

55. See **MSL/YL**, 76:2b; 86:4b; 88:8b; 114:6b-7a; 140:3a; 177:1b-2a;
Wang, **DMB**, I, 654; Hucker (1958), 44-45.

56. See **MSL/YL**, 83:2a-b; 161:4b; 179:2b; Hucker (1958), 59. Vietnamese held the post of commander in the Trấn-di **wei** and the
Giao-châu Rear **wei**. **MSL/YL**, 190:1a-b, gives a number of the
lesser civil and military posts held by Vietnamese, in this
case in Thuận-hóa.

57. **MSL/YL**, 68:10b-11a; 72:1a; 121:4a; 161:4b; 163:1b, 3b; 175:2b;
DMB, I, 146; **TT**, 9:16b; (Hanoi), II, 232. Besides seeking
those Vietnamese with virtue and literary talent, the Chinese
also looked for men who could handle administrative office,
read and figure, speak fluently, farm, handle sea-going ships,
or manufacture bricks, tiles, or incense, not to mention
those who were filial, respectful of elders, of proper physi-
ognomy, and daring. Furthermore, many thousands of artisans,
7,700 in 1407 alone, representing various trades, were sent
north. Woodside (1963), 24; **MSL/YL**, 140:4a; **TT**, 9:21b; (Hanoi), II, 246.

58. **MSL/YL**, 76:2b; 79:1a; Edward L. Farmer and Hok-lam Chan, "Juan
An", **DMB**, I, 687-689..

59. **MSL/YL**, 141:2a; 145:2b; 215:1b; **TT**, 9:16b; (Hanoi), II, 241;
KNLS, 87-88.

60. **MSL/YL**, 114:4b-5a; 115:4b-5a; 192:7a.

61. **MSL/YL**, 115:3b. His conclusions were that only experienced,
honest, and attentive gentlemen be selected, though "the honest are not interested because ruling the people is difficult".

62. **TT**, 9:4a, 6a; (Hanoi), II, 230; **KNLS**, 23-24.

63. These desired qualities are taken from the merit awards noted
in the brief biographies of six Vietnamese officials in the
ANCY (Aurousseau, 205-207). See also **MSL/YL**, 86:1a; 114:6b;
121:4b; 145:2b; 192:7a. An especially good example of the
Yung-lo Emperor's feeling can be seen in his proclamation at

the great awards ceremony of 1416 where he is said to have
stated: "You have been able to offer loyalty and to toil in
the righteous cause. [You] have returned your hearts to the
Court." This was recorded in **TT**, 9:27a-b; (Hanoi), II, 251,
but not in **MSL/YL**, 177:1b-2a.

64. **MSL/YL**, 79:2a; 80:4a; 82:8b; 83:2a-b; 114:6b-7a; 203:1a; **TT**,
9:21a, trans., II, 245; Aurousseau, 206-207. Thúy was also
the great-great-grandfather of the sixteenth-century Vietnamese usurper Mac Đăng Dung who was born deep in the eastern
delta where Thúy's descendants fled following the Ming defeat.
DMB, II, 1030.

65. **MSL/YL**, 83:2a-b; 114:6b-7a; 177:1b-2a; 202:1a; **DMB**, I, 689; Aurousseau, 206; **TT**, 8:53a-b; 9:26b-27a, 28b; (Hanoi), II, 225,
251, 253. The **ANCY** is wrong in listing him as Lý Huân, though
he could have been a descendant of the Lý dynasty, all of
whom were forced to take the Nguyễn name. He was from the
same district as the Mac (Chí-linh).

66. **TT**, 9:53a-b; (Hanoi), II, 225; **TS**, 31:22b; **MSL/YL**, 83:2b; 114:
7a. Viễn was in the third rank of awards in 1411.

67. This is the term used in the **TT**, 9:28b; (Hanoi), II, 253. In
1417, Huang Fu ordered seven Vietnamese to take their families to Peking and to help finance the construction of the
palaces there. The emperor, however, merely rewarded them
and told them to go back home. On the fate of such families,
see Ho Ping-ti, **The Ladder of Success in Imperial China**
(New York, 1962), 69.

68. **MSL/YL**, 114:6b-7a; 177:1b-2a; 192:7a; 202:1a; Aurousseau, 207;
TT, 9:27a, 28b; (Hanoi), II, 251, 253; **TS**, 30:2a-3a. Như Hốt
had served in Nanking after the evaluation of 1411 and before
being promoted into the administrative office. All three were
in the third rank of awards in 1411. Other civil officials
of significance were Lương Sĩ Vĩnh and Dương Cự Giác, assistant prefects of Tuyên-hóa and Thái-nguyễn respectively; both
were in the fourth rank of awards in 1411. See also **MSL/YL**,
149:4b. In 1424, upon his recall to China, Huang Fu recommended more Vietnamese, including Hy Vọng's son, for official
positions and strongly advocated the use of local men, according to the Vietnamese records. **TT**, 10:12b-13a; (Hanoi),
III, 16-17.

69. **MSL/YL**, 73:5a; 83:2b; 85:3a; 161:4b; 182:1b; Aurousseau, 205-

206; **TS**, 30:1a-2a.

70. **MSL/YL**, 215:1b; **KNLS**, 141. Curiously, this man had served Trần Quý Khoáng and upon his surrender became vice-commissioner in the surveillance office and prefect of Nghệ-an; the latter post being taken upon his death by his son who later rebelled.

71. Woodside (1963), 2, 14.

72. Woodside (1963), 24; see also the general comments of Miyakawa Hisayuki, "The Confucianization of South China", in Arthur F. Wright, ed., **The Confucian Persuasion** (Stanford, 1960), 22-23. The pattern described in this essay for earlier times fits the Ming approach of the early fifteenth century very well.

73. Aurousseau, 100-101. In general, see Miyakawa, 32.

74. Aurousseau, 101-102.

75. See the edict sent by the Yung-lo Emperor at the end of 1412 in **TT**, 9:20a-21a; (Hanoi), II, 244-245. Although I have not found it in the **MSL/YL**, this edict appears to be genuine since many of its phrases appear in other edicts and documents of the time.

76. Aurousseau, 244, 251. As the emperor noted in posing a question for the successful graduates in the palace examination of 1415, "the sincerity of the people's customs depends on [our] civilizing mission". **MSL/YL**, 162:1a. Gaspardone, in Aurousseau, 42, n. 4, states that both edicts were drawn up in 1407, but the first makes reference to Trần Ngỗi's rebellion as being in the past (Aurousseau, 248), so it must have come no earlier than 1409 when Ngỗi was captured and it may have appeared in 1410. It is full of warnings against disruptive acts. The second, on the other hand, has no such warnings and deals with what seems to be a peaceful society, perhaps appearing in 1415 or later.

77. Aurousseau, 246, 248, 249.

78. **MSL/YL**, 115:3a-b; Wang, I, 655. The emperor's edict of late 1412 accords well with this approach. **TT**, 9:20a-21a; (Hanoi), II, 244-245.

79. Aurousseau, 246, 252; see also **TT**, 9:20b; (Hanoi), II, 245. Stressing the agricultural situation helped the Confucian ideological push as well; see Miyakawa, 32.

80. Aurousseau, 246-247, 248.

81. Aurousseau, 249, 251, 254-255; **KNLS**, 24; **TT**, 9:21a; (Hanoi),

II, 245.

82. Aurousseau, 244.

83. Aurousseau, 250; see also 246, 248.

84. Aurousseau, 253.

85. Aurousseau, 244, 252; see also 251: "To rule by allowing the
    vulgar to change is truly the fundamental way of civilizing
    a people."

86. Aurousseau, 244, 247-249, 251; **KNLS,** 30. The quotation is from
    Aurousseau, 248.

87. Aurousseau, 247, 253; **TT,** 9:25b; (Hanoi), II, 250; Miyakawa,
    34, 35, 42. Curiously, there is no mention of aberrant mar-
    riage patterns, generally a major concern of Chinese offi-
    cials, as Miyakawa, 31-32, shows. The later Vietnamese ruler
    Lê Thánh-tông would have much to say on this matter. See
    Whitmore, **Transforming Đai Việt** (forthcoming).

88. Aurousseau, 132; pp. 102 and 130 give more brief descriptions
    of local cults and rites. Gaspardone, in Aurousseau, 40, n.
    2, comments on the sources for this information.

89. Aurousseau, 255.

90. Aurousseau, 101-102, 132-133, 208. According to the **ANCY,** there
    were 469 Buddhist temples, ninety-two Taoist temples, forty-
    eight ancestral halls, and 252 shrines at the time of the
    Ming occupation. Of the famous monks listed in the **ANCY** (Au-
    rousseau, 209-212), almost entirely Thiền (Ch'an) in belief,
    six each came from Giao-châu and Bắc-giang, only five from
    the rest of the Red River Delta and one from Nghệ-an to the
    south. The distribution of these figures would reflect not
    so much the fact that the Chinese had a looser control of
    the south than of the Delta as it would indicate the contin-
    ued centrality of the area around Thăng-long and to the north
    for Vietnamese Buddhism.

91. Aurousseau, 253-254; **TT,** 9:25b; (Hanoi), II, 250; **KNLS,** 28. As
    Miyakawa, 34, states, "it appears that the first step towards
    inculcating the principles of Confucianism was to prevail
    upon the native peoples to adopt Chinese dress".

92. Aurousseau, 130, 133; **TT,** 9:25b; (Hanoi), II, 250; Miyakawa,
    40, 44. The **ANCY** (Aurousseau, 131) states that there were
    148 agricultural altars, 148 altars to natural phenomena
    (wind, clouds, thunder, rain, mountains, and rivers), forty-
    six altars attached to the prefectures and subprefectures,

and 102 attached to districts; see also Woodside (1963), 23-24.

93. Hucker (1958), 46; **MSL/YL,,** 131:3b, 4a; 176:2b-3a; 193:1b; 198:2b; 205:2a; Aurousseau, 129; Wang, **DMB,** I, 655. The figures come from the **MSL/YL..** In 1419, according to the Vietnamese **History,** what must have been an official version of the Tripitaka (**Fo-ching**) was distributed by the Buddhist and Taoist offices. **TT,** 10:4a; (Hanoi), III, 8. Toward the end of 1412, seven Buddhist prefectural and eight subprefectural offices appeared throughout the Red River Delta with six Taoist prefectural offices and one in a subprefecture. Only in 1416 would other offices be founded. Buddhist prefectural offices appeared in Tân-an, Thanh-hóa, and Thái-nguyên with the six new Taoist offices making the number equal at the prefectural level. The subprefectural and district levels continued to have more Buddhist than Taoist offices. The upper Delta prefectures of Giao-châu, Bắc-giang, Lạng-giang, and Tam-giang had fourteen subprefectural and twenty-four district Buddhist offices. The southern and eastern Delta prefectures had five and twenty-one, five and seventeen respectively, while only a few existed outside the Red River Delta, mainly in Thanh-hóa, Thái-nguyên, and Tuyên-hóa. A Vietnamese tale from a century later (**TKML,** Saigon, II, 63; Paris, 177-178) comments that the fighting during the resistance had led to a great destruction of Buddhist temples and that "scarcely ten percent" survived.

94. Hucker (1958), 46; **MSL/YL,** 96:4a-b; 106:2b; 132:1b; 176:2a-b; 193:1b; 198:2b; 210:3a; Aurousseau, 129; Wang, **DMB,** I, 655. The figures used come from the **MSL/YL;** see n. 47, above. On these schools, see Tileman Grimm, **Erziehung Und Politik Im Konfuzianischen China Der Ming-Zeit (1368-1644)** (Hamburg, 1960), 156-158. The upper Delta had the highest numbers, thirty and twenty-five, while the eastern and southern Delta had twenty-two and eighteen, with sixteen and eleven spread out in the northern and western mountains and almost nothing in the south. For the Ming efforts to recruit Vietnamese, see **TT,** 9:25b, 26b; (Hanoi), II, 250, 251.

95. Aurousseau, 245; see also 247, 248, 252.

96. Aurousseau, 106, 247, 249-250, 252-253. **MSL/YL,** 115:3b, states that the students (**sheng-yüan**) were to be chosen from among,

first, the sons and kin of the Vietnamese officials, and then,
the "refined and elegant" of the people. Huang Fu's interest
in educational aspects may be seen later in his career (1436)
when he registered complaints about the schools that led to
the establishment of education intendants; see Tileman Grimm,
"Ming Educational Intendants", in Charles O. Hucker, ed.,
Chinese Government in Ming Times (New York, 1969), 131. For
the traditional Chinese approach to education in the south,
see Miyakawa, 33, 37.

97. Aurousseau, 106; **MSL/YL**, 115:3b (in 1412). Liu Pen went on to
say: "Yet [they] have a zeal for honor, profit, [and] pleasure, are boastful, [and] neglect the fundamental [things]."

98. Aurousseau, 106-107; Gaspardone, **"Ngan Nan Tche"**, 171; Hucker
(1958), 46; **Censorial System**, 36-37; **MSL/YL**, 115:3b, 176:1b-
2a; 198:2b; 210:3a; **TT**, 9:19a, 25b, 26b; (Hanoi), II, 243,
250, 251; Chú (Hanoi), I, 318; Woodside (1963), 22; Wang,
DMB, I,, 655. The figures are compiled from the **MSL/YL**. Each
school had living quarters for the teachers and the students,
a kitchen, and a granary. For more detail on the Ming pattern,
see Grimm, **Erziehung**, 65-70. As one Chinese official stated
in a request to the Throne in early 1414, concerning the entire empire, "[in those] prefectures [which] are old barbarian territories, [yet which] have received the Imperial Words,
slowly absorbing [them], [I] request that [there] [we] establish schools and set up teachers to instruct the sons of the
people. [Thus], [we] will transform their barbarian customs"
(**MSL/YL**, 147:3a). At the same time, schools were being set
up in Yünnan and Kweichou in southwestern China, though not
nearly as intensively as in Vietnam. **MSL/YL**, 126:3a; 149:3a;
157:1a; 185:1b; 190:2b; 191:1a; 197:1b, 213:1b; Woodside
(1963), 14. According to Grimm, **Erziehung**, 54, some graduates
of the National College in the Chinese capital were, from the
Hung-wu period on, sent out to such teaching posts; 82-83,
such posts did, however, have low status and the lowest rank
(9b) and were hated by anyone with a chance to go higher.
See also Ho, **Ladder**, 26, 171, where he states that despite
the low rank the early Ming rulers held the teachers in high
regard.

99. **MSL/YL**, 162:1a.

100. Charles O. Hucker (1978), 46-47; **DMB**, I, 125, 388-389, 426, 428;

II, 1302, 1574-1575; **MHY**, 735-737; Grimm, **Erziehung**, 46, 73, 77-84, 140, 162-164 (1382 edict); (1969), 130, 133, 134-135; Ho, **Ladder**, 171-173. There appears to have been no attempt to bring schools to the local level in Vietnam as was done in China (Grimm, **Erziehung**, 139). As Ho indicates, those who could pass local examinations were called **sheng-yüan**, given a stipend, and exempted from corvee with two other males of their family. The quotas fixed for the **sheng-yüan** were forty per prefecture, thirty per subprefecture, and twenty per dis-trict. In 1385, a new category of student was allowed which did not get any stipend. The stipend was set at free board plus one catty of rice per month.

101. **DMB**, I, 389, 430, 627, 957; II, 1226-1229, 1386-1387; Charles O. Hucker, "Confucianism and the Censorial System", in David Nivison and Arthur F. Wright, eds., **Confucianism in Action** (Stanford, 1959), 199; Ku Chieh-kang, "A Study of Literary Persecution during the Ming", trans. by L. C. Goodrich, **Har-vard Journal of Asiatic Studies**, 3 (1938), 293-294, 299-300; Wing-tsit Chan, "The Ch'eng-Chu School of Early Ming", in William T. deBary, ed., **Self and Society in Ming Thought** (New York, 1970), 43-44; Robert B. Crawford, Harry J. Lamley, and A. B. Mann, "Fang Hsiao-ju in the Light of Early Ming So-ciety", **Monumenta Serica**, 15 (1956), 320-321.

102. **MSL/YL**, 158:2a; 168:2b-4a; 170:1b; Wing-tsit Chan, "Introduc-tion", in **Reflections on Things at Hand** (New York, 1967), xxxv, n. 113; **DMB**, I, 362-363, 628, 957; II, 1385, 1387. In his introduction to the collection, the emperor noted that: "If the way of the Six Classics is clear, then the hearts of the sages of Heaven and Earth can be seen and consequently the merit of bringing order can be achieved." Further on he said: "In this way, we will exhaust **li** (the proper pattern) in order to clarify the way, we will establish sincerity in order to gain the fundamental. By reforming oneself, by act-ing within the family, and by utilizing [the result] within the state, we will consequently penetrate everywhere under Heaven. We will cause the family not to be heterodox, we will govern the state in a way that is not different, and the cus-toms will return to the pure forms of old, in order to con-tinue the governance of the former kings, in order to perfect a brilliant rule." **MSL/YL**, 168:3a-b.

103. Chan, **Reflections**, 45. See also Ku, "Literary Persecution",
     295; Sakai Tadao, "Confucianism and Popular Educational Works",
     in deBary, ed., **Self and Society**, 331-332; Grimm, **Erziehung**,
     64, 99; **DMB**, I, 362-363.
104. **MSL/YL**, 186:1b-2a; Ho, **Ladder**, 212. The emperor noted that he
     himself "tirelessly" stayed up nights reading the compilation
     in the palace and claimed to gain great benefit thereby.
105. **TT**, 10:3b-4a; (Hanoi), III, 7-8.
106. Aurousseau, 252.
107. Aurousseau, 247, 253.
108. Aurousseau, 249, 250.
109. Aurousseau, 252. For a translation of the Sacred Edict, see
     Édouard Chavannes, "Les Saintes Instructions de l'empereur
     Hong-wu (1368-1398)", **BEFEO**, 3, 4 (1903), 549-563. The six
     instructions were: (1) Act according to filial piety and
     obey your father and mother; (2) Honor and respect your el-
     ders and superiors; (3) Get along with your neighbors; (4)
     Instruct your sons and grandsons; (5) Be satisfied with your
     occupation; (6) Do not do evil. Grimm, **Erziehung**, 142-143,
     notes that these exhortations became almost a "Confucian ca-
     techism" and were read publicly twice a month.
110. Aurousseau, 247; see also 251 and **MSL/YL**, 115:3b.
111. Aurousseau, 253. All the **sheng-yüan** were to wear headgear like
     the officials whom they were being groomed to join, but dif-
     fered from the latter in the style of robe worn. For Huang
     Fu's son, see Aurousseau, 106; Woodside (1963), 22.
112. Grimm, **Erziehung**, 88-90, 101, 103-107; "Ming Educational Intend-
     ants", 134-135. On the first and fifteenth of each month, of-
     ficials would visit the school and check the students. Early
     each morning, and in the evening as well, students and teach-
     ers were to visit the Confucian temple for ceremonies before
     the sacred personages of Confucianism. The major rites of
     the year were the sacrifices in the second and eighth months.
113. Grimm, **Erziehung**, 93-99, 142-143; Sakai, "Confucianism and Pop-
     ular Educational Works", 331-336, 341-342; Ho, **Ladder**, 171.
     The histories might have included some or all of the twenty
     official histories, with Ssu-ma Ch'ien's **Shih Chi** separate,
     a special place for Ssu-ma Kuang's **Tzu Chih T'ung Chien** (but
     not Chu Hsi's **Kang Mu**), and Ma Tuan-lin's **Wen Hsien T'ung K'ao**.
114. **MSL/YL**, 210:1b-2a; Grimm, **Erziehung**, 98-99; **DMB**, I, 643-644.

The work, entitled **Wei Shan Yin Chih Shu** (Book of the blessings which accrue for good works done in secret), was completed in that year, comprising 165 exemplar biographies from different epochs with the biography, commentary thereon, and a final moralistic poem. The **TT**, 10:3b-4a, (Hanoi), III, 7-8, states that the National College student brought the above text and the **Hsiao Shun Shih Shih** [True occurrences of filial obedience], among other such texts, to Vietnam as well as the official Neo-Confucian works and the Tripitaka. The entry seems, however, a bit early for the imperially sponsored morality text to have reached Vietnam. The Chinese approach on Taiwan several centuries later followed this same basic pattern; see Miyakawa, 43-46.

115. Chú (Hanoi), i, 318.

116. **MSL/YL**, 186:1b; 200:3b; Aurousseau, 107; **TT**, 9:28a; (Hanoi), II, 252-253; Woodside (1963), 23. The students were to be chosen not by the length of time spent in school, but by their degree of knowledge. Giao-châu and Bắc-giang were the only prefectures specifically mentioned as sending students. Curiously, the **ANCY** has one **kung-sheng** per school (161 students and 161 schools). On **kung-sheng** see Hucker (1978), 47; Ho, **Ladder**, 183; Grimm, **Erziehung**, 56-58.

117. Aurousseau, 250.

118. Grimm, **Erziehung**, 61-62. The provincial examinations of 1426 were put off because of the continuing insecurity. **TT**, 10: 18b; (Hanoi), III, 22; Gaspardone (1970), 120. According to J. B. Parsons, "The Ming Dynasty Bureaucracy: Aspects of Background Forces", in Hucker, ed., **Chinese Government**, 223-224, Vietnamese held ten positions in the period 1436-1464, one as Minister of Works (probably the honorary post of Hồ Quý Ly's son, Nguyên Trừng), four provincial, two prefectural, and one district. An eighteenth-century Vietnamese source, Lê Quý Đôn's **Vân Đài Loại Ngữ**, Vietnamese trans. (Saigon, 1973), 238-239, drew on Chinese sources to show that Nguyên Trừng served either as Minister of Finance or as Minister of War in China.

119. Aurousseau, 244-255, **passim**. In 1411, the Yung-lo Emperor announced in his first amnesty edict a three-year restriction on Vietnamese commerce. **MSL/YL**, 113:4a. Foreign trade of a private nature was outlawed throughout the country in any

case. Ray Huang, "Fiscal Administration during the Ming Dynasty", in Hucker, ed., **Chinese Government,** 99.

120. **TT,** 9:25b-26a; (Hanoi), II, 250; **KNLS,** 26. Each **mou** of regular paddy fields was taxed five **sheng** of rice or half a picul. Thus, the large **mou** of private land was taxed 1.5 piculs
as opposed to the Vietnamese maximum of one picul. Aurousseau, 82. Lands on sandy banks were taxed one ounce of silk
per **mou.** See Huang, 85-94, for a basic outline of Ming land
taxes and their collection by tax captains (**liang-chang**),
though it is uncertain how this system was applied in Vietnam. Ho, **Population,** 102-123, discusses the relationships of
actual **mou** to fiscal **mou.** What may have occurred in Vietnam
was that the Chinese wanted to bring a Vietnamese land tax
pattern whose **mẫu** (**mou**) was too large for the degree of fer-
tility in line with the Chinese pattern. This would have been
necessary given the continuing need of the Chinese administration and army for rice, but was in any case extremely severe compared with the taxation system of China proper.

121. Aurousseau, 66-77; Woodside (1963), 25. Paul Wheatley, "Geographical Notes on some Commodities Involved in Sung Maritime
Trade", **Journal of the Malayan Branch, Royal Asiatic Society,**
32, 2 (1959), 45-130, provides descriptions of many of the
products listed.

122. **TT,** 9:26a; (Hanoi), II, 250. See **KNLS,** 27, 88-89; in the eyes
of the Hanoi historians: "During the period of the Ming occupation, these natural resource offices were fearsome hells
on earth for our people." See also **TT,** 10:3b, 10b; (Hanoi),
III, 7, 14. The latter reference makes the odd claim that
the Chinese did not mine silver until 1424. For another val-
id contemporary description, see the **Bình Ngô Đại Cáo** of
1427; Trường Bửu Lâm (1967), 56-57; Woodside (1963), 26.

123. **TT,** 9:26a-b; (Hanoi), II, 250-251; **KNLS,** 26; Huang, **Fiscal Administration,** 94-99. The mountain people were especially
taken advantage of, as soldiers traded salt for rice at a
very unfavorable exchange rate. **TT,** 9:21b; (Hanoi), II, 246;
KNLS, 26.

124. Aurousseau, 82-100. See also **KNLS,** 96-97, for a discussion of
these figures vis-à-vis Thanh-hóa.

125. **MSL/YL,** 183:4a; 195:3b; 207:3a; 219:6b-7a; 232:3a; 244:2a; 254:
2b; 266:3a-b. Gold (thirty-two taels) was sent only once, in

1410. **MSL/YL,** 111:6b. See also Woodside (1963), 27. The tribute ranged from 1,252 to 2,265 rolls of silk per year, 7,535
to 10,000 fans, 2,000 to 3,000 kingfisher skins, 2,000 to
3,000 catties of lacquer (none are recorded for 1419 and
1420), and 1,500 to 5,000 pieces of sapanwood (none in 1417).
Twenty-three different types of incense were sent in 1416,
but the shipment was stopped thereafter. **MSL/YL,** 181:2b. A
MSL/YL entry from 1423 noted: "From the first time in 1416,
the [Vietnamese] supply of goods has increased [annually]
and this year alone [we] had this surplus." **MSL/YL,** 266:3b.
In 1424, the new emperor ended the resource exploitation.
TT, 10:11b; (Hanoi), III, 15; **KNLS,** 165-166.

126. **TT,** 9:26a-b; 10:3a-b; (Hanoi), II, 250-251; III, 7; Woodside
(1963), 26.

127. Woodside (1963), 26-27, 32; Wang, **DMB,** I, 655; **KNLS,** 89-90;
TT, 10:15b-16a, 62a; (Hanoi), III, 19, 65. I wish to thank
Keith W. Taylor for his suggestion about the relationship
between the shrunken administrative structure and potential
peculation.

128. Woodside (1963), 22, 24, 27-28. Essentially the Ming repeated
the weaknesses of earlier Chinese attempts to control various
sections of the south. See Miyakawa, 36.

129. Aurousseau, 245.

130. **MSL/YL,** 214:1b. For this position, see Hucker (1958), 43. As
Miyakawa, 33, points out, the Chinese ideal was that the locally educated would take "the lead in upholding the marriage and burial ceremonies fostered by the governors, establishing a basis upon which local Confucian studies could continue by themselves", hence the seriousness of the act by
the local leaders.

131. **TT,** 10:47b-48a; (Hanoi), III, 51. For translations of the **Bình
Ngô Đại Cáo,** which records the Vietnamese perception in very
strong terms, see Trường Bửu Lâm (1967), 56, and **Vietnamese
Studies** (Hanoi), 21 (1969), 93-94. A recent article is Phạm
Văn Kính, "Nhà Minh xâm-lược nước ta lần thứ nhất và sự thất
bại của nó" [The first Ming invasion of our country and its
defeat], **NCLS,** 210 (1983), 61.

132. Whitmore, **Transforming Đại Việt** (forthcoming), chaps. 4-5.

133. **TT,** 9:6b-7b; (Hanoi), II, 232-233. In their final statements on
the Hồ, both Phan Phu Tiên and Ngô Sĩ Liên reflect the strong

anti-Hồ sentiments of later times. On the one hand, Phu Tiên, while noting in some detail the defiant acts against the Chinese and the efforts at strengthening the state, still could not put aside the evil he saw in the Hồ regime and drew two examples from the Chinese past to illustrate his point. Sĩ Liên, on the other hand, condemned those connected with the Hồ down the line, also drawing on a Chinese case (from the **Chun-ch'iu**). Both certainly put Confucian morality ahead of Vietnamese defense against the Chinese, Sĩ Liên even saying that the Ming had a right to come in and correct the situation if the Vietnamese themselves could not do it: "[If] the men of that country who [wish] to execute [the usurper] do not succeed, [then] the men of a neighboring country may do it, [and if] they cannot, [then] the barbarians should do it. Therefore, the Ming proceeded to execute them." Sĩ Liên did say, however, that the "Law of Heaven" (**Thiên-lý**) worked out correctly in the end as Lê Lợi punished the Ming for their cruelty.

134. G. Coedes, **The Indianized States of Southeast Asia,** trans. (Honolulu, 1968), chaps. 13-14.

135. Whitmore, **Transforming Đại Việt,** chap. 2.

ORIGINAL SOURCES

Aurousseau, L., ed. **An Nan Chih Yüan** [Record of Annan, ca. 1419].
 (French title: **Ngan Nan Tche Yuan**). Hanoi: 1932.

Bùi Huy Bích. **Hoàng Việt Văn Tuyển** [Royal collection of Vietnamese prose, 1825]. Saigon: 1971.

Đại Nam Nhất Thống Chí [Record of the unity of Đại Nam, 1910].
 2 vols. Tokyo: 1941.

Đại Việt Lịch Triều Đăng Khoa Lục [Record of successful examination candidates through the dynasties of Đại Việt]. Vietnamese trans., Saigon: 1962.

Đại Việt Sử Ký Toàn Thư [Complete book of the historical record
 of Đại Việt, 1697]. Original text in Durand Collection, Yale
 University. Vietnamese trans., 4 vols. Hanoi: 1967-68.

Hoàng Cao Khải. **Việt Sử Yếu** [The essence of Vietnamese history,
 1914]. Saigon: 1971.

Hoàng Việt Xuân Thu [Royal Vietnamese spring and autumn annals,
 19th century]. Saigon: 1961.

Hồng Đức Bản Đồ [Atlas of the Hồng-đức period, 1491]. Saigon:
 1962.

Khâm Định Việt Sử Thông Giám Cương Mục [The text and commentary
 of the complete mirror of Vietnamese history as ordered by

the emperor, 1884]. Vietnamese trans., 20 vols. Hanoi:
    1957-60.

Lê Quý Đôn. **Đại Việt Thông Sử** [Complete history of Đại Việt,
    1749]. Document A. 1389, EFEO microfilm 98.

Lê Quý Đôn. **Vân Đài Loại Ngữ**, Vietnamese trans. (Saigon, 1973).

Lê Tắc. **An Nam Chí Lược** [Short record of Annan, 1340]. Hue: 1961.

Lê Trừng. **Nam Ông Mộng Lục** [Recorded dreams of an old man of the
    south, 1438]. In **Chi Lu Hui Pien**, vol. 50 (a Chinese collec-
    tion).

Li Wen-feng. **Yüeh Ch'iao Shu** [Book of the Vietnamese mountains,
    1540]. Canton: 1958.

Ming Hui Yao [Administrative manual of the Ming dynasty, 1887].
    Peking: 1956.

Ming Shih Lu, Yung-lo [The veritable records of the Ming dynasty,
    Yung-lo period, 1420-29]. Taipei: Academia Sinica, 1962.

Ngô Thì Sĩ. **Việt Sử Tiêu Án** [Comments on Vietnamese history, 18th
    century]. Vietnamese trans. Saigon: 1960.

Nguyễn Dữ. **Truyền Kỳ Mạn Lục** [Vast collection of marvelous legends,
    early 16th century]. Vietnamese trans., 2 vols. Saigon: 1963.
    (French trans. by Nguyễn Trần Huân, **Vaste recueil de légendes
    merveilleuses**, Paris: 1962).

Nguyễn Trãi. **Nguyễn Trãi Toàn Tập** [Complete collection of the
    works of ..., 15th century]. Vietnamese trans. by Viện Sử
    Học. Hanoi: 1969.

Phạm Đình Hổ. **Vũ Trung Tùy Bút** [Notes written amidst the rain,
    early 19th century]. Vietnamese trans. Hanoi: 1972.

Phạm Đình Hổ and Nguyễn Án. **Tang Thương Ngẫu Lục** [Random record
    of vicissitudes, early 19th century]. Vietnamese trans.
    Hanoi: 1972.

Phan Huy Chú. **Lịch Triều Hiến Chương Loại Chí** [Annals of the of-
    ficial orders of Vietnam through the dynasties, 1820]. Viet-
    namese trans., 4 vols. Hanoi: 1961.

Ta Ming I T'ung Chih [Record of the unity of the Ming empire,
    1461]. University of Michigan Library.

Thiên Nam Lịch Triều Liệt Huyện Đăng Khoa Bị Khảo [Investigation
    of the successful examination candidates through the dynas-
    ties of the south of heaven listed according to district].
    Document A. 485, EFEO microfilm 253.

Trần Thế Pháp. **Lĩnh Nam Trích Quái** [Wonders plucked from the dust
    south of the passes, late 14th century]. Saigon: 1960.

SECONDARY SOURCES

Bain, Chester. Vietnam: **The Roots of Conflict**. Englewood Cliffs, N.J.: 1967.

Bezacier, Louis. "Conception du plan des anciennes citadelles-capitales du Nord Viet-Nam." **Journal Asiatique 240, 2 (1952)**: 185-195.

Bezacier, Louis. **L'art vietnamien**. Paris: 1954.

Boisselier, Jean. **La statuaire du Champa**. Paris: 1963.

Buttinger, Joseph. **The Smaller Dragon**. New York: 1958.

Buttinger, Joseph. **A Dragon Defiant**. New York: 1972.

Cadière, Léopold, and Pelliot, Paul. "Première étude sur les sources annamites de l'histoire d'Annam." **BEFEO** 4 (1904): 617-671.

Chan, David B. "The Problem of the Princes as Faced by the Ming Emperor Hui (1399-1402)." **Oriens** 11 (1958): 183-193.

Chan, David B. "The Role of the Monk Tao-yen in the Usurpation of the Prince of Yen." **Sinologica** 6 (1959): 83-100.

Chan Hok-lam. "Liu Chi (1311-1375): The Dual Image of a Chinese Imperial Advisor." Ph.D. dissertation, Princeton University, 1967.

Chan, Wing-tsit. **Reflections on Things at Hand. New York, 1967**: xxxv, n. 113.

Chan, Wing-tsit. "The Ch'eng-Chu School of Early Ming." **Self and Society in Ming Thought**, William T. de Bary, ed., New York, 1970.

Chang Kuei-sheng. "Chang Ho." **DMB**, I, 194-200.

Chavannes, Édouard. "Les Saintes Instructions de l'empereur Hong-wu (1368-1398)." **BEFEO** 3, 4 (1903): 549-563.

Chesneaux, Jean. **Contribution à l'histoire de la nation vietnamienne.** Paris: 1955.

Coedes, Georges. **The Indianized States of Southeast Asia.** Translation. Honolulu: 1968.

Couvreur, F. S. **Dictionnaire classique de la langue chinoise.** Reprint. 1963.

Crawford, R. B., Lamley, Harry J., and Mann, A. B.. "Fang Hsiao-ju in the Light of Early Ming Society." **Monumenta Serica** 15 (1956): 320-321.

Dardess, John W. "The Transformation of Messianic Revolt and the Founding of the Ming Dynasty." **Journal of Asian Studies** 29, 3 (1970): 539-558.

Deloustal, Raymond. "La justice dans l'ancien Annam." **BEFEO** 8 (1908): 127-220; 10 (1910): 1-60.

Demiéville, Paul. "Les versions chinoises du Milindapanha." **BEFEO** 24 (1924): 1-253.

Đỗ Văn Ninh. "Tiền cổ thời Hồ [Money in the Hồ period]." **NCLS** 191 (1980), 50-54.

Duncanson, Dennis J. **Government and Revolution in Vietnam.** New York: 1968.

Dưỡng Quảng Hàm. **Leçons d'histoire d'Annam.** Hanoi: 1936.

Durand, Maurice. "Review of **Văn Sử Địa,** nos. 10-20 (Sept.-Oct., 1955, to Aug., 1956)." **BEFEO** 50, 2 (1962): 535-555.

Durand, Maurice, and Nguyễn Trần Huân. **Introduction à la littérature vietnamienne.** Paris: 1969.

Farmer, Edward L. "Juan An." **DMB** I, 687-689.

Farmer, Edward L. **Early Ming Government.** Cambridge, Mass.: 1976.

Franke, Wolfgang. "The Veritable Records of the Ming Dynasty." **Historians of China and Japan,** W. G. Beasley and E. G. Pulleyblank, eds., London, 1961: 60-77.

Gaspardone, Émile. "Deux inscriptions chinoises du Musée de Hanoi." **BEFEO** 32, 2 (1932): 475-480.

Gaspardone, Émile. "Le **Ngan Nan Tche Yuan** et son auteur," in Aurousseau, pp. 7-43.

Gaspardone, Émile. "Bibliographie annamite." **BEFEO** 34 (1934): 1-173.

Gaspardone, Émile. "**Ngan Nan Tchi** and **Ngan Nan Ki Yao.**" **Journal Asiatique,** 233 (1941-1942): 167-180.

Gaspardone, Émile. **Annuaire du Collège de France.** 56 (1956): 290-294; 57 (1957): 358-363; 58 (1958): 393-399.

Gaspardone, Émile. "Le théâtre des Yuan en Annam." **Sinologica 6,** 1 (1959): 1-15.

Gaspardone, Émile. "Deux essais de biographie annamite: I. Lê Quý Ly." **Sinologica** 11, 3-4 (1970): 101-113.

Gaspardone, Émile. "Lê Quý Ly." **DMB** I, 797-801.

Giles, Herbert A. **A Chinese Biographical Dictionary.** London: 1898.

Grimm, Tileman. **Erziehung Und Politik IM Konfuzianischen China Der Ming-Zeit (1368-1644).** Hamburg: 1960.

Grimm, Tileman. "Ming Educational Intendants." **Chinese Government in Ming Times,** Charles O. Hucker, ed., New York, 1969: 131.

Hà Văn Tấn and Phạm Thi Tâm. **Cuộc Kháng Chiến Chống Xâm Lược Nguyên Mông Thế Kỷ XIII** [The resistance against the Yüan/Mongol invasions of the thirteenth century]. Hanoi: 1968.

Hall, Kenneth R. "An Introductory Essay on Southeast Asian State-craft in the Classical Period." **Explorations in Early Southeast Asian History: The Origins of Southeast Asian Statecraft,** Kenneth R. Hall and John K. Whitmore, eds., Ann Arbor, Mich., 1976: 193-203.

Harvey, G. E. **A History of Burma.** London: 1925.

Ho Peng Yoke. "Natural Phenomena Recorded in the **Đại Việt Sử Ký Toàn Thư.**" Journal of the American Oriental Society 84, 2 (1964): 127-149.

Ho Ping-ti. **Studies on the Population of China, 1368-1953.** Cambridge, Mass.: 1959.

Ho Ping-ti. **The Ladder of Success in Imperial China.** New York: 1962.

Honey, Patrick J. **Genesis of a Tragedy.** London: 1968.

Huang, Ray. "Fiscal Administration during the Ming Dynasty." **Chinese Government in Ming Times,** Charles O. Hucker, ed., New York, 1969.

Hucker, Charles O. "Government Organization of the Ming Dynasty." **Harvard Journal** of Asiatic Studies 21 (1958): 1-66.

Hucker, Charles O. "Confucianism and the Censorial System", **Confucianism in Action,** David Nivison and Arthur F. Wright, eds., Stanford, 1959.

Hucker, Charles O. **Traditional China in Ming Times.** Tucson, Ariz.: 1961.

Hucker, Charles O. **The Censorial System of Ming China.** Stanford: 1966.

Hucker, Charles O. **The Ming Dynasty: Its Origins and Evolving In-**

stitutions. Ann Arbor, Mich.: 1978.

Huỳnh Sanh Thông. **The Heritage of Vietnamese Poetry.** New Haven, Conn.: 1979.

Kahn, H. L. **Monarchy in the Emperor's Eyes.** Cambridge, Mass.: 1971.

Ku Chieh-kang. "A Study of Literary Persecution during the Ming." Translated by L. C. Goodrich. **Harvard Journal of Asiatic Studies** 3 (1938): 254-311.

Lê Thành Khôi. **Le Viet-Nam: Histoire et Civilisation.** Paris: 1955.

Le Breton, H. "La province de Thanh-hóa." **Revue Indochinoise** 35, 3-4 (1921): 163, 183-185.

Legge, James. **The Chinese Classics.** Reprint (5 vols.). Hongkong: 1961.

Liu Wu-chi. **An Introduction to Chinese Literature.** Bloomington, Ind.: 1966.

Lo Jung-p'ang. "Policy Formulation and Decision-making on Issues Respecting Peace and War." **Chinese Government in Ming Times,** Charles O. Hucker, ed., New York, 1969: 41-72.

Lo Jung-p'ang. "Intervention in Vietnam: A Case Study of the Foreign Policy of the Early Ming Government." **Tsing Hua Journal** of Chinese Studies, n. s., 8, 1-2 (1970).

Maspero, Georges. **Le royaume de Champa.** Paris: 1928.

Maspero, Georges. "Histoire générale." **L'Indochine,** G. Maspero, ed., Paris, 1929, Vol. I: 93-153.

Maspero, Henri. "La géographie politique de l'Annam sous les Lí, les Trần, et les Hồ (10e-15e s.)." **BEFEO** 16, 1 (1916): 27-48.

Maspero, Henri. "Le royaume de Văn-lang." **BEFEO** 18, 3 (1918): 1-10.

Masson, André. **Histoire du Vietnam.** Paris: 1960.

Miyakawa Hisayuki. "The Confucianization of South China." **The Confucian Persuasion,** Arthur F. Wright, ed., Stanford, 1960: 22-23.

Nghiên Cứu Lịch Sử [Historical research]. Hanoi: 1959-present.

Nguyễn Khắc Viện. "Le Vietnam traditionnel: quelques étapes historiques." **Études vietnamiennes** 21 (1969).

Nguyễn Khắc Viện. **Anthologie de la littérature vietnamienne.** Vol. I. Hanoi: 1972.

Nguyễn Văn Thái and Nguyễn Văn Mừng. **A Short History of Vietnam.** Saigon: 1958.

Parsons, J. B. "The Ming Dynasty Bureaucracy." **Chinese Government** in Ming Times, Charles O. Hucker, ed., New York, 1969: 223-224.

Phạm Thế Ngũ. Việt Nam Văn Học Sử Tân Biên [A new history of Viet-
    namese literature]. Vol. II. Saigon: 1963.

Phạm Văn Kính. "Nhà Minh xâm-lược nước ta lần thứ nhất và sự thất
    bại của nó [The first Ming invasion of our country and its
    defeat]", NCLS, 210 (1983), 61.

Phan Gia Bền. La recherche historique en République Démocratique
    Vietnamienne. Hanoi: 1965.

Phan Huy Lê and Phan Đại Doan. Khởi Nghĩa Lam Sơn [The Lam-sơn
    revolt]. 2nd ed. Hanoi: 1969.

Robequain, Charles. Le Thanh-hóa. Paris: 1929.

Sakai Tadao. "Confucianism and Popular Educational Works." Self
    and Society in Ming Thought, William T. deBary, ed., 1970:
    331-332.

Schurmann, H. F. Economic Structure of the Yuan Dynasty. Cambridge,
    Mass.: 1956.

Smith, R. B. "Thailand and Vietnam: Some Thoughts towards a Com-
    parative Historical Analysis." Journal of the Siam Society 60,
    2 (1972): 1-21.

Taylor, Keith W. The Birth of Vietnam. Berkeley, Calif.: 1983.

Taylor, Romeyn. "Ch'en Yu-liang." DMB, I, 185-188.

"Ten Years of Historical Research in the Democratic Republic of
    Vietnam." Vietnamese Studies 4 (1965).

Trưởng Bửu Lâm. Patterns of Vietnamese Response to Foreign Inter-
    vention. New Haven, Conn.: 167.

Trưởng Bửu Lâm. "Intervention vs. Tribute in Sino-Vietnamese Rela-
    tions, 1788-1790." The Chinese World Order, John K. Fairbank,
    ed., Cambridge, Mass., 1968: 175, 324, n. 53.

Wang Gungwu. "The Opening of Relations between China and Malacca,
    1403-1405." Malayan and Indonesian Studies, J. Bastin and R.
    Roolvink, eds., Oxford, 1964.

Wang Gungwu. "Early Ming Relations with Southeast Asia: A Back-
    ground Essay." The Chinese World Order, John K. Fairbank, ed.,
    Cambridge, Mass., 1968: 34-62.

Wang Gungwu. "China and Southeast Asia, 1402-1424." Studies in the
    Social History of China and Southeast Asia, J. Ch'en and N.
    Tarling, eds., Cambridge, 1970: 375-401.

Wang Gungwu. "Chang Fu." DMB, I, 64-67.

Wang Gungwu. "Huang Fu." DMB, I, 653.

Wechsler, Howard J. Mirror to the Son of Heaven: Wei Cheng at the

Court of T'ang T'ai-tsung. New Haven, Conn.: 1974.

Wheatley, Paul. "Geographical Notes on Some Commodities Involved in Sung Maritime Trade." **Journal of the Malayan Branch, Royal Asiatic Society,** 32, 2 (1959), 45-130.

Whitmore, John K. "Vietnamese Historical Sources for the Reign of Lê Thánh-tông (1460-1497)." **Journal of Asian Studies** 29, 2 (1970): 373-394.

Whitmore, John K. "Note: The Vietnamese Confucian Scholar's View of His Country's Early History." **Explorations in Early Southeast Asian History: The Origins of Southeast Asian Statecraft,** Kenneth R. Hall and John K. Whitmore, eds., Ann Arbor, Mich., 1976: 193-203.

Whitmore, John K. "Chiao-chih and Neo-Confucianism: The Ming Attempt to Transform Vietnam." **Ming Studies** 4 (1977): 51-91.

Whitmore, John K. **Transforming Dai Viet: Politics and Confucianism in the Fifteenth Century** (forthcoming).

Wolters, O. W. "The Khmer King at Basan (1371-1373)." **Asia Major,** n. s., 12, 1 (1966): 44-89.

Wolters, O. W. "Lê Văn Hưu's Treatment of Lý Thần Tông's Reign (1127-1137)." **Southeast Asian History and Historiography,** C. D. Cowan and O. W. Wolters, eds., Ithaca, N.Y.: 203-226.

Wolters, O. W. "Assertions of Cultural Well-Being in Fourteenth-Century Vietnam: Part I", **Journal of Southeast Asian Studies** 10, 2 (1979): 435-450; "Part II", **JSEAS,** 11, 1 (1980): 74-90.

Wolters, O. W. **History, Culture, and Region in Southeast Asian Perspectives.** Singapore: 1982A.

Wolters, O. W. "Phạm Sư Mạnh's Poems Written while Patrolling the Vietnamese Northern Border in the Middle of the Fourteenth Century." **JSEAS,** 13, 1 (1982B); 107-119. Revised version: **The Vietnam Forum,** 4 (1984), 45-69.

Wolters, O. W. "Celebrating the Educated Official: A Reading of Some of Nguyễn Phi Khanh's Poems." **The Vietnam Forum,** 2 (1983), 79-101.

Woodside, Alexander B. "Early Ming Expansionism: China's Abortive Conquest of Vietnam." **Papers on China,** Vol. 17, 1-37. Harvard University: 1963.

Woodside, Alexander B. **Vietnam and the Chinese Model.** Cambridge, Mass.: 1971.

Yamamoto Tatsuro. **Annanshi Kenkyu** [Research on the history of Vietnam]. Tokyo: 1950.

VIETNAMESE STUDIES AT YALE

Welcome to the Lạc-Việt Series

In 1983 we launched THE VIETNAM FORUM, a semi-annual review of Vietnamese culture as part of the Yale Southeast Asian Refugee Project. Today, in the same spirit, and with continued generous assistance from the Henry Luce Foundation, we offer Nguyễn Chí Thiện's **Flowers from Hell** as the first volume in the LẠC-VIỆT Series.

Under the auspices of the Council on Southeast Asia Studies and the editorial direction of Huỳnh Sanh Thông, we are committed to publishing a series of works on Vietnam covering its history, language, literature, folklore, economy, and politics. We hope that men and women of the Vietnamese diaspora will welcome and contribute to this small effort to preserve a precious cultural heritage and a historical experience.

From all readers we invite manuscripts as well as comments and suggestions for the LẠC-VIỆT Series in the hope of making it a vital contribution to Vietnamese refugees and their friends everywhere, and to interested scholars in the humanities and social sciences.

James C. Scott
Chairman
Council on Southeast Asia Studies

YALE SOUTHEAST ASIA STUDIES

ANNOUNCES

THE FIRST VOLUME IN THE Lạc-Việt Series

❋❋

"[Nguyễn Chí Thiện's poems] represent a remarkable legacy. We see no reason to apologize for the strident anticommunist tone of this poetry, which was, after all, nurtured in Vietnamese prisons for twenty years... What is most memorable about these poems is not the target of their cold rage... What is memorable in these poems is the quality of the anger, the apocalyptic vision, the survival of dreams, hope, and love, the minute observation of prison life, and, above all, the survival of poetry in Nguyễn Chí Thiện."—James C. Scott.

US$7.00 (including postage)

Please make your check or money order payable to Yale Southeast Asia Studies and send it to:

Yale Southeast Asia Studies
Box 13A Yale Station
New Haven, CT 06520 USA

ĐẶNG TRẦN CÔN & PHAN HUY ÍCH

THE SONG OF A SOLDIER'S WIFE

a bilingual edition
translated and annotated by HUỲNH SANH THÔNG
illustrated by TRÙNG DƯỜNG

The LẠC-VIỆT Series — No. 3

YALE CENTER FOR INTERNATIONAL AND AREA STUDIES
COUNCIL ON SOUTHEAST ASIA STUDIES

THE VIETNAM FORUM

A REVIEW OF VIETNAMESE CULTURE AND SOCIETY

is published twice a year under the sponsorship of the Yale Council on Southeast Asia Studies and the editorial direction of O. W. Wolters and Huỳnh Sanh Thông.

We welcome contributions (in English, French and Vietnamese) by scholars in the humanities and social sciences, dealing with Vietnam, past and present.

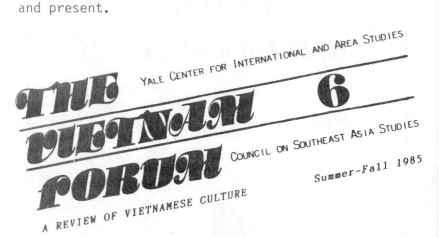

YALE CENTER FOR INTERNATIONAL AND AREA STUDIES

THE VIETNAM FORUM 6

COUNCIL ON SOUTHEAST ASIA STUDIES

Summer-Fall 1985

A REVIEW OF VIETNAMESE CULTURE

Contents: Our land, our home (Á Nam). Limits on state power in traditional China and Vietnam (Nguyễn Ngọc Huy). La proportion occidentale et l'esthétique sino-vietnamienne (Thái Văn Kiểm). The case of "song viết" in archaic Vietnamese (Nguyễn Đình Hòa). Conceptions of change and of human responsibility for change in late traditional Vietnam (Alexander B. Woodside). A mountain home (Huyền Quang). Le maître dhyāna Huyền Quang (Nguyễn Hoàng Anh). The Vietnamese tradition and Võ Đình's woodcuts (Nguyễn Ngọc Bích). Vietnam 1945: some questions (David G. Marr). My milk goes dry (Minh Quân). Les réfugiés originaires du Vietnam et les droits de l'homme (Michel Mignot). The survival of the Vietnamese language in Quebec (Louis-Jacques Dorais, Lise Pilon-Lê & Nguyễn Huy). Economic self-sufficiency among recent Southeast Asian refugees in the United States (John K. Whitmore). Welcome to Trảng Lớn, re-education camp (Hà Thúc Sinh).

Subscription rates:
US$10 a year in the U.S. and Canada; US$12 a year elsewhere.
Address all correspondence to: **The Vietnam Forum**, Box 13A Yale Station, New Haven, CT 06520 USA.

N
G
U
Y
Ễ
N

D
U

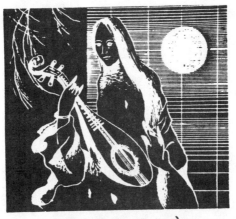

T
R
U
Y
Ệ
N

K
I
Ề
U

The Tale of Kiều

BẢN DỊCH CÓ NGUYÊN-VĂN QUỐC-NGỮ IN SONG-SONG

Sách 250 trang, bìa cứng, in đẹp, giấy bền (không a-xít), với bốn bức vẽ minh-họa độc-đáo của Hồ Đắc Ngọc.

The Heritage of Vietnamese Poetry

GỒM BẢN DỊCH 475 BÀI THƠ

(Nguyễn Trãi, Nguyễn Bỉnh Khiêm, Hồ Xuân Hương, Nguyễn Du, Cao Bá Quát, Nguyễn Công Trứ, Bà huyện Thanh Quan, Nguyễn Đình Chiểu, Nguyễn Khuyến, Trần Tế Xương, **Chinh Phụ Ngâm, Cung Oán Ngâm Khúc, Văn Tế Thập Loại Chúng Sinh, Trê Cóc, Lục Súc Tranh Công, Hoa Điểu Tranh Năng**, vân-vân...). Sách 350 trang, bìa cứng, in đẹp, giấy bền (không a-xít), với bức mộc-bản "Non Nước" của Võ Đình ngoài bìa.

PHIẾU MUA SÁCH

Tôi muốn mua:

[ ] **The Tale of Kiều** ($17.50 + $2.00 cước-phí = $19.50).

[ ] **The Heritage of Vietnamese Poetry** ($32.00 + $2.00 cước-phí = $34.00).

Kèm theo đây chi-phiếu/ngân-phiếu $_____ để trả cho Yale University Press và gởi về: Yale University Press, 92A Yale Station, New Haven, Connecticut 06520, U.S.A.

Gởi sách đến: _____

_____

_____

Yale Southeast Asia Studies
and
Ateneo de Manila University Press

announce the publication

of

Manila 1900-1941: Social Change in a Late Colonial Metropolis

by

DANIEL F. DOEPPERS

This book explores the processes and careers which
produced and changed the structure of Filipino society
in Manila during the early part of the twentieth century.

MONOGRAPH SERIES NO. 27

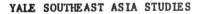 **RECENT PUBLICATIONS**

YALE SOUTHEAST ASIA STUDIES

MANILA 1900-1941: SOCIAL CHANGE IN A LATE COLONIAL METROPOLIS, by Daniel F. Doeppers. Mono. #27. ix, 194 pp. $14.00. With map, figures, tables, photographs, glossary, appendix, index, and bibliography.

CENTERS, SYMBOLS, AND HIERARCHIES: ESSAYS ON THE CLASSICAL STATES OF SOUTHEAST ASIA, edited by Lorraine Gesick with Foreword by Clifford Geertz. Mono.#26. x, 241 pp. $14.00. A collection of six essays which examine the "classical states" of Burma, Thailand, Cambodia, Java and Sulawesi. (1983)

REVOLUTION AND ITS AFTERMATH IN KAMPUCHEA: EIGHT ESSAYS, edited by David P. Chandler and Ben Kiernan. Mono. #25. x, 319 pp. $14.00. Presents a look at some aspects of Kampuchean history in the 1970s during and immediately following the Pol Pot regime. (1983)

MORAL ORDER AND THE QUESTION OF CHANGE: ESSAYS ON SOUTHEAST ASIAN THOUGHT, edited by David K. Wyatt and Alexander Woodside. Mono. #24. vii, 413 pp. $16.00. The intellectual history of Southeast Asia discussed in seven analytical essays which use a wide variety of source materials. (1982)

PEASANT POLITICS AND RELIGIOUS SECTARIANISM: PEASANT AND PRIEST IN THE CAO DAI IN VIET NAM, by Jayne S. Werner. Mono. #23. iv, 123 pp. $10.50. A thought-provoking study of the history of the Cao Dai sect in Viet Nam from its founding in Saigon in 1925. (1981)

SOUTHEAST ASIA UNDER JAPANESE OCCUPATION, edited by Alfred W. McCoy. Mono. #22. vi, 250 pp. $14.00. A collection of nine essays which reassess the thesis that the "Japanese interregnum" formed a distinct and decisive epoch in Southeast Asian history. (1980)

ADDITIONAL PUBLICATIONS CURRENTLY AVAILABLE

Translation Series

SIX INDONESIAN SHORT STORIES, by Rufus Hendon. Trans. #7. viii, 123 pp. $5.50

Bibliography Series

IFUGAO BIBLIOGRAPHY, by Harold C. Conklin. Bibl. #11. vi, 75 pp. $5.50. (1968)

THE INDONESIAN ECONOMY, 1950-1967: BIBLIOGRAPHIC SUPPLEMENT, by George L. Hicks and Geoffrey McNicoll. Bibl. #10. xii, 211 pp. $6.75. (1968)

THE INDONESIAN ECONOMY, 1950-1965: A BIBLIOGRAPHY, by George L. Hicks and Geoffrey McNicoll. Bibl. #11. x, 248 pp. $5.75. (1967)

Monograph Series

PERSPECTIVES ON PHILIPPINE HISTORIOGRAPHY: A SYMPOSIUM, edited by John A. Larkin
Mono. #21. iv, 74 pp. $12.00. (1979)

LANDED ESTATES IN THE COLONIAL PHILIPPINES, by Nicholas P. Cushner, S.J. Mono.
#20. x, 146 pp. $11.50. (1976)

POLITICAL PARTICIPATION IN MODERN INDONESIA, ed. by William R. Liddle. Mono.
#19. x, 206 pp. $9.50. (1973)

FOREIGN POLICY AND NATIONAL INTEGRATION: THE CASE OF INDONESIA, by Jon M.Reinha
Mono. #17. vi, 230 pp. $8.50. (1971)

PHILIPPINE MIGRATION: THE SETTLEMENT OF THE DIGOS-PADADA VALLEY, DAVAO PROVINCE
by Paul D. Simkins and Frederick L. Wernstedt. Mono. #16. x, 147 pp. $8.50. (1

CONFERENCE UNDER THE TAMARIND TREE: THREE ESSAYS IN BURMESE HISTORY, by Paul J.
Bennett. Mono. #15. viii, 153 pp. $8.25. (1971)

THE PEOPLE'S ACTION PARTY OF SINGAPORE: EMERGENCE OF A DOMINANT PARTY SYSTEM, b
Thomas J. Bellows. Mono. #14. xii, 195 pp. $8.25. (1970)

EARLY AMERICAN-PHILIPPINE TRADE: THE JOURNAL OF NATHANIEL BOWDITCH IN MANILA, 1
by Thomas R. and Mary C. McHale. Mono. #2. viii, 63 pp. $4.75. (1962)

SEND ORDERS TO:

Yale University
Southeast Asia Studies
Box 13A Yale Station
New Haven, Connecticut 06520

POSTAGE AND HANDLING:

$1.00 for first volume
$ .50 for each additional volume
Shipment via book rate,
no returns except for damage.

Please make checks payable to Yale University Southeast Asia Studies.

No. of Copies	Description	Total

Postage/handling _____

Total enclosed _____